KU-681-804

Troubled Children/
Troubled Systems

(PGPS-104)

Pergamon Titles of Related Interest

Amabile/Stubbs PSYCHOLOGICAL RESEARCH IN THE CLASSROOM

Cartledge/Milburn TEACHING SOCIAL SKILLS TO CHILDREN: Innovative Approaches

Conoley/Conoley SCHOOL CONSULTATION: A Guide to Practice and Training

Gelfand/Hartmann CHILD BEHAVIOR ANALYSIS AND THERAPY 2nd Edition

Morris/Kratochwill TREATING CHILDREN'S FEARS AND PHOBIAS: Implications for Practice and Research

Webster/Konstantareas/Oxman/Mack AUTISM: New Directions in Research and Education

Related Journals*

CHILD ABUSE AND NEGLECT

CHILDREN AND YOUTH SERVICES REVIEW

JOURNAL OF BEHAVIOR THERAPY AND EXPERIMENTAL PSYCHIATRY

JOURNAL OF CHILD PSYCHOLOGY AND PSYCHIATRY

PERSONALITY AND INDIVIDUAL DIFFERENCES

*Free specimen copies available upon request.

Troubled Children/ Troubled Systems

Steven J. Apter
Syracuse University

PERGAMON PRESS
New York   Oxford   Toronto   Sydney   Paris   Frankfurt

Pergamon Press Offices:

U.S.A.   Pergamon Press Inc., Maxwell House, Fairview Park,
                             Elmsford, New York 10523, U.S.A.

U.K.   Pergamon Press Ltd., Headington Hill Hall,
                             Oxford OX3 0BW, England

CANADA   Pergamon Press Canada Ltd., Suite 104, 150 Consumers Road,
                             Willowdale, Ontario M2J 1P9, Canada

AUSTRALIA   Pergamon Press (Aust.) Pty. Ltd., P.O. Box 544,
                             Potts Point, NSW 2011, Australia

FRANCE   Pergamon Press SARL, 24 rue des Ecoles,
                             75240 Paris, Cedex 05, France

FEDERAL REPUBLIC   Pergamon Press GmbH, Hammerweg 6
OF GERMANY   6242 Kronberg/Taunus, Federal Republic of Germany

Library of Congress Cataloging in Publication Data

Apter, Steven J. (Steven Jeffrey), 1945-
    Troubled children/troubled systems.

    (Pergamon general psychology series ;
v. 104)
        Bibliography: p.
        Includes index.
        1. Mentally ill children--Education.
I. Title. II. Series.
LC4165.A68   1982   371.94   81-12026
ISBN 0-08-027167-7   AACR2
ISBN 0-08-027166-9 (pbk.)

Printed in the United States of America

For the people in my own system—my parents, Connie and Al Apter; my wife, Dianne; and my daughters, Jennie and Rachel—with my love and gratitude for their continual support and encouragement.

Contents

Preface

In a time characterized by anxiety, the destabilization of family life, double-digit inflation combined with increasing unemployment, escalating rates of violence, etc., it should not be surprising that the number of children with emotional problems also seems to be rising steadily. Though not unexpected, such a finding still gives us cause for concern since the continuing increase of emotional stress in children occurs in spite of all of our well-intentioned efforts on behalf of such youngsters.

One unique facet of service to emotionally disturbed children is the diversity of the professionals and the "systems" that attempt to respond to this population. Though for a time efforts were primarily aimed at treatment and psychiatrists were the traditional (sometimes the only) providers, things have changed dramatically in recent years. Psychologists, social workers, family therapists, child-care workers, and teachers have all staked their claims to the territory occupied by children with emotional and behavioral disorders.

While efforts to impact upon such youngsters have emanated from the medical, mental health, judicial-correctional, social service, and religious systems in our communities, the tendency now is for more and more services to be developed and provided in the educational system. Correspondingly, more and more diverse professionals who work with troubled children are doing so from a base in the public schools. In addition, professionals who work with this population of children from other than educational programs soon discover the critical importance of coordinating their efforts with their counterparts in public school settings.

Though the shift from a medical to an educational model for the provision of services to troubled youngsters has probably increased the numbers of children receiving service, the continuing rise of incidence rates indicates that newer efforts may in the long run be no more successful than the older models they replaced. This unhappy conclusion may be due, at least in part, to the narrowness of typical efforts to intervene with troubled children—a characteristic of programs that may be as true for educational programs as it is for medical, mental health, correctional programs, and others.

In fact, narrowness of perspective and of interventions based on such perspectives may be a primary cause of our inability to deal more effectively with troubled children. One point of view which is gaining increasing attention in our field would in fact hypothesize just such a proposition (that narrowness of program perspective reduces chances for successful intervention). This approach, known as the ecological or systems orientation suggests that the failure of narrowly defined programs is the best documentation of the need to consider the contexts surrounding troubled children—the systems in which they live—in our program development and intervention plans.

The ecological perspective, developed in psychology and applied more recently in special education, views emotional disturbance as a "failure-to-match" in the interaction between the child and the system that surrounds him or her. Such a viewpoint assumes that children are *inseparable* parts of mini–social systems and that in order to be maximally effective, interventions must address themselves to the realities of those systems. In short, the ecological or "systems" orientation states that in order to intervene effectively with *troubled children*, we must really think and plan and act in terms of *troubled systems*.

The benefits of an ecological model are many. First, it can serve as an organizing or "umbrella" concept which can help us clarify some of the confusion in efforts to educate troubled children. Issues in diagnosis, the problem of labeling, the comparative usefulness of a variety of interventions, similarities and differences in professional roles and job descriptions, old and new patterns for the delivery of service—all these and more are important elements of work with troubled children that can be clearly conceptualized and perhaps better understood under the ecological umbrella concept.

Second, the ecological model can help us integrate important concepts from the variety of academic disciplines related to the education of children whom we call disturbed. Psychologists in particular have produced much that may be useful but remains unknown to special educators. Sociologists and anthropologists have also contributed greatly to the ecological literature and provided a wealth of ideas for potential application. Finally, the ecological orientation may provide us with important new implications for the training of those who will work with troubled children, guidelines for the development of programs to intervene in the lives of such youngsters, and directions for future research in this area.

In terms of actual practice, the ecological or systems orientation might be translated into two specific kinds of needs for programs for troubled children. First of all, such programs need to develop mechanisms by which they can provide more *comprehensive* and better *coordinated* direct services to the youngsters whom they serve. Services that are delivered in piecemeal fashion and in isolation from other important elements of a given child's system stack the deck against success.

Second, professionals involved in such programs must find ways to increase their committments of time and energy to *indirect services*. The now agreed-upon conclusion that there will never be enough trained personnel to provide effective direct services to troubled youngsters demands our attention to making the most of our efforts. Working with families of identified children, consultation with other adults who work with such youngsters, providing formal or informal inservice to professional and paraprofessional colleagues, and developing programs with representatives of community agencies are all potentially valid activities that may yield a geometric increase in results.

The purpose of this book is to demonstrate the utility of an ecological approach to troubled children. Specifically, we shall try to demonstrate the importance of thinking in terms of troubled systems and to describe ways in which the goals of providing more comprehensive and coordinated direct services and increasing our committment to indirect services can be met.

We shall attempt to do this in the context of the systems in which most of us spend our professional lives. By considering the realities of such matters as current job descriptions, role definitions, and financial necessities, our hope is that this book will provide both a better understanding of troubled systems as well as some clearer directions for the application of that understanding to those children we call emotionally disturbed or behaviorally disordered. It is hoped that special educators, psychologists, social workers, and therapists who work in school programs or whose work connects them to school programs for troubled children will all find something of use in these pages.

Acknowledgments

For permission to reprint from copyrighted materials, the author is indebted to the following:

Allyn and Bacon for excerpts from *Teaching Children with learning and behavior problems* by D.D. Hamill and N.R. Bartell, Copyright 1978; for excerpts from *The emotionally disturbed child in the classroom: The orchestration of success* by F.M. Hewett and F.D. Taylor, Copyright 1980; for excerpts from *Understanding and teaching emotionally disturbed children* by P.L. Newcomer, Copyright 1980; for excerpts from *Educational assessment of learning problems: Testing for teaching* by G. Wallace and S.L. Larsen, Copyright 1978; and for excepts from *The resource teacher: A guide to effective practices* by J.L. Weiderholt, D.D. Hamill, and V. Brown, Copyright 1978.

American Orthopsychiatric Association and Morton Silverman for excerpts from "Beyond the mainstream: The special needs of the chronic child patient" by M. Silverman, *Amer. Journal of Orthopsychiatry*, 1979, *49* (1), 62-8, Copyright 1979 by the American Orthopsychiatric Association, Inc. Reproduced by permission.

American Psychological Association for permission to reprint one figure from "Helping disturbed children: Psychological and ecological strategies" by N. Hobbs, *American Psychologist*, 1966, *21*, 1105-15. Copyright 1966 by the American Psychological Association. Reprinted by permission.

Basic Books, Inc. for excerpts from *Current concepts of positive mental health* by Marie Jahoda. Copyright 1958 by Basic Books, Inc., New York.

Behavioral Publications, Inc. for excerpts from "Strategies for the prevention of mental disorders" by B.L. Bloom in *Issues in community psychology and preventive mental health* by the Task Force on Community

Mental Health of Division 27 of the American Psychological Association. Copyright 1971 by Behavioral Publications, Inc.

Professor S. Cohen, Hunter College for excerpts from *Family reactions to the handicapped child* by S. Cohen. Hunter College of the City University of New York, 1974.

Council for Children with Behavioral Disorders for excerpts from "Ecological disturbance: A test of the matching hypothesis" by T.J. Curran and B. Algozzine, *Behavioral Disorders*, 1980, *5* (3), 169–174; for excerpts from "Perspectives on re-education" by N. Hobbs, *Behavioral Disorders*, 1978, *3* (2), 65–66; for excerpts from "Strategies for diagnosis and identification of children with behavior and learning problems" by E.M. Koppitz, *Behavioral Disorders*, 1977, *2* (3), 136–140; for excerpts from "Competency in teaching socio-emotional impaired" by W. Morse, *Behavioral Disorders*, 1976, *1* (2), 83–87; for excerpts from "Teacher behaviors and ecological balance" by S.I. Mour, *Behavioral Disorders*, 1977, *3* (1), 55–58; from "Forum" by T.M. Stephens, *Behavioral Disorders*, 1976, *1* (2), 146–147; and for excerpts from "The ecological model of emotional disturbance in children: A status report and proposed synthesis" by S. Swap, *Behavioral Disorders*, 1978, *3* (3), 186–196. All reprinted by permission.

Council for Exceptional Children for permission to adapt one figure ("The Cascade System") from "Special education as development capital" by E. Deno, *Exceptional Children*, 1970, *37*, (3), 229–237, Copyright 1970 by the Council for Exceptional Children; and for one figure ("Major Theories in emotional disturbance") by W.C. Morse and J.M. Smith, copyright 1980 by the Council for Exceptional Children. Reprinted with permission.

Family Process for excerpts from "Interdisciplinary versus ecological approach," by E.H. Averswald, *Family Process*, 1968, *7* (2), 202–215. Reprinted by permission.

Grune and Stratton, Inc. for excerpts from "A review of critical issues underlying mainstreaming" by C. Meisgeier. In L. Mann and D. Sabatino (Eds.), *The third review of special education*. New York: Grune and Stratton, 1976. Reprinted by permission.

Harcourt, Brace, Jovanovich, Inc. for excerpts from *All our children: The American family under pressure* by K. Kenniston and the Carnegie Council on Children, New York: Harcourt, Brace, Jovanovich, 1977. Reprinted by permission.

Professor K. Heller, Department of Psychology, Indiana University, for excerpts from *Psychology and community change* by K. Heller and J. Monahan. Homewood (Ill.): Dorsey Press, 1977. Reprinted by permission.

Human Policy Press for excerpts from *Teach and reach: An alternative guide to resources for the classroom* by E. Barnes, W. Eyman, and M.

Bragar. Syracuse (N.Y.): Human Policy Press, 1977. Reprinted by permission.

Institute for Response Education for excerpts from "Family-school relationships" by S.L. Lightfoot, *Citizen Action in Education*, 1981, *8* (1), 6–7. Reprinted by permission.

Jossey-Bass, Inc. for excerpts from "Effect on parents" by K. Gorham, C. DesJardins, R. Page, E. Pettis, and B. Scheiber. In N. Hobbs (Ed.), *Issues in the classification of children* (Vol. II), San Fran.: Jossey-Bass, 1975; and for excerpts from *The futures of children* by N. Hobbs. San Francisco: Jossey-Bass, 1975. Reprinted by permission.

Professor M. Lay-Dopyera, School of Education, Syracuse University for excerpts from *Mainstreaming children with special needs: An independent study guide* by M. Lay-Dopyera, Division for the Study of Teaching, School of Education, Syracuse University, 1981. Reprinted by permission.

Professor J. Mallan, School of Education, Syracuse University for excerpts from *Anonymous letter to a teacher*, undated. Reprinted by permission.

Department of Educational and Psychological Research, School of Education, Malmo, Sweden, for excerpts from *Educational and psychological interactions: Models of remediation for behavior disordered children* by K.D. Joul. Bulletin #62, July 1977. Reprinted by permission.

Department of Special Education, University of Missouri-Columbia, for excerpts from *National needs analysis in behavior disorders* by J.K. Grosenick and S.L. Huntze, 1979. Reprinted by permission.

C.V. Mosby Co. for excerpts from *Children in conflict* (Ed. 2) by H.R. Reinert, St. Louis: C.V. Mosby Co., 1980, and for excerpts from *Teaching strategies for children in conflict* by H.L. Swanson and H.R. Reinert. St. Louis: C.V. Mosby Co., 1979. Reprinted by permission.

National Support Systems Project, Univ. of Minnesota for excerpts from *Observations on the course in special education planning held at the Federal University in Rio de Janeiro (Brazil)* by M. Reynolds, 1977. Reprinted by permission.

Professor S.R. Newbrough, L.S. Walker, and S. Abril for excerpts from their "Workshop on ecological assessment" presented to the National Association of School Psychologists annual meeting on March 23, 1978, New York, New York. Reprinted by permission.

Plenum Publishing Corp. for excerpts from "The ecology of child treatment: A developmental educational approach to the therapeutic milieu" by J. Whittaker, *Journal of Autism and Child Schizophrenia*, 1975, *5* (3), 223–237. Reprinted by permission.

Prentice-Hall, Inc. for excerpts from *A psychological approach to abnormal behavior* by L. Ullman and L. Krasner, 1969. Reprinted by permission of Prentice-Hall, Inc., Englewood Cliffs, N.J.

Random House, Inc. for excerpts from *Mental health in the schools* by

1
Overview/Introductory Concepts

A child is born into a world of phenomena all equal in their power to enslave. It sniffs—it sucks—it strokes its eyes over the whole uncountable range. Suddenly one strikes. Why? [Peter Shaffer, *Equus*, 1975, p. 88].

Why? What is emotional disturbance, what is mental health? What kinds of programs have been developed for youngsters identified as having emotional or behavioral difficulties? Are these interventions effective? Will Public Law 94:142 (The Education of All Handicapped Children Act of 1975) bring troubled children closer to all of us who work in schools? What are the implications of "mainstreaming"? Who are the adults who work with troubled youngsters? Can they work together productively— cooperate—in their efforts to serve children who are labeled emotionally disturbed?

The broad and undefined field that revolves around work with troubled children is complicated, often confusing, certainly frustrating, perhaps even chaotic at times. Above are just some of the questions which will be addressed in the following pages. Though answers are hard to find, it is hoped that our efforts will bring some clarity to the field. Before starting, however, it is important to describe the point of view that permeates this effort.

Ecological

The ecological orientation which forms the basis of this book views issues, concerns, and concepts related to emotionally disturbed children from a broader perspective than is usual. From this outlook, emotional disturbance is not seen simply as the necessary result of intrapsychic conflict nor as the inevitable product of inappropriate social learning. Instead, according to the ecological model, disturbance resides in the interaction between a child and critical aspects of that child's surrounding environment, that is, the child's system. More specifically, ecological theorists believe that what we know as emotional disturbances or behavior disorders actually result from discrepancies between a given child's skills and abilities and the demands or expectations of that child's environment.

We shall try to consider the ramifications and implications of a systems-centered (as opposed to more individual-focused) view of emotional disturbance. Further, the ecological perspective can serve as an "integrating" overview, as an umbrella concept that helps us understand the chaotic nature of the field.

Comprehensive

This work is also based on an acceptance of the need for fuller participation in the process of developing and implementing programs for youngsters with special emotional needs. When we recognize that the problems presented by troubled children really represent more complex troubled systems, we also acknowledge the need for more comprehensive intervention strategies. Consequently, while developing skill at working directly with a youngster is an important and necessary task for professionals who work with troubled children, it is not sufficient. We must also be concerned with increasing our ability to work with parents, learning how to function as members of interdisciplinary teams, refining our consultation skills, and perhaps most importantly, developing a coordination focus in each of our professional roles. All are important elements of a comprehensive approach to troubled youngsters.

Preventive

Our efforts are also based on a recognition of the ultimate impossibility of a direct-service-only approach for the scope of the emotional disturbance problem. We must come to terms with the fact that there will never be enough trained professionals to meet the needs of the number of troubled children in current society. In addition to providing direct service for troubled children, then, we must also strive to prevent the development of emotional disturbances. We must continue to consider the psychological well-being of *all* children and the implications for "regular" educators of the need to intervene *before* emotional disturbances are created or exacerbated.

Taken together, these three points combine to define a recent movement in the human-services field—the shift from a more "clinical" individualistic approach to human problems to an effort more oriented toward total community life. As Whittaker (1975) has noted: "Child treatment programs should focus on growth and development in the child's total life sphere, rather than on the amelioration of psychiatrically defined syndromes or the extinction of certain problematic behaviors" (p. 225). In the field of psychology, this shift is represented by the community psychology movement which is described in the following section.

COMMUNITY PSYCHOLOGY

Community psychology may be described as a relatively new approach to dealing with human behavior problems. It stresses the environment's role in causing adjustment difficulties and consequently emphasizes the necessity of developing interventions that impact on environments or systems as well as on individuals. According to Heller and Monahan (1977), two recurrent themes that the community psychology perspective brings to the mental health field are (1) a concern for prevention, and (2) the need to focus on broader ecological levels. Both themes are based on the following general findings:

1. Questionable effectiveness of traditional mental health functions.
2. Dissatisfaction with inequities in service delivery systems.
3. Staggeringly high need for mental health services in general population.
4. Ominous shortages in projected available mental health "manpower."
5. Inappropriateness of the medical model.

The case of psychotherapy might be seen as an example. In the early 1960s, studies by Eysenck (1961) and others raised serious questions about the effectiveness of psychotherapy. More importantly for our concerns here, people began to realize that even if psychotherapy proved to be *very* effective, it did not represent a very feasible solution to the large-scale mental health problems of modern society. In 1962, Eisenberg stated:

> The limitations of present therapeutic methods dooms us to training caretakers at a rate that ever lags behind the growing legions of the ill, unless we strike out successfully in new directions in the search for cause and treatment. . . . Society can ill afford todays precious overspecialization in which trainees may learn one method even superbly well but a method that ever lags behind the demands placed upon it, while they remain abysmally unaware of the problems besetting the bulk of the mentally ill [p. 825].

Community psychologists, regardless of the position they hold on psychotherapy's effectiveness, believe that there is a need for new approaches to our mental health problems. For some, that could mean wide-scale preventive programs aimed at reducing the number of persons who need psychotherapy. For others, it could mean making psychotherapy more available by enabling less formally trained people to become providers. More generally, unmet mental health needs suggest to community psychologists that change is needed both in the manner in which services are delivered and in the types of services offered.

The essence of community psychology may be the focus on individuals in the context of the systems in which they live. This is in contrast to the more traditional individualistic psychological viewpoint. Such a perspective implies new areas for mental health intervention and research—the study of organizations and institutions, the development of effective systems of service delivery, group dynamics, etc.

For example, Heller and Monahan (1977) have pointed to the importance of intervening at a number of ecological levels (individual or small group, organization, community) and discussed the need for change strategies aimed at increasing competence (instead of reducing deficits). Table 1.1 depicts the kinds of intervention programs that might be included in Heller and Monahan's framework.

Heller and Monahan conclude:

> The impact of the community perspectives can be conceptualized best in terms of emphasis and orientation that highlight a few key concepts: prevention; intervention at organizational and community levels; and procedures to foster skills and competencies. In contrast, the traditional perspectives in clinical psychology emphasize the remediation of deficits in individuals that are developed sufficiently to warrant a visit to the office of a mental health professional—the helping resource usually called upon last in time of trouble. The distinctions between the two orientations are important [p. 19].

As we shall see in later chapters, this sort of perspective—a focus on strengths as well as weaknesses—represents one critical aspect of an ecological orientation.

COMMUNITY PSYCHOLOGY AND SPECIAL EDUCATION

What does the community psychology perspective have to do with the education of troubled children? First of all, it highlights the very real needs of children as a group in America. The following findings provide additional documentation for this gloomy perspective.

Table 1.1. Strategies for Change: Deficit and Competency Orientations

Ecological Level	Focus on Deficits Point of Intervention		Focus on Competencies Point of Intervention	
	Earlier	Later	Earlier	Later
Individual or Small Group	1. Identify high-risk children 2. Crisis intervention 3. Polio vaccination	1. Much of individual psychotherapy 2. Much of group therapy 3. Medication	1. Well-baby clinics 2. Parent effectiveness training 3. Skill building (athletics, public speaking, etc.)	1. Behavior shaping 2. Occupational therapy 3. Women's or gay support groups
Organizational	1. Staff sensitivity groups 2. Case-centered consultation 3. Special education programs	1. Remedial reading classes 2. Hospital token economies 3. Continuation schools	1. Police selection and training 2. English-as-a-second-language programs 3. Sex education classes in schools 4. Consultee-centered consultation	1. Achievement Place 2. Fairweather's Lodge program 3. Organizational Development training groups
Community	1. Media program on the "early warning signs of mental illness" 2. Street lighting to reduce crime 3. Seat belts in cars	1. Welfare programs 2. Building mental hospitals 3. Building prisons	1. Community development programs 2. Fostering support networks 3. Anticipatory guidance through community-wide media	1. Social advocacy strategies 2. Job banks for displaced workers

Source: Based on Heller and Monahan (1977), pp. 15–18.

Item: The report of the Foundation for Child Development's National Survey of Children concluded that one-third of the 1.25 million children in America with an emotional, behavioral, mental, or learning problem serious enough for parents to seek outside help, did not receive any counseling or care (APA *Monitor*, 1977).

Item: All Our Children (1977), the report of a five-year study by the Carnegie Corporations' Council on Children found that between one-quarter and one-third of all American children grow up in conditions of poverty that significantly damage their development. Further, the council declared that the United States needs a comprehensive family policy to begin shifting the myth of equal opportunity to a reality.

Item: "8.1 million of the 54 million children and youth of school age, or 15 percent of that population, need help for psychological disorders. . . . One of every three thousand children has an autistic disorder. There are 200,000 cases of child abuse reported every year, and surveys indicate the total number may be at least 10 times greater. Adolescents show an alarming increase in suicide, depression, and alcohol and drug misuse." (President's Commission on Mental Health, 1977, p. 8).

Item: "For the past few years, the most commonly used estimate is that at any one time, 10 percent of the population need some form of mental health care. . . . There is new evidence that this figure may be nearer 15 percent of the population" (President's Commission on Mental Health, 1978, p. 8).

Item: Recent New York State estimates indicate that approximately 36,946 (20 percent of the 182,299 special education) students served in public-, private-, or state-supported schools in 1979–80 were emotionally disturbed. Unfortunately, the number of youngsters labeled emotionally disturbed does not include all those who experience severe emotional distress at any given time. For example, the state of New York estimated that, during the 1978–79 school year there were an additional 6,000 children with handicapping conditions served by other state agencies, and more than 500,000 students designated not as handicapped but as pupils with special educational needs. If we use the same percentage figure (20 percent) for these two populations, it is possible that there were an additional 100,000+ emotionally troubled children in New York State schools during the 1978–79 academic year.

Item: The state of New York has indicated the following needs for additional teachers of seriously emotionally disturbed children (Division for the Education of Pupils with Handicapping Conditions, 1980–81 State Plan):

- Projected number of personnel needed to meet the full educational op-portunities goal for seriously emotionally disturbed children in 1980–81 is 223 teachers (more than 1/4 of the total of 802 needed special education teachers).

- The same projection for the 1981–82 year is 396 teachers. For the 1982–83 year, there is a projected need for 578 teachers of seriously emo-tionally disturbed youngsters.

- These figures do not include (and the data are not yet available for) pro-jected teachers needed to serve less seriously (mildly and moderately) disturbed children, or regular classroom teachers who need additional training to serve troubled children.

Item: A recent review of federally funded personnel preparation programs in emotional disturbance (Brown & Palmer, 1977) points out that the need for more teachers may be magnified by the need for differently trained teachers:

> With Public Law 94-142, most special class teachers will be confronted with a greatly changed teaching situation. Most mildly to moderately emotionally disturbed pupils now in special classes will in all likelihood be mainstreamed, while more severely disturbed pupils will be placed in public school special classes. However, most special class teachers of emotionally disturbed children have little or no experience with the most severely disturbed population. Special educators also are likely to assume more of a consulting role with regular class teachers who have exceptional pupils mainstreamed into their classrooms. Yet, there are few inservice training programs to help special educators develop the necessary consulting skills for this new role [p. 174].

Item: According to the *National Needs Analysis in Behavior Disorders* (Grosenick & Huntze, 1979), "The most glaring concern that exists in the area of behavior disorders is the staggering number of children with behavior problems who remain unserved" (p. 6).

Clearly, the state of the art in the provision of services to troubled children reflects Heller and Monahan's (1977) community psychology themes: the need for prevention, and the necessity for focusing intervention efforts on broader ecological levels. The findings cited by Heller and Monahan (1977)—questionable effectiveness of mental health services, in-equities in service delivery, staggeringly high needs for service, critical shortages of trained personnel, etc.—apply directly to our efforts with troubled children as cited in the above items.

In summary, we can look once again at the recent *National Needs Analysis in Behavior Disorders* conducted by Grosenick and Huntze (1979).

Based on their review of pertinent findings from the *Report to the President from the President's Commission on Mental Health* (1978), *Children in Adult Jails* (Children's Defense Fund, 1978), the annual *Gallup Poll* of public attitudes toward public schools (as reported in the *Phi Delta Kappan*, September 1979), and other sources, Grosenick and Huntze noted:

> Granting the diversity of this data, it appears reasonable to assume that the phenomenon of emotional disturbance is widespread throughout the United States. If one narrows the focus to only children and youth ages 3 to 21, the size of the problem is still formidable. Looking only at seriously emotionally disturbed children, as delineated by the Bureau of Education for the Handicapped (BEH), it is *conservatively* estimated that two percent of children and youth ages 3 to 21 require special education because of their emotional disturbance. The current estimate of school age population (5 to 17) is 51,317,000. Using the conservative figure of two percent of the school age population as having a serious emotional disturbance so as to require special education, then 1,026,340 of these children and youth would need this special education. Data from State Plans and from Public Law 89-313 programs indicate there are 284,645 seriously emotionally disturbed children who are receiving special education. *This means that there are approximately 741,000 seriously emotionally disturbed children not currently receiving special education* [pp. 9-10, emphasis added].

The fact that a conservative estimate indicates that nearly three-quarters of a million seriously disturbed children are not receiving a special education is certainly cause for alarm. It must be emphasized that the figures presented by Grosenick and Huntze (1979) above do not include youngsters who are believed to be mildly or moderately disturbed, making the gap between the need for service and the provision of service even wider. The need for an ecological approach that stresses comprehensive services and prevention is certainly supported by the figures cited above and by the following summary conclusion reached by Grosenick and Huntze (1979):

> Conceptualization, identification, and treatment of children with behavior disorders is a fragmented and formidable problem. As previously indicated, manpower shortages are massive. Consensus has not been reached regarding who is disordered, much less what constitutes severe disorders. Professionals have not resolved the issue of appropriate educational programming for secondary students with behavior disorders, and the interdisciplinary collaboration that has occurred has been insufficient to determine overall, unified ways of providing services to behavior disordered children and youth. [p. 16]

As noted above, one of the major areas of confusion has to do with definitions of emotional disturbance or behavior disorders. The next section of this chapter will focus on the problem of definitions more completely.

DEFINITIONS OF EMOTIONAL DISTURBANCE

Ironically, despite the prevalence of youngsters labeled "emotionally disturbed" in schools and mental health centers around the country, it is exceedingly difficult to agree on a definition for that term. Hobbs (1975) describes the range of meanings that we give to emotional disturbance:

> Emotional disturbance is a generic term referring to conditions ranging from mild and temporary reactions to profound and prolonged disabilities. There are numerous related terms: adjustment problems of childhood, behavior disorders, mental illness, neurosis, childhood schizophrenia, infantile autism. In each instance, what is observed and classified is the child's behavior, although inferences are frequently made about underlying physical or psychological processes [p. 55].

Public Law 94:142 defines serious emotional disturbance in the following way:

> Seriously emotionally disturbed is defined as follows: (i) The term means a condition exhibiting one or more of the following characteristics over a long period of time and to a marked degree, which adversely affects educational performance: (a) an inability to learn which cannot be explained by intellectual, sensory, or health factors; (b) an inability to build or maintain satisfactory interpersonal relationships with peers and teachers; (c) inappropriate types of behavior or feelings under normal circumstances; (d) a general pervasive mood of unhappiness or depression, or (e) a tendency to develop physical symptoms or fears associated with personal or school problems (ii) The term includes children who are schizophrenic or autistic. The term does not include children who are socially maladjusted, unless it is determined that they are seriously emotionally disturbed [Federal Register, 8/23/77 p. 42478].

This definition, which has created considerable controversy in the field (Raiser & Van Nagel, 1980; Kauffman, 1980), is based on a definition developed by Bower and Lambert (1971) who described emotional disturbance as the involvement of a youngster in one or more of the following behavior patterns.

1. An inability to learn which cannot be traced to other factors;
2. An inability to relate satisfactorily with peers or adults;
3. Inappropriate reactions to normal stimuli and events;
4. Pervasive unhappiness;
5. The development of physical symptoms as a frequent response to stress.

Bower and Lambert pointed out that if a youngster is to be identified as emotionally disturbed, according to this definition, he or she should demonstrate more than one of these behavior patterns to a *marked degree* over a *prolonged period* of time.

The confusion caused by the Public Law 94:142 definition relates to the clause appended to the Bower and Lambert description that stipulates the noninclusion of youngsters who are socially maladjusted but not emotionally disturbed. Kauffman (1980) has noted that "The addition of that clause makes the definition nonsensical by any conventional logic" (p. 524), and has decried the bureaucratic entanglements that the definition will bring on: "That is the kind of ambiguity of language and frailty of logic that keeps lawyers busy and drives decent people insane" (p. 524).

Raiser and Van Nagel (1980) point out that the term "behavior disorders" is used by many to include both emotionally disturbed and socially maladjusted youngsters, though it may be difficult to separate the groups on the basis of overt behavior. Since special education has always responded to the full range of behavior-disordered children, Raiser and Van Nagel see their exclusion as a serious problem for the delivery of services to such youngsters.

Cowen (1978) has stated that children need to do two things in school: they must learn, and they must adjust (p. 51). In fact, many children do not learn, countless others do not adjust, and all too many youngsters fail to meet either demand. Often such youngsters also fail to get the help they need from our woefully inadequate service-delivery system. Raiser and Van Nagel's point is that we must continue to try to meet the needs of the full range of behavior-disordered children; Cowen's point is that we need to increase our efforts to prevent the development of "crystallized 'end-state' conditions" (p. 52) with such a poor prognosis for change.

Reinert (1980) has compiled a list of definitions of emotional disturbance including:

A child is disturbed when his behavior is so inappropriate that regular class attendance (a) would be disrupting for the rest of the class, (b) would place undue pressure on the teacher, or (c) further the disturbance of the pupil. (Pate, 1963, p. 242)

Behavioral disabilities are defined as a variety of excessive, chronic, deviant behaviors ranging from impulsive and aggressive to depressive and withdrawal acts (a) which violate the perceiver's expectations of appropriateness and (b) which the perceiver wishes to see stopped. (Graubard, 1973, p. 246)

A behavior deviation is that behavior of a child which (a) has a detrimental effect on his development and adjustment and/or (b) interferes with the lives of other people. (Kirk, 1962, p. 330)

One who because of organic and/or environmental influences, chronically displays: (a) inability to learn at a rate commensurate with his intellectual, sensory-motor and physical development, (b) inability to establish and maintain adequate social relationships, (c) inability to respond appropriately in day to day life situations, and (d) a variety of excessive behavior ranging from hyperactive, impulsive responses to depression and withdrawal. (Haring, 1963, p. 291)

The child who cannot or will not adjust to the socially acceptable norms for behavior and consequently disrupts his own academic progress, the learning efforts of his classmates, and interpersonal relations (Woody, 1969, p. 7) [Reinert, 1977, pp. 3-4].

Clearly, as can be seen in the definitions cited above and as Grosenick and Huntze (1979) noted, there is little agreement as to what constitutes an emotional disturbance. One useful definition comes from Reinert (1977), who does not use the label "emotionally disturbed" but defines "children in conflict" as follows:

The child whose manifest behavior has a deleterious effort on his personal or educational development and/or the personal or educational development of his peers. Negative effects may vary considerably from one child to another in terms of severity and prognosis [p. 5].

Reinert (1977) cites four major behaviors that are subsumed under his definition; acting-out, withdrawing, defensive, and disorganized.

Obviously, as Kauffman (1980) has pointed out, "A definition does not remove the need for clinical judgment" (p. 524). We still need to give careful consideration to the ways in which children meet the demands of their environments. Some of the major areas in which youngsters might demonstrate distress include a variety of day-to-day activities: eating, playing, sleeping, etc. Some general signs of emotional disturbance might include an inability to have fun, unidimensional or rigid behavior, and tension (which may be evidenced in a variety of ways). Specifically, we would want to examine a child's capacity to relate effectively to peers and adults, function satisfactorily in school settings, adapt to everyday demands, find aspects of life to enjoy, and make informed judgments.

It is important to examine the ways in which a youngster meets the demands of everyday life. Does he withdraw into himself when faced with a dilemma? Does she vent her anger on inappropriate and innocent targets? Do they regress to earlier developmental stages, falling ever farther behind their peers? Children who end up being labeled emotionally disturbed or behavior disordered may fit the "empty bucket syndrome" described by Whittaker (1975, p. 227). That is, such youngsters may be characterized by the following common clusters of problems:

1. Poorly developed impulse control—low frustration tolerance, inability to delay gratification, disruptive outbursts, temper tantrums, aggression as

characteristic way to deal with problems, propensity for "contagion," etc.

2. *Low self-image*—view of self as bad or stupid or trouble, fatalistically negative view of future, lack of success experiences, etc.
3. *Poorly developed modulation of emotion*—inability to deal appropriately with own or others' feelings, difficulty in expressing and/or understanding emotions, emotional lability.
4. *Relationship deficits*—fear of closeness and of adults, avoidance of contact, overdependence on others, manipulation of others, overdemandingness, difficulty in entering peer groups, lack of social skills, stereotypic reactions to others.
5. *Family pain and strain*—upsets in family system, guilt, divided loyalties, parental effect on children and children's impact on parents.
6. *Special learning disabilities*—specific problems in learning of undetermined origin, negative academic and/or interpersonal school experiences, etc.
7. *Limited play skills*—limited repertoire and overload on one or two activities, inability to play alone or in groups, behavioral disruptions, etc.

Whittaker notes that youngsters who fit the "empty bucket" syndrome have failed to develop emotional, social, and physical competence and confidence intrapersonally, interpersonally, and externally. Such children may seem like buckets whose bottoms are filled with holes; no matter how much water one pours into it, the bucket remains empty.

Another useful framework for consideration of troubled youngsters stems from Reinert's (1980) description:

> Most of the behaviors attributed to children in conflict are normal behaviors; at least they are normal if one considers that normal children will sometimes cheat, or lie, or act out aggressive feelings by hitting other children. What often makes these behaviors deviant, and the children who exhibit them in conflict, is the fact that the behaviors *are exhibited* in the wrong places, at the wrong time, in the presence of the wrong people, and to an inappropriate degree [p. 18].

Such a definition calls to mind the perspective of Ullman and Krasner (1969) on abnormal behavior:

> Behavior which is called abnormal must be studied as the interaction of three variables: the behavior itself, its social context, and an observer who is in a position of power. *No specific behavior is abnormal in itself.* Rather, an individual may do something (e.g., verbalize hallucinations, hit a person, collect rolls of toilet paper, refuse to eat, stutter, stare into space, or dress sloppily) under a set of circumstances (e.g. during a school class, while working at his desk, during a church service) which upsets, annoys, angers or strongly

disturbs somebody (e.g. employer, teacher, parent, or the individual himself) sufficiently that some action results (e.g. a policeman is called, seeing a psychiatrist is recommended, commitment proceedings are started) so that the society's professional labelers (e.g. physicians, psychiatrists, psychologists, judges, social workers) come into contact with the individual and determine which of the current sets of labels (e.g. schizophrenic reaction, sociopathic personality, anxiety reaction) is most appropriate. Finally, there follow attempts to change the emission of the offending behavior (e.g. institutionalization, psychotherapy, medication) [p. 21, emphasis added].

While the perspective cited above serves as the basis for Ullman and Krasner's behavioral orientation to abnormal behavior, we can also find it useful ecologically. It is important to recognize the interactional process involving an identified child, his or her "system," and a powerful representative of society (professional labeler), in the production of emotional disturbances. From an ecological viewpoint, the entire interactional process and all its elements—not the child alone—should be seen as potential targets for intervention plans.

It is important to recognize the confusing reality of diagnosing emotional disturbance. In Hobbs' (1975) words,

A particular child, for example, may be regarded as mentally ill by a psychiatrist, as emotionally disturbed by a psychologist, and as behavior disordered by a special educator [p. 57].

In a discussion of early infantile autism, Schopler (1978) points out the confusion created by overlapping diagnostic categories and notes how this dilemma may have led to our overdependence on the all-encompassing "emotional disturbance" category:

If a child was evaluated at the Putnam Center in Boston, he would be called atypical (Rank, 1949). Mahler (1952) introduced symbiotic psychosis in New York. In the same city, Goldfarb (1961) and Bender (1953) used childhood schizophrenia, and Ekstein (1954) on the west coast referred to borderline psychosis. . . . This lack of consensus among leading professionals resulted in the use of a catch-all category—like emotionally disturbed, in which normal misbehavior was no longer distinguished from any other form [p. 83].

Difficult as it is to agree on a definition of emotional disturbance, it is even harder to communicate what we mean by mental health. We can define it negatively of course, as the absence of emotional disturbance, but that is not a very productive or useful concept in our efforts with troubled youngsters. Perhaps most useful is the definition provided by Ringness (1968); "Mental Health consists of being able to function successfully in terms of one's own goals, abilities, and opportunities within the context of one's social and physical environment." (p. 12)

According to Ringness (1968), then, a mentally healthy person:

1) is self-acceptant and has reasonably high self-esteem, feels generally adequate, but recognizes his own shortcomings and seeks to improve;
2) has a realistic evaluation of himself and sets his aspirations accordingly;
3) accepts responsibility for managing his own life and making his own decisions and does not vacillate or lean upon others;
4) is well-balanced, flexible, and consistent in his attitudes, goals, and ideals;
5) can withstand stress, tolerate some anxiety, and overcome the effects of trauma and frustration;
6) can relate well to others and has the good of society at heart;
7) seeks independence, autonomy, and self-direction and is neither completely conforming nor completely selfish;
8) attempts to solve his problems, rather than to escape them or to employ defense mechanisms excessively [Ringness, 1968, p. 16].

While confusion about definitions of emotional disturbance and mental health will undoubtedly continue for some time, there have been some recent efforts to conceptualize the major approaches to work with disturbed children more clearly, as discussed in the next section of this chapter.

MAJOR PERSPECTIVES IN THE EDUCATION OF DISTURBED CHILDREN

Some years back Bill Rhodes and a number of colleagues undertook an extensive study of the major theoretical and programmatic approaches to the education of troubled children in America. The results of their work (The Conceptual Project on Child Variance) were published throughout the 1970s and have become the basis for the consideration of approaches to special educators' work with troubled children. Capsule descriptions of the approaches are presented here. Later chapters will describe some of the approaches in more detail.

Biophysical

Behavioral deviation results solely or primarily from biological and physical factors and has many of the same characteristics as physical illness. There may be necessary biogenetic predispositions that result in emotional disturbances if triggered by particular environmental conditions. Applications of the theory are focused primarily on supporting the "medical model" of intervention, consulting with pediatricians, supporting children undergoing physiological changes (surgery, special diets, new glasses), and planning educational programs to include children on medication.

Psychodynamic

The disturbed child has not successfully "worked through" the intrapsychic conflicts that he faced in the process of psychological and physical development. Personality is composed of id, ego, and superego, three hypothetical systems that work together in supportive harmony in mentally healthy children but which are in conflict within the psyche of a maladjusted child. Children must pass through a series of difficult developmental stages on the way to mature adulthood.

Psychodynamic theory has had a very significant influence on work with troubled children. Some applications include milieu therapy, life-space interviewing, play therapy, the use of art, music, and dance in therapy, classrooms in psychiatric clinics, and many more.

Behavioral

Behavioral deviance is maladaptive behavior that has been learned and maintained through the effects of reinforcement and punishment. Behaviorists generally believe that it is nonproductive to look for causes of behavior or to use the label "emotionally disturbed." They prefer to observe the deviant behavior and the environment in which it occurs and describe it as completely as possible as the first step in change.

Applications of behavioral therapy are based on the notion that any behavior that is learned can be "unlearned" and that new, more appropriate behavior can be learned to replace that which was deviant. A variety of behavioral systems exist for this purpose, including operant conditioning, contingency management, and modeling.

Both the behavioral and psychodynamic models will be described more completely in Chapter 3.

Counter Theory

Counter theorists do not accept any of the major theories as satisfactory. Though they represent a broad range of viewpoints, they hold in common a strong belief that traditional approaches to the education of "troubled children" have by and large failed. Some particular concerns are the irrelevancy of the school curriculum, the damaging effects of "labeling" children, and the inability of traditional school organization to allow children more of a voice in their own education. There are a multitude of diverse applications of counter-theoretical thought, but one major example focuses on the "Free School" movement as espoused by A.S. Neill and others.

Sociological/Ecological

In sociological theory, deviance is regarded from a much broader social context that examines the effects of social forces on individuals, rule breaking in society, the process of labeling. Ecological theory sees disturbance in the interaction between a child and his community, since the child's behavior is only part of the problem. Both theories recognize the totality and comprehensiveness of the "emotional disturbance" problem. Although it might be neater and quicker to look for deviance within the individual, interventions based on these theories must focus on the interactions between individual and community as well.

While all of the major models utilized in work with troubled children (psychodynamic, behavioral, biophysical, and sociological) agree that internal and external forces operate together to produce human behavior, they differ significantly in emphasis. Both the psychodynamic and the biophysical models are primarily concerned with the definition and understanding of internal forces. Psychodynamic theorists focus primarily on "needs" and "drive" while biophysical theorists emphasize physiological conditions which may lead to certain typical behavior patterns.

The behavioral and sociological models, on the other hand, are concerned mainly with external forces. The behavior theorists work to understand the stimulus-response patterns and to describe the reinforcing and punishing conditions in the environment which produce particular patterns of behavior. Sociologists are more concerned with the wider environment (including institutions, communities, culture, and society) in their efforts to understand forces which can produce particular behaviors by individuals and groups of individuals. More recently, ecological theory has been used as a way to understand emotional disturbance that is conceptually broader than the more traditional models described above. Contrary to the narrower models, ecologists insist that both internal and external forces must be acknowledged, and further, that it is the interaction between them which always accounts for behavior.

Figure 1.1 graphically depicts the relationship of these five major models.

The ecological orientation stresses the importance of examining a child's entire "life space" for the sources of disturbance. Disturbance is seen as a mismatch between a child's abilities and the demands of his or her environment. Consequently, either an increase in a child's skills or a decrease in environmental pressures can prevent the ocurrence of school situations that produce or exacerbate disturbance. Ecological intervention programs for troubled children are based on the following assumptions.

1. Each child is an inseparable part of a small social system. The context in which youngsters live is important and children cannot be arbitrarily

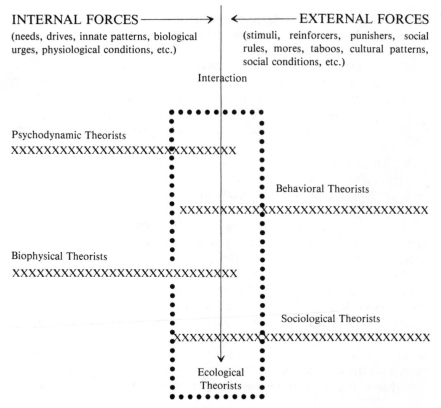

Fig. 1.1. Major theories in emotional disturbance (After Morse, Smith, & Acker, 1978).

separated out of systems for intervention purposes. Working with children in isolation from their environments is not likely to be very successful.

2. Disturbance is not viewed as a disease located within the body of the child, but rather as discordance (a lack of balance) in the system. When a child's behavior is congruent or in harmony with the norms of his or her system, disturbance does not exist. Disruption in the system equals emotional disturbance.

3. Discordance may be defined as a disparity between an individual's abilities and the demands or expectations of the environment—a "failure to match" between child and system. It is not the child alone or the environment alone that causes emotional disturbance. Rather it is the interaction between them that creates discordance and disrupts the system.

4. The goal of any intervention is to make the system work, and to make it work, ultimately, without the intervention. There is no disturbance when

systems are in balance. Interventions should be planned to help systems correct and ultimately maintain themselves.

5. Improvement in any part of the system can benefit the entire system. Since all elements of the system impact on one another, it is possible to intervene in one area and see results in another. Consequently, the way to help a child is not necessarily to focus on the youngster him or herself. It may be more productive to direct efforts to another part of the system.

6. This broader view of disturbance gives rise to three major areas for intervention:
   a. changing the child;
   b. changing the environment; and
   c. changing attitudes and expectations.

Clearly, there are options in our choice of intervention targets. If we believe we are faced with a systems problem, we must direct our efforts and energies to any and all aspects of the systems that confront us.

While specific, uniquely ecological intervention techniques do not really exist, it is possible to adapt methods developed in other conceptual models to fit into an ecological framework. What is unique about ecological intervention strategies is their constant focus on improving the fit between a given youngster's behavior and the surrounding setting(s). Interventions may focus on any system element but in all cases, as Morse, Smith, and Acker (1978) point out, the goal of such efforts is not to cure a child of his emotional disturbance, but rather to increase the concordance in the child's system.

SUMMARY AND CONCLUSIONS

To summarize, the need for more, and more effective, educational programs for children labeled emotionally disturbed continues to increase. If we expect to make progress in our efforts to serve such youngsters, the needs for new kinds of service-delivery systems and new training programs for the people who will staff such systems must be filled. An ecological approach has much to offer in this regard. Further, the ecological orientation has been utilized increasingly frequently by professionals in a wide range of human services, as more and more people recognize the applicability of this broader conceptual framework to the complex problems of troubled children in today's world.

For example, Hartman (1974) has noted

That the generic stance in social work practice could be highly congruent with the goals, objectives, and functions of the family agency and that students educated to practice across methods, boundaries, and with systems of different sizes are well suited for creative family agency practice [p. 200].

Auerswald (1970) described both interdisciplinary and ecological systems approaches and found the latter to have the following advantages:

> It focuses precisely on the interfaces and communication processes taking place there . . . it insists that the structure, sources, pathways, repository sites and integratial functions of messages became clear in addition to their content . . . this, plus the holistic non-exclusive nature of the approach, minimizes the dangers of excessive selectivity in the collection of data and allows for much more clarity in the contextual contributions to its analysis [p. 204].

In the same article, Auerswald describes his efforts to develop a neighborhood health services system, the main aim of which was to

> Find ways to avoid the fragmentation of service delivery which occurs when a person's problem is defined as belonging primarily to himself, and he is sent to a specialist who is trained to deal primarily with that type of problem [p. 206].

Auerswald contrasts this developing program with the usual result of a referral to a "specialist":

> The specialist naturally sees the problem not only as an individual matter, but defines it still further according to the professional sector he inhabits. He is not accustomed to looking at the total set of systems surrounding the individual with the symptom or to noticing the ways in which the symptom, the person, his family, and his community interlock, and he is often in the position of a man desperately trying to replace a fuse when it is the entire community power line that has broken down [pp. 206–07].

Finally, Auerswald describes the use of an ecological systems approach to the problems presented by a 12-year-old girl, Maria, and her family and concludes:

> The "ecological systems" approach literally changed the name of the game. By focusing on the nature of the transactions taking place between Maria and the identifiable systems that influenced her growth, it was possible for the "systems" psychiatrist to ascertain what strengths, lacks, and distortions existed at each interface. Two things happened when this was done.
>
> The first was that Maria's behavior began to make sense as a healthy adaptation to a set of circumstances that did not allow her to develop more socially acceptable or better differentiated means of seeking a response to her needs as a developing child. Thus, the aura of pathology was immediately left behind.
>
> The second was that the identification of lacks and distortions in the transactional arena of each interface automatically suggested what needed to be added

or changed. Thus the tasks of the helping person were automatically defined. Rigidity of technique in accomplishing these tasks could not, under those circumstances, survive. Flexibility, ingenuity, and innovation were demanded [pp. 211–12].

Although the importance of "focusing on transactions" is a critical aspect of the ecological systems approach as described by Auerswald and others, specific models for the application of such a focus to the problems of troubled children and families are not yet very well developed. Nick Hobbs (1978) pointed out:

In many ways, the most original, powerful, and as yet not fully exploited idea is the notion of the ecosystem, of the child as the defining member of a small social system made up of parents and siblings, peers, teachers, a case worker, an adult friend, and, for a limited period of time, the staff of the Re-Ed school. Our task is to help the people in the system learn how to order the system in the interest of the long-term development of the child. . . . (A) good question for a Re-ED school staff to ask itself is this: How sensitive are we to the requirements of the child's ecological system and how effective are we in helping that system to work well in the service of the child? [p. 65].

Cantrell (1974) put it another way:

Ecological psychology has attempted to look at human behavior as the product of past and current interactions of the individual with all the social-physical units within which that person exists; the view seems rich in analyzing human behavior as a part of a complex system, but it is weak in methodology for prediction or change [p. 1].

A truly ecological view of child treatment requires intervention in a number of different supporting systems to ensure continuity of care (Taylor & Alpert, 1973). In developing children's services the goal should be the development of a service net, rather than an aggregate of isolated services. In effect, what happens to a child once he or she leaves a treatment program will probably be more important than anything that happened to him while in residence. Cavior, Schmidt, and Karacki (1972, p. 3) say essentially this in explaining the discrepancy between in-program and follow-up adjustment of juvenile offenders from a sophisticated behavior modification treatment program.

In fact, what happens within any particular program for troubled children may in the long run be less important than the linkages developed between programs. According to Whittaker (1975): "(S)uccessful treatment programs will be those that actively seek to develop linkages with the other major systems in which the child participates, school, peer group, juvenile justice system, recreation/occupational system'' (p. 225).

Finally, it may be instructive to return for a moment to our discussion of definitions of emotional disturbance. Kauffman (1980) concluded:

> (T)hat there is no clear unambiguous definition of emotional disturbance. It is time we faced the fact that disordered behavior is whatever we choose to make it; it is not an objective thing that exists outside our arbitrary sociocultural rules [p. 524].

Unfortunately, the way we have "chosen" to operationalize emotional disturbance has often occurred in the manner described by Dunn (1973); "There has been a tendency to take pupils the regular teacher cannot handle and find something wrong with them so that they can be given a disability label" (p. 5).

The process Dunn describes has certainly been applied to children whose behavior is disturbing to significant others in schools. While the ecological orientation can surely incorporate a strong focus on providing comprehensive and coordinated services to troubled youngsters, it suggests that identified children do not "own" the disturbance and should not be the sole targets of intervention. As long as they are, to the extent that we continue to believe that the only appropriate intervention strategies are those that modify children to fit environments, we are engaged in a self-defeating enterprise which is destined for failure. The dilemmas posed by troubled children and troubled systems require broader, more comprehensive ecological and preventive strategies. The following chapters discuss critical aspects of such an approach in more detail.

2
Systems

According to Rhodes and Gibbins (1972), the prevailing conception of emotional disorders before the 14th century was a demonic one; it was believed that disturbed people were probably possessed and that religious interventions were necessary to exorcise the demons that controlled them. Thus, the church was responsibile for warding off evil.

Later, the church-state gave way to municipal governments and "city councils" took over the responsibility for disturbed people. This responsibility was affected through a variety of "relief" measures, especially the creation of asylums. Such institutions served two purposes. First, they provided care for those citizens who were unable to care for themselves. Second, they protected communities from the dangers presented by the behavior of deranged persons.

It was still later, according to Rhodes and Gibbins, that prominent physicians involved themselves with the problems of disturbed people and started the rise of the "medical model." Now, emotional disturbance was viewed as sickness and consequently, like other illnesses, was best met by a diagnostic-treatment medical response.

Though the medical model has retained much of its preeminence even now, Rhodes and Gibbins (1972) note:

Even though this latter frame of reference has a high value in community thinking today, each of the other perceptions of the problem are still active within society and influence its programs with respect to such children. They can be observed to exist side-by-side in the community and to provide alternate routes for children whom we might call emotionally disturbed. A child who repeatedly attacks other people might be called delinquent, referred to a juvenile court, and placed in a correctional facility. He might be seen as sick, diagnosed as "acting-out" or "sociopathic," and hospitalized in a mental institution. He might be seen as socially maladjusted and he and his family referred to a child service agency or family agency for intensive casework. Conceivably, he can travel each route at different times or even be caught at some stage within each route simultaneously [p. 361].

Indeed, a number of systems through which troubled children may pass do exist, depending upon both the specific nature of the youngster's behavior and the availability and accessibility of resources to that youngster and his or her family. This chapter will discuss some of the major systems that impact on the lives of troubled youngsters and families, describe the roles of the professionals who work in agencies within these systems, and raise some implications of our confused and confusing service-delivery systems for work with troubled children.

The four major systems to be discussed include: social-welfare, legal-correctional, mental health, and education. According to Rhodes and Gibbins (1972), each system creates its own network of unique elements, its own structure for delivering services. Four critical elements common to all these systems, as applied to problems of emotional disturbance, are:

1. A systematic philosophy, body of knowledge, and set of assumptions about child behavior.
2. A related group of intervention techniques.
3. A work force that has learned the philosophy and the techniques.
4. Operational patterns that bring the first three components to bear on threat-excited situations.

Figure 2.1 graphically depicts the impact on troubled youngsters of the four systems being discussed in this chapter.

SOCIAL-WELFARE SYSTEM

While not really geared up to respond to the special needs of troubled youngsters, the social-welfare system has frequent contact with disturbed children and youth. Such contacts frequently occur when the social-welfare system, through its case workers, attempts to provide aid and protection to youngsters believed to be in need of such services.

Social-welfare agencies are required to provide a variety of services to eligible clients. According to Unger (1974), there are three major types of services: follow-up of initial referral to determine eligibility and acceptance into the system, on-going short-term service delivery, and responses to emergency or crisis requests that demand immediate action. Unger (1974) also lists ten major specific services for children offered by the Michigan

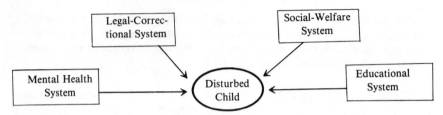

Fig. 2.1. Systems impacting on troubled children.

Department of Social Services as representative of the typical range of social-welfare services available:

1. Adoption;
2. Alternate care for children (foster, relative or group house or half-way house);
3. Comprehensive services for youth (services for youth with emotional, behavioral, or retardation problems; alternative treatment and placement methods and on-going services for delinquents);
4. Day care services (individual placement for less than a twenty-four hour period in a substitute home placement);
5. Education services (compensation for lack of formal education and support for a child experiencing school difficulties);
6. Family planning services (social, educational and medical service to help voluntarily limit family size);
7. Health services (mental and physical health information and resources from specialized professionals);
8. Home and family management services (services to strengthen the family);
9. Protective services for children (services to correct conditions of neglect, abuse, and exploitation, including legal home removal if necessary);
10. Services to children with special needs (information and specialized rehabilitative services for eligible handicapped individuals) [Unger, 1974, pp. 378-79].

In addition, the Michigan Department of Social Services provides seven major services primarily relating to adults or relating equally to both adults and children. These include alternate care for adults, emergency services (temporary shelter, food, etc.), employment services (for counseling and training opportunities), housing services, protective services for adults (to compensate for conditions caused by age, handicap, illness, neglect, abuse, etc.), transportation services, and volunteer services.

System Operations

The delivery of services through the social-welfare system usually works according to the following general sequence of steps.

1. The eligibility of the client is determined (in an "Intake Interview") and a case manager is assigned. The case manager becomes the coordinator of all services delivered to the client and works with the client to analyze the current difficulties and develop an appropriate intervention plan (a process known as service planning).
2. When the initial service-planning process has been completed, the case manager works to facilitate the fast and effective delivery of agreed-upon services to the client.
3. The client continues to receive service until:
   a. The goal(s) of the service plan has been reached and service is no longer required;
   b. The goal has not been reached, but the client has made progress and services have been exhausted; or
   c. The client no longer desires service. At this point, service is terminated.
4. If the client requires further service and is still eligible, the process begins again with a new intake interview.

Staff Functions

While there are a variety of staff service specialists (Unger lists ten; intake, employment, family and youth self-support, family and youth self-care, family and youth community-based care, family and youth institutional care, adult self-support, adult self-care, adult community-based care, adult institutional care) involved in this system, the critical staff role in the social-welfare system is that of social worker or case worker.

Social workers may respond to the needs of their clients in a variety of ways. They may provide direct service, acting in the role of counselor or therapist. They may offer more indirect assistance as well, by acting as a consultant to other professionals or by assisting efforts to organize communities and bring about improved environmental conditions. Unger describes four major approaches to social casework. They are capsulized in Table 2.1.

Problems in the System

Troubled children are frequently less than adequately served by the social-welfare system. Youngsters with emotional and behavioral difficulties often also become designated as "hard to place" and case workers may become very frustrated in their efforts to find suitable placements for such children.

Protective services are designed to prevent youngsters from suffering physical or emotional harm and are available on an around-the-clock basis. Issues related to emotional disturbance are also intimately involved in this area in a number of ways. Clearly, youngsters who are subjected to physical

Table 2.1.   Approaches to Social Casework

Functional

The client is the source of change. The caseworker is a helper (not a "treater") whose goal is to enable the client to discover and utilize his or her own power for positive change. When such individual changes occur, society will benefit and ultimately the relationship between man and society will be improved.

Problem Solving

Life is comprised of a continual series of problems to be resolved and clients need help to improve their problem-solving skills. The case worker provides help by adding motivation, capacities, and opportunities, with the goal of helping clients change from being "problem-victims" to become "problem solvers."

Psychosocial

Problems are located in the interactions between the client and his or her surrounding system, especially the family. The case worker tries to help clients change unhealthy interactions and thereby restore their systems to some semblance of balance and harmony.

Behavior Modification

The case worker is trained in skills of behavior modification and uses the laws of learning to help clients change their deviant behavior. Workers catalogue clients' observable responses, identify problem areas, elicit client cooperation, and formulate treatment plans that strengthen selected positive behavior and extinguish negative behavior.

Source: After Unger, 1974.

and psychological abuse are at high risk for developing serious emotional disturbances. Interestingly, some parents may resort to abusive tactics in response to their children's otherwise uncontrollable behaviors. That is to say, the difficulties presented by unserved disturbed youngsters may in some cases lead to a very inappropriate parental reaction which only serves to complicate the problems of the children.

Levinson (1969) reported that the longer a family received assistance, the more likely it was that it would have children with serious emotional problems. Such a finding may be due in large part to the problems in the social-welfare system. In addition to the typical weaknesses of a variety of large and institutionalized systems (confusion about staff roles and responsibilities, inefficient administration, continual breakdowns in communication, inaccessible records, inadequate numbers of staff, etc.) the social-welfare system may be particularly vulnerable to what Unger (1974) has called "fragmentation of the client" (p. 390):

Not only do workers not know what is expected of them, but no economical, fair, and high quality methods have ever been developed to deliver adequate services to child and adult clients when they need them. One of the largest obstacles to effective improvement has been client "fragmentation": the fact that no single worker has had overall responsibility for the coordination of all services received by a client.

The practical effects of client fragmentation may mean that a child might wait for much needed services for months. . . .

The result of this delay, no matter what the reason, is often a worsening of the problem or the creation of additional problems, including, in both instances, emotional disturbance [p. 348].

LEGAL-CORRECTIONAL SYSTEM

For troubled youngsters who come in contact with the law, society's response is usually correctional; children and youth found to be in violation of the law are often incarcerated in the hope that enforced attendance in a correctional institution will help them change their inappropriate behavior.

Currently, such behavior change objectives must be seen as part of an overall goal of rehabilitation of the young offender. Previously, the purpose of incarceration might have been viewed as punishment or even as the formal mechanism by which society revenges its wrongs. In other periods, it was hoped that legal-correctional system interventions would prevent future violations; deterrence was the primary goal.

A great many of the rehabilitation programs currently in use are based on principles of behavior modification and group counseling efforts. Individual psychotherapy has not been particularly effective with this population.

SYSTEM OPERATIONS

A number of stages in the legal-correctional process have been identified. Here we can briefly examine four major elements: "station-house adjudication"; petition and authorization; detection, waiver hearings, preliminary exam; and adjudication and disposition.

Station-house adjudication is the term used to describe the official or informal warnings given by police to youngsters, usually in the station house. The critical aspect of these warnings is that they represent the only action of the system with regard to this particular violation; no further steps are taken. Station-house adjudications are *very* common. In one recent year in Chicago, such warnings outnumbered court referrals by about two to one (26,000 station-house adjudications: 13,000 court referrals [Atkinson, 1974]).

Petition and authorization is the next step and represents the beginning of the more formal court referral process. In this phase, court intake staff (varying from a contingent of highly trained social workers to a judge's clerical assistant) contact the petitioner (frequently the police), parents and child, friends, school authorities, and others, in an effort to gather appropriate information concerning the complaint or violation. While the court cannot compel the cooperation of any individual in this process, it is empowered to begin unofficial interventions at this time.

The next phase includes a variety of potential dispositions that the court may make in preliminary stages of the case. Should the child be examined? Should treatment as a juvenile offender be waived so that the youngster may be tried as an adult? What further information might be needed based on the data provided in a preliminary examination?

For example, the court may need to decide if a particular youngster needs to be confined to a correctional facility immediately. In Michigan, such a decision might be made if the following conditions applied:

1. No other placement was available or appropriate for the youngster.
2. Home conditions require immediate removal.
3. The youngster is a runaway or other evader of legal custody.
4. The youngster presents a danger to public safety.
5. The youngster is in need of observation and/or treatment by experts [Atkinson, 1974].

Finally, during the adjudication phase, the intake department presents the case to the court. The judge may act on the case in a variety of ways: by issuing a warning; by placing the child in any one of a number of settings (group home, training school, private setting); by putting the youngster on probation, etc. Once the adjudication has been made, the case is moved from the intake department to the appropriate arm of the court for disposition.

Facilities and Programs

The legal-correctional system utilizes a variety of programs and facilities to rehabilitate the youngsters in its charge. Training schools (previously known as reform schools) are one of the basic longstanding programs in this system. Typically located relatively near urban centers, training schools are usually very regimented and controlled settings. Though staffed by people known as counselors, the atmosphere in the setting may effectively change their role to that of "guard." There is usually a shortage of clinical and educational services and many training schools have been phased out in recent years.

Group homes are becoming more common as the training school approach loses favor. These programs represent a critical aspect of the deinstitutionalization movement as they provide the basis for maintaining a variety of previously institutionalized people in local communities. Group counseling and interaction form the core of the treatment program. Often, behavioral contracts such as point systems serve as the basic management plan in the home.

Probation is another mainstay of the legal-correctional system's programs. Simply defined, probation is the maintenance of a youthful offender in the community under the supervision of the court (in the person of a probation officer). As part of the conditions of probation, a youngster may be requested to:

1. Report to his or her probation officer on a regular basis.
2. Attend job training, counseling, and placement activities.
3. Participate in appropriate community activities.

Problems in the System

As with all systems, a number of problems can be identified in the operations of the legal-correctional system. For example, training of staff at all levels varies widely. The judge may be a political appointee, totally unfamiliar with the needs of troubled youth, or a highly trained and experienced jurist in this area. The court staff might vary from one part-time clerk/bailiff/probation officer to a full complement of trained and experienced workers divided into appropriate departments and divisions (intake, probation, detention, after-care, etc.).

The attorneys appointed to serve as legal advocates for youngsters referred to court may have little knowledge of the system's programs and facilities. In turn, each program has particular issues to contend with as well: probation officers are often saddled with case loads that make attention to individual needs nearly impossible in most cases; group home programs have difficulty avoiding the overuse of coercion and threats of "going back to the institution"; training schools are burdened by the usual problems built into institutional models. Even excellent residential programs face the "deviant subgroup" dilemma; what chances do even "model" trainees have to stay out of difficulty when they leave the training school and return to the same environment which proved so problematic for them in the past?

MENTAL HEALTH SYSTEM

According to Sagor (1974):

> If a child has to be "sent away" because of his or her deviant behavior, parents favor entrusting the child to a system which is ideologically committed

to the development of human potential and individual aspirations (mental health), rather than to a system whose operational implications are the necessities and protection of the body-politic (legal-correctional system). Whether or not this dichotomy is actual as some insist, or a polite fiction as others suggest, the mental health system advertises its ideological commitment as an advocate for the individual [p. 224].

Sagor goes on to point out four major aspects of mental health ideology:

1. Mental illness can be identified, treated, and cured.
2. All problems of living which affect mental well-being are appropriate concerns of the mental health system.
3. The mental health approach to deviant behavior is the most humane and scientific available.
4. The treatment and prevention of Mental Illness should move beyond the hospital and clinic to the community at large [p. 276].

The concept of "mental health" may be one of the fuzziest and most difficult notions to define. As Jahoda (1958) has noted:

There is hardly a term in current psychological thought as vague, elusive, and ambiguous as the term "mental health." That it means many things to many people is bad enough. That many people use it without even attempting to specify the idiosyncratic meaning the term has for them makes the situation worse, both for those who wish to promote mental health and for those who wish to introduce concern with mental health into systematic psychological theory and research [p. 3].

Despite the confusion and ambiguity over the concept, the mental health system has become an exceedingly popular source of service. In fact, one of the major problems in the system is the serious lack of trained personnel to meet the mental health demands of the population. This inability to meet mental health needs adequately can be traced to two obvious factors. First, demand for service has risen dramatically as the stigma of seeking help has declined. A very successful mental health information campaign has contributed to the reduced hesitancy to seek psychological services and to a revolution in the creation and public discussion of a host of therapeutic systems.

Second, the supply of trained personnel has been decreased by strict licensing and certification procedures. More importantly, the popularity of the individual psychotherapy model (one therapist: one patient) has perpetuated a very ineffective use of psychological resources.

Personnel

Psychiatry. Almost since the time that physicians took over responsibility for the treatment of insane and feebleminded people, psychiatry has been the predominant discipline in the mental health system. In addition to their responsibility in state institutions, psychiatrists' influence soon spread to clinics and other programs for less severely disturbed individuals and ultimately to the wider conception of social psychiatry and community mental health.

Sagor (1974) reports that although child psychiatry was not a formally established medical specialty until 1960, psychiatric techniques for treating children have a much longer history. Dating back to the work of Anna Freud and the early years of the child guidance clinic movement, such techniques include psychoanalysis, play therapy, group therapy, the "open approach" (open discussion by therapists with child and parents in a manner suggestive of modern family therapy), relationship therapy, and social treatment (an early form of consultation).

Psychology. The involvement of psychologists in the mental health system was changed dramatically by World War II. Before that time, psychologists were very academically oriented, involved in the measurement of mental abilities and individual differences. The trauma of the war created severe needs for direct service and psychologists were pressed into new roles as psychodiagnosticians and psychotherapists. Immediately after the war, the discipline of clinical psychology was born. Clinical psychologists are now trained to provide services very similar to those offered by psychiatrists, in the same kinds of settings (primarily mental hospitals and psychiatric clinics).

Social Work. Social workers usually represent the final element of the interdisciplinary mental health team. Though originally developed as part of the "settlement movement" in an effort to reduce social dysfunction, social workers now provide many of the same kinds of services offered by their colleagues in psychiatry and psychology. Many elements of social workers' roles are described in detail in the above section of this chapter on the social-welfare system.

Others. In recent years, psychiatric nursing has become another core specialty in the mental health system service-delivery model. Rehabilitation counselors are found more and more frequently in mental health systems as well. Therapy aides, activities therapists, and educators also play critical roles in the mental health system.

Interventions

Psychotherapy, in a variety of formats, has been the basis of many mental health system interventions. Some basic assumptions of a psychotherapy model include (according to Sagor):

1. The notion that it is emotionally relieving to tell a nonjudgmental empathic "other" about your troubles.
2. The possibility that the process will help a "patient" understand relationships between current problems and past events and his or her emotional responses to those events; in other words, the patient may develop *insight.*
3. Psychotherapy may be a corrective emotional experience, enabling the patient to have a stable relationship with a trusted figure who responds differently than others have in the past.
4. The therapist' careful choice of behaviors may facilitate changes in the patient's thinking, feeling, or behaving.

Psychotherapy with children often takes the form of play therapy. In this format, youngsters are encouraged to express their feelings through their play activities in a specially designated "play room." Art and music therapies are similar formats that employ different modes of expression.

Family therapy has become an increasingly popular form of treatment as therapists of all professional persuasions have come to realize the importance of working with each troubled youngster's family system. In this format, therapists see parents and children together and attempt to help them understand their roles and contributions to the family. By meeting together, the therapist and family can examine their communication patterns and, when appropriate, change these in favor of more productive models.

There are, of course, a number of problems with reliance on the psychotherapy model. For example, critics have charged that therapy takes too long, focuses too much on the past, provides little assistance to youngsters who need help with here-and-now problems, and has failed to document its long-range effectiveness.

Behavior Modification

As a result of the criticism detailed above, new formats for helping youngsters through the mental health system have developed in recent years. Foremost among these is the revolutionary increase in interventions based on learning theory; programs that everyone knows as behavior modification. Such programs begin with the observation and recording of target behaviors, continue with the determination and implementation of appropriate reinforcers, and complete the cycle by measuring the change that occurs and making appropriate revisions. The process is described more completely in the next chapter.

Chemotherapy

Another dramatically changing aspect of the mental health system has been

the so-called "pharmaceutical revolution." The development of tran-
quilizers has had a major impact on the atmosphere of state institutions, as
much of the violently aggressive behavior has been "medicated" away.

For youngsters, as with adults, chemotherapy involves the attempt to
change behavior by introducing chemicals into the body. Essentially,
chemotherapy reduces symptoms, thereby serving as a holding action
against the secondary problems that result when those symptoms (e.g.,
hyperactivity) are displayed.

Prevention

In recent years, the mental health system has become more "prevention-
oriented" (see Chapter 10). Activities in this area have been primarily
consultation- and education-oriented. For troubled youngsters, consultation with schools may be the most critical program.

Facilities and Programs

Residential treatment centers are primarily privately owned settings that
provide inpatient services mostly to seriously emotionally disturbed
youngsters. State mental hospitals also continue to provide inpatient treatment for troubled children, though their populations have been decreasing
steadily with the deinstitutionalization movement.

Outpatient clinics, based on the child-guidance model, continue to exist
and provide diagnostic and treatment services to disturbed children and
their families. Community mental health centers provide comprehensive
mental health services to a wide range of clients. Services included are: inpatient care, outpatient care, partial hospitalization, emergency services, and
community consultation and education. Community mental health centers
provide inpatient care to children and adolescents, though not very frequently to young children. When inpatient care is required, it is frequently
because the child simply has no other more "normal" place to go.

EDUCATIONAL SYSTEM

Since their initial efforts to focus on troubled children, public schools have
provided services to such youngsters through special education teachers and
school psychologists. For many years, the primary program for disturbed
children in public school was the self-contained classroom. One teacher
"taught" a small class (usually about ten children) of youngsters, all of
whom had been identified as having emotional or behavioral disorders.
Morse, Cutler, and Fink (1965) described those programs as falling into the
following seven categories:

1. *Psychiatric dynamic*—based on an individual psychotherapy model with only secondary attention to education.
2. *Psychoeducational*—a more equal focus on psychological and educational concerns.
3. *Behavioral*—systematic applications of learning theory with an emphasis on changing inappropriate behaviors.
4. *Educational*—traditional classroom routines in a controlled environment.
5. *Naturalistic*—spontaneous teacher-centered atmosphere.
6. *Primitive*—rigid, "law-and-order" approach.
7. *Chaotic*—limited classroom order and stability, frequent behavioral eruptions.

In the earlier years, self-contained classrooms were primarily based on psychodynamic principles. More recently, behavior modification has been the predominant philosophical orientation. In both cases, two things became clear: youngsters assigned to self-contained classrooms were totally segregated from their typical peers—a fact that may well have led to *increased* social isolation and alienation—and second, self-contained classrooms never did document their effectiveness in educating children who were placed there for that very purpose.

There were other educational programs existing outside the public schools at that time, primarily in day-treatment centers or residential institutions. Since the passage of Public Law 94:142, efforts to develop appropriate educational programs for disturbed youngsters in least restrictive settings have increased dramatically. Now educational systems try to provide a range of programs suitable to the needs of mildly, moderately, and seriously troubled children.

Self-contained classrooms no longer stand as the only major format for the education of troubled youngsters. More and more, such children are spending their days with their peers, participating and learning in regular classrooms with help, when appropriate, from one or more of a variety of specialists. Resource teachers (sometimes known as crisis or helping teachers) represent one critical new special education role (see Chapter 5).

Another educational system role critical to programs for troubled children is that of school psychologist. Though school psychologists have traditionally been primarily involved in diagnostic testing and evaluation, that responsibility has received a "bad press" in recent years. Serious questions about bias in psychological testing (especially intelligence tests) and the overrepresentation of minority groups in special education classes (placements typically made on the basis of those questionable tests) have combined with the discrepancy between the staggering number of youngsters potentially in need of service and the minimal number of school psychologists available to serve them to produce the following negative descriptions of school psychology:

- School Psychologists do evaluations for the purpose of producing a score that will lead to a child's removal from the regular classroom [Bersoff, 1971].

- School Psychologists serve as gatekeepers on the border between classroom teachers and special educators, though they have little communication with either group [Sabatino, 1972].

- The traditional school psychology role centers on testing. School Psychologists make infrequent classroom visits and offer impractical suggestions to teachers [Forness, 1972].

Despite the negative attitudes about what has become a stereotyped role description, school psychologists in many schools have been changing their roles in a variety of ways. In many places, psychologists have been doing less testing and more productive consultation with teachers; taking on more coordination responsibility for troubled children; developing in-service education programs for their schools, and so on.

Involvement with Other Systems

One critical aspect of the educational system's work revolves around its involvement with other systems. The great majority of youngsters identified as emotionally disturbed in school have at least some contact (official or unofficial) with at least one of the other major service-delivery systems.

For example, seriously troubled students would in all likelihood be referred by the school (preferably through contact with the family though sometimes unfortunately not) to the appropriate agency in the mental health system. After a mental health system evaluation, it might be deemed necessary to remove the child from the school (and possibly the home) so that he or she could receive more intensive assistance from the mental health system. Usually, however, this would not be necessary and the mental health and educational systems would instead develop an appropriate format for working together in the child's best interests.

Similarly, the school social worker or guidance counselor or principal or teacher might be involved in coordinated efforts with representatives of the social-welfare or legal-correctional systems. Specifically, school personnel might be involved in the referral of students to other systems, providing information for intake investigations conducted by other systems, working with agencies to provide follow-up information on youngsters returning from more restrictive settings to public school programs, and in other ways.

CHANGES NEEDED ACROSS SYSTEMS

While each of the systems which intervene with troubled youngsters has particular problems specific to its idiosyncratic concerns, all of the systems share some more general dilemmas. Following are some major areas where change is needed across systems.

More Effective Use of Resources

The tremendous number of youngsters with continuing unmet emotional needs, in spite of the conglomerate of efforts by all systems, demands that existing resources be utilized more effectively. In mental health this may be seen in a variety of efforts to develop programs that will lead to the *prevention* of emotional disturbances by reorganizing the ways in which professionals spend their time. Cowen (1978), for example, has noted that one critical element in the success of his Primary Mental Health Project in Rochester, New York, has been changing the role of school psychologist from a direct service to a "quarterbacking" function. Caplan (1964) provided a model of consultation that has changed the nature of many psychiatrists' (and others') work from one-to-one efforts with patients to consultation with others who work with similar clients.

A consultation model can help "spread the effects" by enabling a single professional to reach many more troubled people through the appropriate sharing of his or her expertise—a process that has been called "giving psychology away" (Albee, 1967). Such models might operate from a mental health base or from a school base. The Psycho-Educational Clinic developed at Yale by Sarason and his colleagues (Kaplan and Sarason, 1967), the Jowonio School Program in Syracuse, New York (Knoblock, 1978), and the Rose School in Washington, D.C. (Long, Morse, & Newman, 1965) are all examples of school-based efforts with critical consultation aspects.

Systems Reorganization

The notion that systems need to be reorganized in order to provide better service to youngsters is not new. The striking movement of a variety of educational, correctional, and mental health programs to a behavior modification philosophy and format is representative of the recognition of this need. The CASE (Contingencies Applicable to Special Education) Project conducted when the National Training School for Boys was still located in Washington, D.C. (Cohen, Filipczak, and Bis, 1967) is one example of systems reorganization at a single site. In this case, an entire program for some very difficult adolescents was redeveloped as a totally individualized token economy system. All appropriate behaviors earned points for residents and *all* rewards were purchasable for points. Rewards included the usual tangibles like food and cigarettes but points were also needed for entrance to the residents' social area, and could be used to rent more private living space on the unit.

The South Shore Mental Health Center in Quincy, Massachusetts also operates from a systems-reorganization viewpoint. In addition to the typical community mental health center's responsibility for treatment of disturbed persons, South Shore has also developed a program aimed at preventing mental disorders through consultation and education, participating in community-planned change efforts, training of professionals and of nonprofessional staff, and conducting research in their community (Rosenblum, 1968). South Shore is one mental health center focused on contributing to the reorganization of its community in ways that will improve the psychological well-being of its constituents.

Examples within the legal-correctional system include the Federal Bureau of Prison's efforts to match juvenile offenders with treatment-relevant correctional programs (Gerard, 1970). The state of New York's decision to separate the legal system's operations with juveniles into two separate tracks, one for "Persons in Need of Supervision" (PINS—youngsters who may be viewed as ungovernable by their families or schools but who may not have committed any serious crimes), and the other for juvenile delinquents, is a recent example of systems reorganization.

Systems can also be reorganized as the result of outside pressures. Perhaps the best example is the recent passage of Public Law 94:142, the Education for All Handicapped Children Act of 1975. Just a few years ago, great numbers of children in America were not receiving an education in the public schools. Many of these youngsters were denied access to school because of a particular handicapping condition. Youngsters who were thought to be emotionally disturbed or behaviorally disordered or youngsters whose actions violated formal laws or informal standards of school conduct formed one of the largest components of the unserved group.

This state of affairs continued to exist until a small number of parents coalesced into groups and began the process of seeking rights for their children. Lawyers and advocates were soon involved, the movement spread and deepened and Public Law 94:142 was the ultimate result. There remain many children today who do not go to school or who do not receive an appropriate education, but the educational system's responsibilities for troubled and other disabled children have certainly been clarified. Further, the need for all systems that respond to troubled youngsters to develop and have in place an appropriate educational component to their program has also been made clear.

Communication

In a discussion of the social-welfare system, Unger (1974) comments that

> It should be clear that a lack of communication within the social welfare
> bureaucracy and between the system and other suppliers of services (agencies,
> groups, individuals) is a problem which creates many other problems. But
> what is not clear from the above is that communication between the system
> and the client is also frequently poor. The client may wait for months for a
> much needed service and not once hear from a worker that something is being
> done and that he has not been simply forgotten or ignored [p. 398].

While the "communication problem" has become a cliché in modern
times, it is no less real in relationships between the systems we've been
discussing and troubled children and families. It is imperative that systems
find ways to overcome the rigidity that always develops in small or large
bureaucracies and that they respond to the real needs of clients. Children
and families need information about available services and if communication is to improve, such data probably need to come from a single, and what
one hopes is a trustworthy source. More and more programs and agencies
are using the role of advocate or coordinator or primary worker as a more
effective way to build a partnership between client and program.

Project Re-Ed (Hobbs, 1966), discussed in more detail in a later chapter,
paid special attention to the communication issue. By developing a new professional role—liaison-teacher—the project was able to ease the problems
associated with the movement of troubled youngsters from residential settings back to public school and community life. By recognizing the
likelihood of difficulties arising during that critical period and by proactively planning to address those problems through the new staff role, Re-Ed
was able to demonstrate considerable success in reintegrating its youngsters.

Professionalism

Professionals at work in each of the systems face similar dilemmas daily. In
light of the existing demand for their services and the inadequate time and
staff to provide adequately for youngsters' needs, how can they act as responsible members of their own profession? Nonprofessional staff, who represent the front line of all programs, except schools, face the same concerns.

Shakow (1978) has defined a good profession as being (among other
things):

1. Guided by a sense of social responsibility;
2. Less focused on building "guild" strength;
3. Honest in the representation of its abilities;

4. Ethical in relationships with clients;
5. Cooperative in relationships with other professions;
6. Continually concerned with improving its techniques and procedures.

How many professionals at work in the systems that serve troubled youngsters believe that their own professional roles match Shakow's description of a good profession? If we are to have an impact on the problems of troubled children and systems, it is imperative that professionals adopt a proactive stance about their roles in light of the qualities described by Shakow above.

CONCLUSIONS AND IMPLICATIONS

The ways in which we provide services to troubled children today are greatly influenced by the practices and programs of earlier times. The lasting effect of buildings is especially powerful, as Rhodes and Gibbins (1972) noted:

> Any social institutional form that includes buildings and facilities has a tenacious capacity for maintaining itself within the social body. These edifices have a powerful influence on the way in which communities continue to handle human problems no matter what new discoveries or methods may evolve. Institutions have an uncanny ability to coopt and absorb new discoveries of orientation and procedures into their old forms. Even when society makes a radical shift to a new major frame of reference about the human problem of "disturbance," the old institutional form persists. Under such conditions, even if new structures and edifices evolve to fit the new conceptions, the old institution may continue to exist side-by-side with the new operational pattern.

> Society seems very reluctant to fully abandon either a frame or reference or a facility that it has brought into existence to handle a human problem. Most characteristically, the new dominating frame of reference is imposed on the old one, like a new archaeological layer on an older deposit [p. 362].

Historically, intervention efforts have focused on correcting the deficit(s) in the disturbed child. This strategy of intervention may have come about because disturbed children threaten the community and require a corrective response; the dominance of the medical model made such individual-focused treatment the logical response; political action is taken to remedy the problems presented by these individuals, or other reasons. Whatever the reason, as Rhodes and Gibbins noted, once established, a frame of reference for responding to social problems is not easily replaced.

In recent years, however, there has been an increasing emphasis on environmental and interactional responses to the troubled-child problem. Perhaps as a result of the overload of cases in all the systems described above combined with the continuing scarcity of appropriately trained personnel, the focus of many intervention programs has shifted from "exciter-centered" interventions such as psychotherapy or behavior modification to "respondent-centered" efforts ranging from neighborhood organization to milieu therapy.

Both of those categories, however, are unilateral measures; they deal with only one part of the person-environment interchange. What Rhodes and Gibbins (1972) term "exchange-centered" interventions are more interaction-based. Strategies included in this category try to recognize the ecological nature of disturbance and affect a positive change in the interaction between a youngster and his or her environment.

Exchange-centered interventions represent a new format for intervention and consequently there are as yet few programs based specifically on this point of view. Some examples are provided in later chapters but a useful model to discuss here is that of *educateur* (Linton, 1971). Linton describes the educateur approach as follows:

> The educateur approach to the handicapped child emphasizes the importance of change in the child's social system, which, it is assumed, affects his condition. Our *national credo is geared heavily toward individualism* and the exploitation of those who for various reasons are unable to play a competitive role in the economy. *Our system condemns the deviant individual* to a systematic process of rejection, isolation, and dehumanization. *Surprisingly*, in light of our denigration of the handicapped, *we have chosen the most expensive and inappropriate approaches* in providing services for them.

> Educateur training would provide the trainees with an awareness of the role of the child's social system in effecting positive change. Unlike the traditional mental health specialist, the graduate educateur is expected to utilize directly the natural supportive forces in the child's environment and to effect change in the negative aspects of the child's social system in order to assist him in making a successful reentry into his natural community. In this sense the educateur is expected to be an advocate for his group of handicapped children and a change agent in the child's social system [p. 171, emphasis added].

Linton points out how the heavy stock we place on individualism in this country causes us to see the locus of problems in individual children and prevents us from focusing our attention on the interactions of children with the systems that surround them. The educateur, however, is trained specifically to focus on the interface between child and environment and to utilize natural support systems in order to effect change. Such a strategy represents the essence of the ecological approach—the development of interventions aimed at enabling systems to reduce discordance and return to a balanced and harmonious state and the withdrawal of outside interventions when that goal is reached.

Interchange-centered interventions and the ecological model on which they are based present the best opportunity for the development of programs that can cross system lines and discipline boundaries. This can be done through the efforts of trained generalists (i.e., the educateur model described above) but also through more informed "systems-oriented" specialists in a variety of program settings and facilities. Case workers in the social-welfare system, psychologists in the mental health system, court personnel in the legal-correctional system, and, of course, all who work in educational systems might improve their understanding and increase the effectiveness of their interventions by adopting an ecological basis for their efforts.

3

Psychodynamic and Behavioral Models

Over the years, innumerable theories have been proposed and countless programs developed in efforts to serve troubled children. According to Kauffman (1977), "throughout history persons in every culture have sought to conceptualize unusual or disturbing human behavior in terms of causal factors and to draw implications of those factors for eliminating, controlling, and preventing deviant acts. . . . humans have been variously conceptualized, for example, as spiritual beings, biological organisms, rational and feeling persons, and as products of their environments" (p. 42).

While efforts to understand and intervene effectively with troubled people do indeed have a long history, events of the past 35 years have had a dramatic impact on the treatment of disturbed children. For example, the increased popularity of psychoanalysis in the years after World War II, the equally dramatic rise of behavior therapy in the 1960s and 1970s, the pharmaceutical revolution in mental hospitals and the deinstitutionalization movement that followed, and the increasing attention to the concept of learning disabilities, have all occurred in recent years. While many of these events have had considerable impact on work with troubled youngsters, they have also contributed to the continual confusion that permeates the study of emotional disturbance in children.

One effort to bring order to this confusion began in the early 1970s when Bill Rhodes and his colleagues at the University of Michigan at Ann Arbor began work on what became known as the "Conceptual Project in Child Variance." The goal of that endeavor was to clarify, on the basis of comprehensive research and study, the major conceptual perspectives on emotional disturbance in children, the types of interventions that followed from each of these perspectives, and the ways in which the various systems in our culture became involved with troubled youngsters.

The conceptual project produced voluminous materials documenting the information described above. In many ways those materials have served as the basis for efforts to develop services, plan research programs, train special educators and others who will work with disturbed children, and especially to describe the field of emotional disturbance to students in a variety of disciplines.

This chapter will draw on the experience of the Conceptual Project and some of the writings that followed from it in order to present two of the major models of thinking about emotional disturbance. Chapter 1 touched upon each of the models described by the Conceptual Project. Here we will examine in particular two of the most critical perspectives in our field: the psychodynamic and behavioral points of view. Each has had an enormous impact on efforts to serve troubled children and both need to be understood clearly before we can move on to a more detailed discussion of the ecological perspective that serves as the basis for this book.

Table 3.1 provides capsule descriptions of both the psychodynamic and behavioral perspectives on emotional disturbance.

PSYCHODYNAMIC MODEL

This orientation, which originated in the conceptualizations of Freud and his colleagues and has since divided into many camps with somewhat different perspectives, includes the following common aspects:

1. All children have some basic needs that must be met in order to develop a healthy personality. They include the need for love, security, belonging, success, etc.
2. Feelings are of primary importance in the life and behavior of the child.
3. Each child goes through several stages of emotional growth. Traumatic experiences and deprivations may interfere with this growth and result in lasting personality disturbances.
4. The quality of the emotional relationship a child has with his family and other significant people in his life is of crucial significance.
5. Anxiety over unmet needs and inner conflicts is an important determinant in behavior disorders [Juul, 1978, p. 9].

Newcomer (1980) adds the following characteristics:

1. Behaviors that reflect a state of emotional disturbance are caused primarily by internal psychic pathology.
2. Both biological forces and early environmental influences contribute to the pathological condition.

Table 3.1. Capsule Descriptions of the Psychodynamic and Behavioral Models.

Psychodynamic

The disturbed child has not successfully "worked through" the intrapsychic conflicts that he faced in the process of psychological and physical development. Personality is composed of id, ego, and superego, three hypothetical systems that work together in supportive harmony in mentally healthy children but conflict within the psyche of a maladjusted child. Children must pass through a series of difficult developmental stages on the way to mature adulthood.

Psychodynamic theory has had a very significant influence on work with troubled children. Some applications include: milieu therapy, life-space interviewing, play therapy, the use of art and music and dance in therapy, classrooms in psychiatric clinics, and many more.

Behavioral

Behavioral deviance is maladaptive behavior that has been learned and maintained through the effects of reinforcement and punishment. Behaviorists generally believe that it is not productive to look for causes of behavior or to use the label "emotionally disturbed." They prefer to observe the deviant behavior and the environment in which it occurs and describe it as completely as possible as the first step in change.

Applications of behavioral therapy are based on the notion that any behavior that is learned can be "unlearned" and that new, more appropriate behavior can be learned to replace that which was deviant. A variety of behavioral systems exist for this purpose including operant conditioning, contingency management, and modeling.

---

3. Etiology must be identified if effective treatment is to be undertaken.
4. The individual is not consciously aware of the source of the problem.
5. Changing overt behavior is less important than dealing with the underlying conflicts that cause the behavior, since surface treatment only results in symptom substitution.
6. Treatment involves changing the person by providing insight into past conflicts unearthed from the unconscious.
7. Treatment through psychoanalysis can reverse certain pathological behaviors, but the process is long and difficult [p. 39].

Reinert (1980) summarizes it this way:

From a psychodynamic point of view the child in conflict has not negotiated, at a successful level, the various intrapsychic and external conflicts faced in the process of psychological and physiological maturation [p. 40].

In order to understand psychoanalytic thought fully, one must be cognizant of the three major personality systems: the id, ego, and superego—three hypothetical constructs that form the basis of psychological development.

The id represents instinctual energy (it is the only system present at birth) and its power is used in the service of the "pleasure principle" (the constant effort to achieve gratification and to avoid pain).

The superego represents societal values and often conflicts directly with the id. The ego serves as the mediating system, walking through the conflicts between id and superego by the use of logic and rationality (the "reality principle").

When the three systems work together productively, the person is able to meet his needs without trespassing on others' rights or society's rules and he is said to be well adjusted. When the systems are in conflict—if, for example, the id's impulses are too strong to control—then the child is maladjusted.

In addition to the three major personality systems, psychoanalytic thought is also based on a sequence of five psychosexual developmental stages. Beginning from birth, the stages are: oral, anal, phallic, latency, and genital. Each child passes relatively systematically through the developmental stages, though some overlapping of stages does occur. Though it is not uncommon for problems to occur even in the development of typical children, disturbed youngsters often fail to resolve the dilemmas presented by one or another of the psychosexual stages.

Table 3.2 summarizes the events of each of the developmental stages.

From a psychodynamic perspective, the first three stages are critical, as

Table 3.2. Psychosexual Development Stages.

Stage	Description
Oral	From Birth to about two years. Mouth is center of gratification. Child tries to put everything into mouth—"swallow the world."
Anal	From two to four years of age, anal area is center of gratification.
Anal-expulsive	Child derives great satisfaction from expelling feces.
Anal-retentive	Child derives most satisfaction by holding feces.
	Conflicts in this stage can lead to children becoming too orderly or not orderly at all. Defiant, obstinate behavior.
Phallic	From four to six years of age, children demonstrate preoccupation with genital area; masturbation; sex play with others; learning where babies come from, etc., in effort to work out sexual identity. Problems include inappropriate sexual identification and attitudes.
Latency	From six years old to puberty—rest period between phallic and genital stages. Little sex interest, identification with same-sex parent and peers for activities.
Genital	From puberty to adulthood—Phallic stage conflicts resume, but sexual interest is now outside the family and child (now young adult) has physiological capability to act out feelings toward others.

by the time the youngster has completed the phallic stage the basic personality components have been established. If problems have been resolved successfully in those early years, later difficulties are less likely. Problem behaviors might develop because a child invests too much psychic energy in one stage and has insufficient resources to meet the next, or youngsters who have difficulty at later stages may regress to behavior characteristics of earlier times.

For many years, at the beginning of the short history of educating disturbed children, the psychodynamic model represented the only point of view in the field. Juul (1978) reports that the exclusive usage of the model in that early time has created the following lasting impact:

1. With its revelations of the rich and complex inner life of children, it has created in parents and teachers a new sensitivity to children's feelings and needs.

2. The discoveries of the devastating effects emotional deprivation in early childhood has on personality development have led to major reforms in child care institutions and agencies.

3. Teachers have become conscious about their importance to their pupils as models and as objects of identification. They also realize that through their relations with their children they can alleviate many emotional problems and create security and confidence [pp. 13, 14].

After a while criticisms of the dynamic viewpoint increased, its effectiveness was questioned, and its application in educational settings began to decline. Some of the specific reasons for the loss of enthusiasm for the psychodynamic orientation are listed below:

1. It presents an extremely pessimistic view of human beings (Newcomer, 1980).

2. Its description of human behavior is based on hypothetical constructs and operations (Newcomer, 1980). Many practitioners have abandoned this hypothetical system in favor of more observable answers (Reinert, 1980).

3. It emphasizes the examination of the unconscious as the way to mental health despite the lack of evidence for such a position (Newcomer, 1980). Follow-up studies of children who had received psychodynamic treatment have shown a very low success rate (Juul, 1978).

4. Teachers may have been encouraged to allow the same freedom in the classroom that was practiced in the therapeutic hours. In turn, such practices created so much aggression and destructiveness that chaos was the result. Juul (1978) reports on one such setting:

Once I visited a public school class for emotionally disturbed children which was under the supervision of a psychiatrist. There were only two boys in the class. One was constantly trying to cut the teacher's hair with a pair of scissors. The other repeatedly dug a tomahawk into the teacher's back. Fortunately the weapon was made of rubber. The harrassed and unhappy pedagogue—a middle aged lady—explained apologetically that she was under instructions not to inhibit the children's self-expression [p. 15].

5. The psychiatric professions tended to look upon the schools and upon education with hostility and suspicion and downgraded the role of the teacher and the classroom in the therapeutic program (Juul, 1978).
6. In therapeutic practice, there was a preoccupation with a child's pathology and limitations and a lack of appreciation for his capabilities and strengths (Juul, 1978).
7. There was a tendency to ignore the powerful impact of the environment on a child's behavior. Thus, not enough efforts were made to elicit the support of the significant people in the child's daily life. Again, Juul notes:

During the late 1940's I worked in a metropolitan child guidance clinic. Many of the children had school and learning problems. Our time was spent almost entirely on expressive and insight therapy. Never did we visit the schools or consult with the teachers about the children's difficulties [Juul, 1978, p. 16].

Educational Implications

One basic premise of the psychodynamic model is that disturbed behavior is determined by psychological processes. Psychopathology is determined by the way in which the individual's psychological make-up—thoughts, feelings, perceptions, needs, etc.—responds to the events of everyday life. Though everyone brings inherited potentialities to life situations, it is the specific manner in which those genetic or biological factors interact with particular aspects of the individual's own life space that results in the development of maladaptive or disturbed behavior.

Nick Long (1966) has developed a framework for understanding the interaction between biological potential and environmental influences described above. According to Long's cycle (Figure 3.1), each child's innate inherited potential is soon subjected to the stresses and strains of the youngster's environment with anxiety the likely result. The youngster's efforts to ward off the anxiety by employing one or another of the defense mechanisms usually results in increased conflicts, especially in school settings. Consequently, that conflict produces more anxiety and the cycle is repeated continuously.

When a child's

> *Innate Biological Potentials* such as:
>   Intelligence-maturational rate,
>   Energy level-congenital anomaly,
>   Sensitivity-capacity for adaptation

are subjected to

> *Early Environmental Forces* such as:
>   Insufficient affection and acceptance
>   Inconsistent management
>   Overprotection
>   Communication of fears
>   Parental dissension
>   Nurtural deprivation
>   Physical damage

the

leads to an attempt to
regain balance by
developing

> *Resulting Anxiety*
>
> *Rigid Defense Mechanisms* such as:
>   compulsion, regression, projection, conversion,
>   withdrawal, denial repression, displacement

These symptoms usually
result in further social
emotional disturbances in
school with

> *Authorities* —
> *Peers*
> *Self*   which perpetuate the psychopathological
> *Learning*   cycle

Fig. 3.1. Framework for understanding children with social and emotional disturbances (After Long, 1966).

According to Newcomer (1980), the psychodynamic model has made several important contributions to educational programming for disturbed children. First, it has emphasized the premise that personality characteristics are determined by early childhood events. For disturbed youngsters, this implies that emotional distress is caused in early family relationships and that school problems are simply repeat manifestations of those early disturbances. As Baruch (1949) has noted:

> If a child misbehaves, we must recognize that he must have unmet emotional needs or that he is still expressing hurt, fear, or anger for lacks in the past [quoted in Juul, 1978, p. 25].

As a result, psychodynamic thinking has focused considerably on child and family—not school—intervention strategies.

Second, psychodynamic models are based on the notion "that abnormal behaviors are symptoms of unconscious conflict" (Newcomer, 1980, p. 38). Consequently, educators must realize that troubled children are frequently not conscious of the rationale or motivation for their inappropriate behavior, nor are they able to control that behavior consciously. An additional implication is that treatment of symptoms (overt behavior) may simply result in the substitution of another more problematic symptom and should thus be avoided. Instead, youngsters should be encouraged to express these feelings and educators should be trained to provide environments that do not repress youngster's symptomatology and their opportunities to express the underlying conflicts.

Newcomer (1980) summarizes the positive contributions of the psychodynamic model as follows:

1. Children do not always consciously plan and cannot always consciously control disruptive behaviors, therefore when they misbehave they should not be treated punitively;
2. Hostility directed to the teacher should not be viewed as a personal insult since it might stem from a variety of motivations and does not necessarily mean that the child dislikes the teacher;
3. Children respond to internal conflicts, therefore, inconsistencies in behavior should be expected [p. 38].

Some of the most important work based on this model includes Aichorn's early efforts with antisocial adolescents, the rational-emotive therapy developed by Albert Ellis, Bruno Bettelheim's Orthogenic School for emotionally disturbed children, Victor Frankel's logotherapy, and transactional analysis popularized by Eric Berne.

One application of psychodynamic therapy, the "psychoeducational" approach, may have started with the work of Fritz Redl whose efforts with delinquent youngsters in the 1940s and 1950s still apply today (Redl & Wineman, 1951). That same psychoeducational perspective served as the basis for the development of the life-space interview technique by Fritz Redl (1959) and by William Morse (1965).

The concept of life space stems from the work of Kurt Lewin who noted that Behavior (B) was a joint function of personal factors (P) and the perceived environment (E), $(B = f[P,E])$. A person's life space then represents the continual interaction between inner and outer forces and equals the individual's psychological world at any given moment.

A life space must be viewed through the eyes of its "owner." The realities of the situation are less important than the individual's interpretation or perception of the surrounding environment, since perceptions serve as guides to behavior.

The life-space interview tries to discover the meaning of specific behaviors by examining the reasoning that led up to them. The operating assumption here is that if the reasoning process can be understood, then new and more appropriate concluding behaviors can be developed and incorporated into the child's repertoire.

We can see then that life-space interviewing deals with both feelings and actions. When well executed, such an interview can legitimize a troubled youngster's feeling ("You were right to feel angry"), help him or her understand the inappropriateness of the action that followed the feeling ("But it's not okay to try to stab him with your pencil"), and finally, move to the consideration of new behaviors ("What else do you think you could do when you're feeling angry?"). This focus on both feelings and actions should follow real-life events as soon as possible so that youngsters can get assistance when they most need it and when it is likely to be most meaningful.

Life-space interviewing represents a way in which adults can assist youngsters to understand the effects of their unconscious thoughts, feelings, and actions on others. It also serves as a model for the application of psychodynamic thinking to the real-life situations encountered by educators and clinicians.

BEHAVIORAL MODEL

Learning theory moved out of the laboratory and into the classrooms in the early 1960s. Suddenly the dynamic model had competition and in a very short time, behavior modification developed an immense following. For many educators and psychologists who work with troubled children, it has taken the place of the psychodynamic model as the *only* point of view.

Some of the most critical reasons for the rapid rise in the behavioral orientation's popularity are:

1. It is a very practical approach that deals with concrete and observable issues and concerns.
2. The theories themselves are simple to understand and can be easily learned.
3. Specific behavior modification techniques quickly demonstrated effectiveness with many populations and problems.
4. The need to be specific regarding a child's behavior and the focus on observation has helped teachers become more aware of children's qualities and more conscious of their own capabilities.
5. There is a general emphasis on praise and rewards and on attention to the child's positive behavior.

Newcomer (1980) has noted that the behavioral model attempts to make psychology a science by advocating the study of *observable* human behavior, especially behavior associated with learning. Behaviorists believe that human behavior is learned, or as Newcomer says: "Children are not born speaking, walking, or, for that matter, punching classmates" (p. 39). In order to understand behavior, it is necessary to study the interactions between individuals and environments and the stimulus-response patterns therein.

Some of the most critical assumptions of the behavioral model include:

1. All behavior is learned and can be unlearned through the application of principles of learning.
2. Inappropriate behaviors can be altered (extinguished and/or replaced by more acceptable alternative behaviors) through the use of reinforcement procedures.
3. It is possible to predict and ultimately to control behavior if all the pertinent environmental characteristics are known.

Clearly the most popular behavioral methodology is operant conditioning. First introduced by Skinner (1953), operant learning is based on the principle that all behavior is determined by its consequences.

The notion that pleasant consequences reinforce behavior has had an overwhelming impact on program planning for troubled children. Stated more specifically by Gentry and Parks (1977), "Behavior which is followed by pleasant consequences will tend to increase in rate or maintain itself at present level" (p. 73), this simple law has given rise to an entire new technology of behavior change. Table 3.3 provides capsule descriptions of some of the most important and popular behavioral techniques.

The notion of reinforcement is central to a behavioral perspective. We can see in Table 3.3 that positive reinforcement (an environmental response that has the effect of maintaining or increasing the level of behavior that it follows) may be delivered according to a number of different reinforcement schedules (fixed interval, variable interval, fixed ratio, and variable ratio). Fixed schedules are considered most effective for learning new behaviors while variable schedules are more useful for maintaining behaviors.

The Premack Principle is also related to reinforcement; a behavior that usually occurs often (e.g., watching television) can be used as a reinforcer for behavior that occurs less frequently (cleaning your room). Thus, a parent might tell a child that he or she can watch television *after* he or she has cleaned his or her room.

It is also important to note that reinforcers should be just strong enough to effect the desired change in behavior and that the choice of reward must be considered on an individual basis. For every child, factors such as age, goals, interests, and relative strength of a variety of reinforcers must be considered when deciding what reward to offer.

Table 3.3. Behavioral Techniques and Terms.

Premack Principle	Given two responses A + B, if B occurs with greater frequency than A, it can be used as a reinforcer for A.
Contingency Contracting	The development of an agreement between two or more parties that stipulates the responsibilities of each as related to a specific item or activity; i.e., the relationship between a child's appropriate behavior and the provision of an agreed-upon reward.
Positive Reinforcement	Environmental response with effect of maintaining or increasing level of the behavior that it follows. (i.e., praise for good work)
Negative Reinforcement	Environmental response that, when removed, causes increase in strength of behavior. (i.e., removal from time-out room increases appropriate behavior in classroom)
Schedules of Reinforcement	Rates at which positive reinforcers are delivered.
Fixed Interval	Reinforcement is delivered according to specific and consistent periods of time (one every five seconds, one every ten minutes, etc).
Variable Interval	Reinforcers are provided after varying amounts of time.
Fixed Ratio	Reinforcers are consistently delivered after a fixed number of behavioral acts (one every two acts, one every twenty acts, etc.).
Variable Ratio	Reinforcers are provided after varying numbers of acts.
Punishment	Removal of a positive reinforcer or the presentation of a negative reinforcer with the aim of decreasing specific behaviors. Punishment may involve the direct presentation of an aversive stimulus and it should not be used until more positive approaches have been tried.
Extinction	The withholding of reinforcement from undesired behaviors in an effort to decrease the frequency of such behaviors. The removal of adult attention, planned ignoring of specific inappropriate behaviors, can be very powerful, though some behaviors can't be ignored. It is also likely that targeted behavior will increase at start of the program before extinction can take hold.
Overcorrection Restitution	Correcting the results of the inappropriate behavior thoroughly (Clean up the paint you splashed *and* wash the entire wall.)
Repeat Positive Practice	Close the door properly *several* times.

Table 3.3. (Cont.)

Reinforcing Incompatible Behavior	Reduce frequency of undesired behavior by rewarding a more appropriate incompatible response (reinforce sharing instead of taking toys).
Time Out	Reducing inappropriate behavior by removing the child from the reinforcing situation (class, play yard, etc.) to a space where no opportunities for reinforcement are available.
Shaping	Procedure used to move child through small steps or successive approximations to a terminal goal. Example: Dressing, putting on coat Full physical prompt — Give child complete assistance Partial physical prompt — Get coat ready for child. Gestural prompt — Show coat to child. Verbal prompt — "Time to get your coat on."
Fading	Slow removal of cues until child can perform behavior with no prompts.
Chaining	Moving from one step (behavior) to next in learning a sequence of skills.
Forward Chaining	Start with first step (one foot forward) and work up to "walking."
Reverse Chaining	Start with last step (making a bow) and work up to "shoe-tying."
Generalization	Process by which children learn to transfer skills learned in educational programs to real-world settings. Can be eased by; efforts to make training setting resemble living/working settings, training in many different settings with multiple trainers, teaching different forms of same skill or concept.
Task Analysis	Procedure used to develop efficient skill sequences for shaping new behaviors. Careful programming of complexity and sequence of skills to be learned according to following outline: 1. *Determine Behavioral Objective* (Terminal Behavior — what child will end up doing). A statement of the skill the child will attain, the level of performance expected, and the conditions under which the skill will be performed. 2. *Identify Sequence of Skills* Break terminal objective into small, discernible steps. 3. *Identify Prerequisite Entry Behaviors* What specific cognitive, verbal, social, motor skills are needed as basis for learning new target behaviors? 4. *Determine the Order for Teaching the Subtasks*

Table 3.3. (Cont.)

Modeling	Provision of a simple appropriate behavior for the purpose of encouraging the patterning of a child's behavior. Three major positive effects may occur:

1. *The modeling effect*:
   Children may acquire behaviors from the model that were not previously a part of their repertoire.

2. *The inhibitory effect*:
   Unacceptable behaviors for which the model is punished may be inhibited in the child.

3. *The eliciting effect*:
   Behavior is elicited from within the child's repertoire that approximates the model.

Contingency contracting is a very popular technique and will be described more completely in Chapter 7. Extinction is really the flip side of reinforcement and is used frequently in attempts to help youngsters reduce inappropriate behaviors. The effects of punishment are less clearly positive and methods based on a punishment model are therefore used less often today.

Overcorrection and the reinforcement of incompatible behaviors are also important elements of standard behavioral approaches to troubled youngsters, as is the technique called "Time Out." Time out can help reduce inappropriate behavior by removing the child from the reinforcing situation and confining him or her to a space where no opportunity for reinforcement exists, but caution must be used. Children must always be supervised and less intensive measures should be tried first. Time outs should also be short; there is no evidence to indicate that long periods are more effective than shorter ones.

Shaping, fading, chaining, and task analysis all pertain to the ways in which new behaviors can be learned and combined to reach a terminal objective. Modeling is increasingly becoming a major aspect of behavioral programming, the basis upon which a number of programs and models are being built. Finally, generalization has to do with the ability to transfer skills learned in one setting (school) to another setting (home, neighborhood). This area has been problematic for behavioral programs, as generalization has not proven easy to attain.

Criticisms of the Behavioral Orientation

Despite its dramatic rise in popularity and the success it has been able to demonstrate, the use of a behavioral model has also created a wealth of criticism and controversy. Some of the most serious criticisms are listed below:

1. The behavioral model focuses on simple behaviors and is not as useful when applied to more complex human problems.
2. Behaviorists sometimes display disregard for elementary principles of maturation and development. Their rejection of the importance of inner cognitive and affective processes is subject to serious implications. For example, Juul (1978) quoted a teacher who said: "We don't explain things anymore. We only reward them when they emit the appropriate behaviors."
3. The modification of another person's behavior involves serious questions about values that have not yet been dealt with adequately.
4. Some positive results of behavioral programs do not hold up over time. Programs based on the behavioral model have demonstrated severe difficulty in the area of generalization or "transfer of training," enabling clients to use their skills in other than program settings.
5. There has been, on the part of some individuals and some systems, a tendency toward overcommitment to the model and a corresponding refusal to consider alternative strategies.
6. Perhaps the most serious criticism about the behavioral orientation is that it is so open to ethical abuse. For example, there has been considerable controversy generated (appropriately) about the use of aversive conditioning in programs for troubled children.

Juul (1978) reports two examples of inappropriate, inhumane, and perhaps illegal "behavioral" programs.

One teacher locked a psychotic boy in a closet while she took the other children swimming. By chance the boy's mother came to visit and found her son all alone, screaming and banging on the door.

Another teacher in a similar class had a boy sit in a corner and watch while the rest of the group enjoyed a Thanksgiving dinner the teacher had prepared for them. The class was on a token economy, and the unlucky boy did not have enough tokens for the meal. He came from a very impoverished home, and had used some of the tokens to get some food when he came to school in the morning [p. 38].

There is little doubt that the behavioral model will continue to be a center of controversy. This orientation to work with troubled children touches upon values and ideologies where agreements cannot be reached easily. Its major limitation may be that it lends itself so easily to misuse, but if applied in a positive context, behavioral techniques can be effective and constructive instruments in work with troubled children.

NEED FOR UNIFYING PERSPECTIVE

While both of the major models described in this chapter have demonstrated some positive impact on efforts with troubled children, neither has produced the level of results needed to "make a dent" in the "disturbed child problem." Although psychodynamic theory has increased the sensitivity of educators and clinicians (and, to some degree, the lay public) to the psychological needs of troubled children and the critical importance of early development, and despite the phenomenal rise of "proven" behavioral techniques and their widespread adoption in programs for disturbed children, there are more troubled children in America today than ever before.

In fact, the rapid developments in the field over the past 30 to 40 years and the (understandably) exaggerated, but as yet unfulfilled, promise of new models may have obfuscated the ever-clearer critical issue in work with troubled children. In our search for the perfect model, we have refused to accept the possibility that no such model exists or at least that our present level of sophistication is simply inadequate to the task of developing such a universally applicable theory.

Our efforts to develop models, like our efforts to intervene with troubled youngsters, are simply not precise enough or successful enough to allow unwavering commitment to any one school of thought or to dismiss out of hand anything that works. The model that may be most useful may be the one that provides clinicians and educators with a conceptual framework that enables us to match the needs of children with appropriate intervention strategies. This kind of matching-model perspective is best exemplified by the ecological approach to troubled children—an orientation which is described more completely in the following chapter.

4

The Ecological
Orientation

One of the biggest needs identified in the education and treatment of emotionally troubled children today is for some unifying theory to serve as the
basis for currently developing programs and to help define a model with
which to approach the future. In the past few years, ecological theory,
which is concerned with the interaction between organism and environment,
has reappeared and seems to have great potential for application to this
area. Instead of focusing only on individuals, ecological theorists are more
interested in examining ecosystems—interaction systems comprised of living things and the nonliving habitat. In order to do this, ecologists engage in
naturalistic research in an attempt to understand human behavior in its
natural setting. Ecologists typically do not consider emotional disturbance a
physical disease located solely within a child, but prefer to look at a disturbed ecosystem, in which disturbance can be more profitably viewed as a
"failure to match."

The ecological orientation to emotional disturbance is based on the
assumption that each child must be viewed as a complete entity surrounded
by a unique mini–social system or ecosystem. When the various aspects of a
child's system are working together harmoniously, ecologists say that the
ecosystem is congruent or balanced, and the child appears to be "normal."
Thurman (1977) explains:

> Most individuals whom we judge as normal are operating in a behavioral
> ecology which may be defined as congruent. That is, the individual's behavior
> is in harmony with the social norms of his environmental context [p. 329].

On the other hand when such congruence does not exist, the child is likely to be considered deviant (out of harmony with social norms) or incompetent (unable to perform purposefully in the unchanged setting). When this is the case, ecologists say that the system is not balanced, that particular elements are in conflict with one another. Such conflicts are termed "points of discordance," specific places where there is a failure to match between the child and his or her ecosystem. According to ecologists, the search for solutions to the problem of emotional disturbance must focus on these points of discordance and the resulting failure to match.

When the failure to match is resolved and the ecosystem is once more congruent or balanced, Thurman (1977) states:

> the stage has been set for maximization of his function and adjustment. Competent function brings along with it human dignity, acceptance within the setting, and provides the basis for developing higher levels of competency [p. 332].

Finally, Thomas and Marshall (1977) summarize this brief introduction to the ecological orientation and highlight the importance of a balanced ecosystem when they state that "The success with which a person meets life's challenges is dependent upon his ability to reach a desired functional balance between his physical and social habitats, and himself" (p. 16).

ECOLOGICAL THEORY

But what exactly is ecological theory? What are the key concepts and principles? What are the implications for work with troubled youngsters? This chapter will focus on the above questions, looking in turn at the history and development of the theory, some definitions of critical aspects, descriptions of particularly important principles and assumptions, examples of intervention programs based on this theoretical point of view, and some general implications for practice.

The words "ecological orientation" carry a number of meanings, depending upon the perspective and viewpoint of the persons involved. In its most general sense, ecology can be defined as the biologist saw it, "the study of living things in their natural habitat." While this may not appear to be a particularly useful definition for those of us interested in the development of psychological and educational programs for children with special emotional and behavioral needs, consider the contrast between this definition and the following quotation: "Much of American developmental psychology is the science of the strange behavior of children in strange situations with strange adults" (Bronfenbrenner, 1977a).

Bronfenbrenner refers, of course, to the predominant tendency of modern psychology to attempt to improve understanding of children's development and behavior by studying very small bits of information usually produced under artificial laboratory surroundings. What is missing from the picture gained in this manner is any understanding of what *really* happens to children within the context of the systems in which they live. Can we understand the experience of being a child in a family, a neighborhood, a school, a community?

Such knowledge has an impact on our work with troubled youngsters as well; the ways in which we study children affect the kinds of programs we develop for them. Small studies lead to narrow programs, and the ecological viewpoint stresses the need to go beyond such narrow visions of behavior and development and to find ways to focus on the interactions of children with critical aspects of their environments. We must increase our knowledge of the actual conditions in which children live, according to the ecologists, before we can use what we learn from such experiences as the basis for our intervention programs. Without such comprehensive knowledge, it could not be reasonable to expect our efforts to impact on children within the context of their systems. What we learn in the laboratory, at this point, may simply be too far removed from reality to be of much use in the construction of programs for children with special emotional and behavioral needs.

How will ecological theory help us in this regard? Let us begin by examining some of the key concepts. Table 4.1 contains definitions of critical ecological terms.

The terms defined in Table 4.1 all point to the importance of studying persons in the context of their interactions with environments. The "ecological niche" (the role or roles of the organism in the environment), "niche breadth" (the range of roles), and "goodness of fit" (congruence between individual and environment) are all critical interaction-based ecological terms. Adaptation is the term used to describe the adjustment of an individual or species to new environments. Individual differences or the wide variations among people represent an important reality incorporated into the ecological perspective.

While the above definitions come from what we might call general ecology, those below (see Table 4.2) are taken from a somewhat more specified field known as human ecology. More specifically, some of them come from the work of Bronfenbrenner (1977a) and his colleagues, who have been concerned with building an experimental psychology of human development. Here, however, we find the terminology useful as a bridge between the general area of ecology and our more specific concern with the application of ecological principles to the education of troubled children.

The ecological environment defined above is graphically depicted in

Table 4.1. Definitions of Ecological Terms.

Ecology: The study of relationships between organisms and environment.
Ecosystem: The interaction between living organisms and their physical environment.
Natural Habitat: The place or places (social and physical environments) in which a species lives.
Ecological Niche: The role the organism plays in the environment.
Niche Breadth: The range of roles which the organism is able to carry out.
Goodness of Fit: The congruence (match) between the organism's individual characteristics and the environment in which he is placed.
Naturalistic Research: The research method in which observation and classification of natural phenomenon are used to describe an ecosystem.
Adaptation: The rate of adjustment to a new niche or habitat, and the range of environments to which the species can adjust. (More adaptable species can adjust to a greater variety of different environments and niches and can do so more quickly than less adaptable species.)
Individual Differences: The wide variations that are basic among people and must be taken into account when evaluating a given system. The person alone is not a good predictor of future behavior. Neither is environment alone. The interaction between person and the environment is the important factor.

Table 4.2. Definition of Terms From Human Ecology.

1. *Ecology of Human Development*: The scientific study of the progressive, mutual accommodation, throughout the lifespan, between a growing human organism and the changing immediate environments in which it lives; this process is affected by relations obtained within and between these immediate settings, as well as the larger social contexts, both formal and informal, in which the settings are embedded.
2. *Ecological Environment*: A nested arrangement of structures, each contained within the next.
    a. *microsystem*: The complex of relations between the developing person and environment in an immediate setting containing that person (i.e., home, school, work, etc.).
    b. *mesosystem*: The interrelations among major settings containing the developing person at a particular point in his or her life. A mesosystem is a system of microsystems.
    c. *exosystem*: An extension of the mesosystem embracing other specific social structures, both formal and informal, that do not themselves contain the developing person but impinge upon or encompass the immediate settings in which that person is found, and thereby influence, delimit, or even determine what goes on there. These structures include the major institutions of the society, both deliberately structured and spontaneously evolving, as they operate at a concrete local level.
    d. *macrosystem:* The over arching institutional patterns of the culture or subculture, such as the economic, social, educational, legal, and political systems, of which micro, meso, and exosystems are the concrete manifestations.
3. *Ecological Validity*: The extent to which the environment experienced by the subjects in a scientific investigation has the properties it is supposed to or assumed to have by the investigator.

Source: Based on Bronfenbrenner (1977a).

Figure 4.1. Sometimes this concept might be described as the ecological system or ecological network, but in most cases, the reference is to a nested arrangement of systems in which each individual lives. Swap (1978) describes it as follows:

> It seems useful to picture the ecological network as consisting of three nested systems or levels. The first level and the most basic environmental unit or system is the behavior setting, initially explained by Barker (1968) and summarized in Gump (1975). The behavior setting consists of a physical milieu, a program of activities, inhabitants, and a location in time and space. A child in a behavior setting (such as a classroom) is a component of the setting and is also significantly influenced by the expectations, constraints and opportunities available in that setting. Behavior settings can be described with various degrees of inclusiveness: the kindergarten class or the whole school; the family at breakfast or the home.

In any behavior setting, disturbing behavior is seen as the product of the interaction between the child and elements of the setting. Any of the elements of

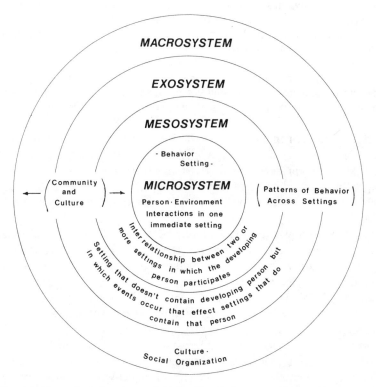

Fig. 4.1. The ecological environment (after Bronfenbrenner, 1977a and Swap, 1978).

a setting (and/or their interactions) may be involved in the initiation of a potentially disturbing behavior; significant inhabitants of the setting are usually involved in classifying the behavior as disturbing and responding to it in an agitated manner. The reciprocal nature of the interaction between child and behavior settings is a fundamental concept in the ecological model.

The second level of analysis in this nested model is patterns of behavior across settings. At this level, behavior settings comprise the building blocks for studies of more complex child-environment interactions, including for example, the behavior of the same child at home and school or the behaviors of children labeled disturbed and non-disturbed in different settings.

The community and culture influence the design and meaning of simple behavior settings and the relationships among them. Community and culture as the third and most complex level of analysis includes formal and informal structures at local and supra-local levels as well as characteristics of the physical environment. For example, formal structures created to respond to deviance and which affect the milieus and programs which are provided for children include educational, mental health, social-welfare, legal-correctional and religious systems (Rhodes & Head, 1974). Informal transmission of cultural values (e.g., through social networks, local newspapers, television programs) affects expectations and goals for children's behaviors by creating standards of normal or appropriate behavior, defining patterns of abnormal behavior, and determining who gets access to which formal structures. Finally, physical characteristics of the community environment such as population density and characteristic housing design may affect the incidence of disturbance and access of children to particular service delivery systems [p. 187].

As may be seen in Figure 4.1, the innermost circle represents a given child's immediate environment, a specific microsystem or behavior setting. The next circle represents the mesosystem which may be seen as the locus of Swap's "analysis of behavior across settings." Finally, the two outermost circles, the exosystem and macrosystem, represent community and cultural influences.

While the ecological perspective may be most useful in its conceptualization of a given youngster's entire ecosystem, it can also help us understand a specific behavior setting more completely. Figure 4.2 depicts one representation of the varying aspects of the school "system" that surround a child (Fox et al., 1975). In this figure, the child (or "learner") is represented by the innermost core circle. The surrounding circles represent ever more distant individuals and groups with potential for impact on the child in school. The closest circles represent the microsystem while those furthest from the youngster represent macrosystem influences.

Finally, to concretize even further the ecological view, we can examine a model for looking at the ecosystem of a given child (Hobbs, 1966, 1975,

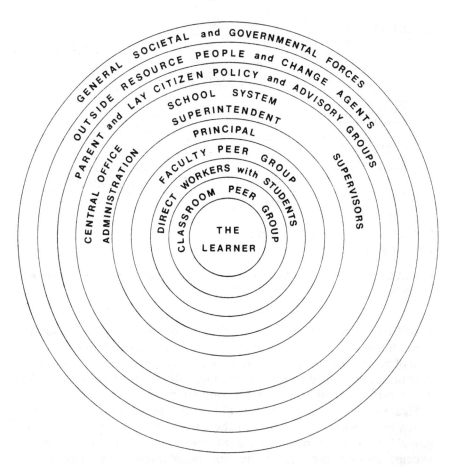

Fig. 4.2. Subsystems of a school system (After Fox et al., 1975, p. 4).

1978). Figures 4.3, 4.4., and 4.5 depict three variations of an ecosystem diagram which was first formulated by Hobbs in 1966.

In the uppermost representation (Fig. 4.3) we can see Hobbs' conceptualization of the way in which Project Re-Ed (described later in this chapter) was integrated into the system of a particular child. In Figure 4.4, we see a more detailed version of the systems (school, family, neighborhood, community) and the people within each of those systems (teachers, parents, friends, physician, etc.) contained within a youngster's ecosystem.

Just as every child is considered unique, so is every ecosystem. When there is too much discordance for the ecosystem to function harmoniously, the system is considered troubled (though the youngster will probably be

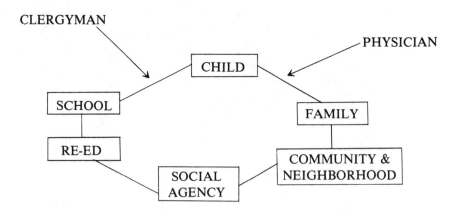

GOAL: Make the system work
without Re-ED

Fig. 4.3. Chart of ecological system, the smallest unit in a systems approach to working with a disturbed child (After Hobbs, 1966, p. 1108).

identified as the disturbed party). Efforts to help "troubled children," then, should be addressed to the problems of "troubled systems," with the goal of making the system work in the interests of the child. Systems change over time (as indicated by the arrow in Fig. 4.4) and interventions should be matched to the ecosystem's current configuration.

Figure 4.5 represents Hobbs' description of a more idealized ecosystem in which the family is represented as the unit of primary responsibility, the school is viewed as a somewhat less influential but still very significant sub-system, and the two spheres overlap considerably. The community is depicted in this diagram as actively caring and assisting both family and school in their efforts on behalf of children.

The situation depicted in Figure 4.5 according to Hobbs (1978) would enable us "to provide an optimum array of resources for the rearing of our children" (p. 765).

APPLICATIONS OF ECOLOGICAL THEORY TO TROUBLED CHILDREN

Since ecology is not usually seen as a separate discipline, but rather an area of study within several disciplines, the basic concepts in research methodologies of ecology have come from a variety of other fields. There are ecological biologists, sociologists, anthropologists, behavioral ecologists, psychoanalytical ecologists, etc. Although the ecological posi-

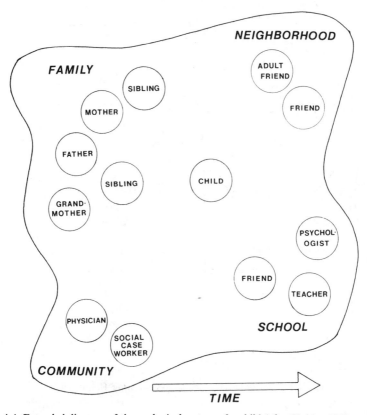

Fig. 4.4. Extended diagram of the ecological system of a child (after Hobbs, 1978, p. 797).

tion is shared by scientists with distinct professional interests, they have in common their concern for the relationship of individuals to settings, and their use of similar methodologies in their research. All human ecologists would agree that behavior is a product of the interaction between internal forces and the circumstances of the environment. An ecologist's primary discipline would be likely, however, to determine the way that he or she interprets such individual setting interactions.

According to Morse, Smith, and Acker (1978), anthropologists may have been the "original Human ecologists," and their contributions to the field, beginning in the early 1900s, have concerned the cultural context in which deviant behaviors occur. Sociologists have also added to our knowledge of human ecology with significant studies of the social conditions which tend to be associated with high rates of deviance. Farris and Dunham (1939) published their classic work, *Mental Disorders in Urban Areas*, which described their conception of "Concentric Zone Theory," social disorganiza-

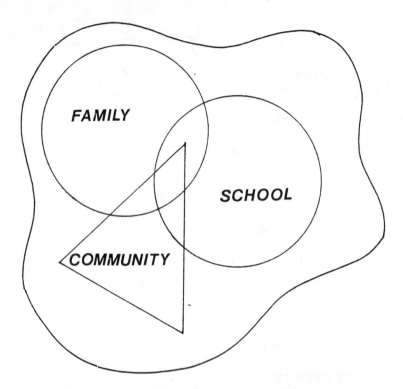

Fig. 4.5. Diagram of idealized ecosystem (after Hobbs, 1978).

tion, and the relationship of those concepts to mental illness. They postulated that in order to have a mentally healthy child, three things are necessary: (1) intimacy and affection between the child and some permanent group; (2) a consistency of influence on a child; and (3) some harmony between home and outside situations. They also stated that their definition of insanity is not a list of actions, but consists of a lack of fitness between actions and situations.

Ecological psychologists such as Barker, Lewin, and others have looked at the environment in terms of both psychological and nonpsychological forces. Ecological psychologists define mental illness as behavior which is poorly fitted to the circumstances of the setting. Barker and his colleagues have developed an especially useful and very comprehensive research program designed to operationalize the concept of life space developed by Kurt Lewin. In their work on behavior settings (small ecosystems that call forth particular behaviors), they have discovered the importance of "synomorphy" (the fit of individual behavior to the particular setting) and concluded, among other findings, that deviance is tolerated more in "undermanned" settings than in optimally or "overmanned" settings. Their studies have also resulted in the conclusion that since behavior is flexible and can be so different in different settings, it would seem invalid to diagnose deviance on the basis of only one setting (e.g., school).

Medical ecologists, such as Dubos, have contributed to the field with their research into the interaction between individual genetic determinants and environmental differences. Thomas, Chess, and Birch (1968) have found that infants are born with varying levels of nine tempermental dimensions (activity level, approach/withdrawal, intensity of reaction, quality of mood, attention span and persistence, rhythmicity, adaptability, threshold of responsiveness, and distractibility). They suggest that any level of these qualities can result in emotional disturbance under the "right" environmental conditions; that is, that the temperament (and consequently the behavior) of some children fits better into their environment than do the temperaments or behaviors of other children.

Finally, we turn to a group who might be called psychoanalytic ecologists, persons with traditional psychiatric or psychological training who now view emotional disturbance as a malfunction in interaction. Notable in this group are the family interactionists (Vogel & Bell, 1960; Mischler & Waxler, 1968; Ackerman, 1970) who have suggested that the emotional disturbance of individual children is one aspect of a much larger pattern of family relationships. The work of this group of ecologists stems from their efforts to apply a psychoanalytic explanation of individual personality to the interaction patterns within a given individual's family.

With regard to the application of ecological theory to the education of troubled children, Feagans (1972) drew three basic conclusions:

1. There is no formalized ecological theory of emotional disturbance at the present time.
2. Ecology is an inter-disciplinary concept with roots in ethology, anthropology, sociology, psychology, and medicine. This diversity of views is a strength, but the lack of unity is a weakness.
3. A systematic attempt to combine all of this into a general theory to account for emotional disturbance is needed [p. 379].

Although Feagans accurately represents the state of the field, there have been some beginning efforts to apply what we know about ecological theory to the problems presented by emotional disturbance in children. Some of the most important work in this area has been done by William Rhodes, who suggested as early as 1967 that special educators had borrowed a physiological model and applied it to emotional disturbance. Thus, Rhodes said, educators had come to view disturbance as residing totally and completely within the child, and their intervention efforts consequently were based on finding and correcting the neurological, chemical, genetic, and/or psychological flaws within the youngster. At the time, Rhodes proposed an alternative view of emotional disturbance, an ecological view that emphasized the reciprocal nature of the disturbance phenomenon and focused on the interchange between a child and the environment as the locus of disturbance. Though he did not deny the importance of intrapsychic, behavioral, or biophysical theory analyses of human behavior, Rhodes suggested that they left an incomplete picture. Ecological theory, he pointed out, supplied a more comprehensive view by recognizing the contact between child and community as the point of disturbance and developing interventions more appropriately addressed to both of those elements.

Rhodes (1967, 1970) has also conceptualized emotional disturbance as the outcome of an aggravated interaction between a behaver or excitor (the child) and the responder (family, school, community). In this view, the behavior of a "disturbed child" violates standards of the responders and consequently elicits "reciprocating emotive reactions." From this perspective it becomes imperative to study emotional disturbance in the context of the interaction between the child (excitor) and the environment (responder).

Hewett and Taylor (1980) have noted that even the most serious biological problems of youngsters can be exaggerated or reduced by the nature of the child's environmental experiences (p. 36). They also point to the compatibility between the ecological orientation and the two major systems of theory and interventions with troubled children—the psychodynamic and behavioral perspectives.

Some logical conclusions to be drawn about the ecological perspective, then, are:

1. Ecological theory can be a useful basis for conceptualizing issues and planning intervention programs for even the most severely disabled youngsters, and
2. Ecological theory can embrace useful aspects of all the other major perspectives on emotional disturbance.

In 1970, Rhodes concluded:

The time has come to begin to concentrate attention upon changing the ecological conditions under which children have to live and grow, and thus reduce the number of occasions of disturbance and the number of children who are extruded or alienated from their living units. This is the only way in which our society can come to terms with the magnitude of the problem called emotional disturbance [p. 314].

If, as Morse (1977), Hewett and Taylor (1980), and others have so clearly stated, the breakthrough in serving troubled children is likely to be found in the more sophisticated matching of individual children's needs with appropriate teaching strategies and materials, ecological theory may be the most appropriate and useful basis upon which to conceptualize such an approach. While a number of investigators including Swap (1974, 1978), Apter (1977), Kounin (1970, 1975), Hobbs (1966, 1975), and others have continued to work in this area, Feagan's assertion that there is no unified theory by which to apply ecological principles to emotional disturbance still holds true at this time. There have been, however, a number of intervention programs based on our developing ecological understanding of emotional disturbance, and the following section of this chapter will focus more specifically on ways to utilize an ecological perspective in the creation and implementation of programs for troubled youngsters.

OVERVIEW OF ECOLOGICAL INTERVENTIONS AND PROGRAMS

Let us begin by reviewing some of the major assumptions made by persons who develop intervention programs based upon ecological principles:

1. Each child is an inseparable part of a small social system.
2. Disturbance is not viewed as a disease located within the body of the child, but rather as discordance (a lack of balance) in the system.
3. Discordance may be defined as a disparity between an individual's abilities and the demands or expectations of the environment—"failure to match" between child and system.
4. The goal of any intervention is to make the system work, and to make it work ultimately without the intervention.
5. Improvement in any part of the system can benefit the entire system.
6. This broader view of disturbance gives rise to three major areas for intervention:
   a. Changing the child.
   b. Changing the environment.
   c. Changing attitudes and expectations.

According to Bricker (1966), deviancy "reflects a discrepancy between what the individual is capable of doing (his repertoire) and the demands made upon that repertoire by the various environmental situations in which the individual is located" (p. 6). Bricker points out that deviance is a relative, not an absolute, concept dependent upon the unavoidable interaction between behavior and the demands of various environments.

In reviewing his work with a number of seriously troubled youngsters, Bricker (1966) notes:

In every case the deviant behavior could be traced to either skill deficits or an undemanding environment. By reducing the discrepancy between environmental demands and behavior, the deviancies of those children were reduced substantially without ever focusing directly on them [p. 4].

As Bricker has described, behavior is the result of the interaction between skills and competencies that an individual already has and the demands or expectations of others in a given situation. The bigger the discrepancy between abilities and expectations, the more likely it is that "deviant" behavior will result.

At these times when the ecological system is disrupted (points of discordance), intervention is called for. The ecological viewpoint allows a variety of interventions (including those that may follow from behavioral, biophysical, or psychodynamic beliefs) but demands that all intervention be examined with regard to potential effect on the entire ecosystem. Intervention can focus on any element or combination of elements within a particular ecosystem, and all interventions must strive to be as comprehensive, coordinated, and functional as possible.

Such a perspective raises a number of important implications, some of which are listed below.

1. Emotional disturbance must be viewed, at least in part, as culturally relative. Behavior that is "normal" in one environment may be viewed as deviant in a different behavior setting.
2. Interventions must focus on all elements of a given ecosystem—not only on the identified child.
3. Interventions must focus on the realities existent in a given ecosystem. While it is obviously difficult to change the environmental conditions which surround many of the youngsters labeled emotionally disturbed, ignoring those conditions is not likely to "cure" emotional disturbance.
4. Especially in schools where the focus for so long has been on changing the child to fit the system, this perspective advocates considerable change in program planning. As Newcomer (1980) has noted:

The ecological position assumes that effecting behavioral change requires modification of the school setting as well as alteration of the child's reactions to the school [p. 337].

For example, the following is a list of interventions that might be developed in response to a troubled system. Clearly, targeting intervention on the identified child is just one of many strategies:

- *Work with the child*
  - Build new competencies.

- Change priorities.
- Obtain necessary resources.
- Find more appropriate environments.

- *Work with the adults*
  - Alter perceptions.
  - Raise or lower expectations.
  - Increase understanding or knowledge.
  - Restructure activities.

- *Work with the community*
  - Bring more resources in to school.
  - Allow more entry into community.
  - Develop coordinating ties.

- *Develop new roles*
  - Resource teacher.
  - Diagnostic-prescriptive teacher.
  - "Linking" person.

- *Develop new program models*
  - Community education/schools.
  - Outdoor education.
  - Alternative public schools.
  - Focus on prevention.
  - Teach "mental health."
  - Preventive mainstreaming.

5. Finally, one major implication of an ecological orientation is that we must give up our search for a magical answer to the problems presented by troubled children. Instead we must learn to think in terms of troubled systems and increase our understanding of the reciprocal person-environment interaction patterns. If we can move in this direction, perhaps we can approach the goal set by Hewett and Taylor (1980):

One hundred years from now we will more likely have learned to use what we presently know in a wiser and more individualized manner rather than have discovered a breakthrough approach that will be appropriate for every disturbed child. Matching the individual child and his or her individual needs with the teaching strategy and instructional materials that will do the best possible job—whether this means walking a balance beam, engaging in a Life Space Interview, providing M & M's for appropriate behavior, or enrolling the child, the family, and the community into a total treatment effort—should be our continuing goal [p. 88].

We can see, then, that as Morse, Smith, and Acker (1978) state, the general goal of an ecological intervention is not a particular state of mental health, nor a particular set of behavior patterns, but rather an increased concordance between the behavior of the child and the setting in which he resides. Since it is generally recognized that there are no pure ecological intervention techniques currently in use, most intervention programs attempt to utilize methods developed from other theoretical models but in an ecological manner.

Sometimes the immediate goal is to change the child's behavior, and then the ecologist may try to teach the child behaviors which are positively viewed by the surrounding culture, and at the same time discourage behaviors which are viewed negatively. At other times a short-term goal is to change the setting. In such cases, attempts are made to change environments by removing aspects which promote negative behaviors and by increasing environmental characteristics believed to promote positive behaviors. In still other circumstances it may be impractical or inadvisable to attempt to change either the child or the environment directly. Instead, an effort is made to improve concordance by changing the attitudes of those who perceive a child's behavior as a problem. Here the ecologist might work with family members, school personnel, and others to help them reinterpret the child's behavior and perhaps to change their requirements and expectancies regarding that behavior. Hewett and Taylor (1980) provide a dramatic example of a discordant ecosystem:

> We worked with an adolescent boy with an IQ of approximately 80. He had the misfortune to be born into a family of extremely high achievers who expected him to follow in his father's footsteps and go to Princeton University. He was attempting an academic program in high school and failing miserably. From the father's point of view, he was just lazy. His mother babied him. His older brother teased him. His teachers criticized and demeaned him. He stayed up long hours to study but still couldn't keep up. His health began to suffer. Finally, he became deeply depressed and attempted suicide. Fortunately, following this episode, a careful examination of this boy's eco-system resulted in greater understanding and acceptance on the part of all parties concerned [p. 75].

In all of these cases, ecological interventions have the common goal of adapting the fit between behavior and setting. The specific procedures used, however, may be drastically different, depending on: (1) whether the intervention is aimed at changing the child, changing the environment, or changing the perception of the child's behavior, and (2) depending upon the particular point of view of the ecological interveners—do their techniques stem from psychodynamic, behavioral, biophysical, or sociological theory? The following section will describe some particularly effective intervention programs that could be incorporated into an ecological framework.

Ecological Programs

Psychoeducation. Based on the concepts of life space, as developed by Kurt Lewin, and therapeutic milieu originally developed by Maxwell Jones (1953), as applied to the education of troubled children by Fritz Redl, William Morse, and others, the psychoeducational approach demands awareness of each child's total environment. Consequently, affective development is considered to be as important as cognitive development and educational efforts are deemed equally necessary in both areas.

Psychoeducators believe that classrooms can be utilized as therapeutic milieus by integrating all aspects of school—physical characteristics, special activities, children's peer and adult relationships, time schedules, and the like. All elements of a given classroom setting, of course, are aimed at enhancing therapeutic growth in each child.

An additional ecological basis of psychoeducational programs is the notion that teachers must be aware of children's life outside of school (at home, in the neighborhood, etc.) and of the effect of the child's life in the world on his behavior in the classroom (and vice-versa). In some cases, psychoeducators go even further with this idea, suggesting that the traditional role of teacher should be broadened to maximize the possibilities of impacting on a child's total environment. Morse (1967) has described a way in which an educator's mental health function can be enhanced by special training in a manner that enables the teacher to translate mental health principles into direct classroom action. He also suggests that teachers take upon themselves the task of improving the coordination between various parts of a child's life.

Similarly, Rhodes (1967, 1969) has proposed that teachers enter into the whole life situation of each child and in effect become "reeducators" of both the child and the important persons in the child's environment. Finally, Apter (1977) has suggested that a model of "community special education," in which educators' roles are broadened considerably, be adopted. He has further suggested, for example, that resource teachers be prepared not only as competent direct-service personnel, but also as consultants, in-service educators, and community educators.

Family Interaction. Based on the need to approach the problems of troubled children through the notion of disordered family systems, a variety of human-service professionals have developed programs that use the family as the point of intervention. Often this means that the families are seen at home instead of or in addition to being seen at schools and clinics.

Beyond the army of "family therapists" currently engaged in these kinds of efforts, some individuals (Attneave, 1976; Gatti & Coleman, 1976) have proposed an ecologically logical next step, a process called family network therapy. As currently practiced, family network therapy consists of gathering a large group of people, as much of the given individual's social system as possible, in an effort to use the network to understand interaction patterns and ultimately to intervene on behalf of the troubled person at the center of the network. Network meetings have been held with up to 100 people and family network therapists report considerable success.

Many other programs have described efforts to work effectively with family networks, though less completely than the family network therapists described above. Schopler and colleagues detailed the importance of parents to their work with severely troubled youngsters in North Carolina. Hobbs (1966) has discussed how an ecological orientation helped lead his Re-Ed program (discussed below) to the idea that parents and professionals must work in partnership. Apter et al. (1979) have documented the development of a new role—that of "family advocate"—as a successful means of achieving such parent/professional cooperation.

Physical Space Interventions. In recent years, one of the most intriguing areas of intervention based on ecological thinking has been the focus on the use of space. The increasing attention to the affects of architectural design in general, and recent legislation on architectural barriers in particular, are excellent examples of ecological interventions destined to have very broad impact on our culture and the individuals who live within it. In this area of physical space intervention, we see perhaps the best examples of ecological interventions that focus on changing the environment as the means to improve the interaction between troubled children and the systems that surround them.

With specific regard to education, Bednar and Haviland (1969) have discussed the need for classroom environments to fulfill psychological needs and to facilitate special instructional methods. Hewett's (1968) "engineered classroom" was an effort to structure the educational environment in a way that would maximize each individual's progress through a series of educational goals. This was done by designing sections of the classroom for special levels in the sequence of learning activities and by requiring the teacher to structure time, place, and specific activities for each child for each lesson.

Project Re-Education. Beginning in the early 1960s, Nicholas Hobbs and his colleagues developed and implemented a program designed to move away from the medical model (and "cure" as a goal) toward an ecological model ("making the system work") for intervention with troubled children. The idea behind Project Re-Ed was to shift the focus of work with troubled children from "treatment" by clinicians to reeducation by teachers. As described in his presidential address to the American Psychological Association (1966), Hobbs discussed reeducation as an attempt to form an educational base for intervention with children labeled disturbed and more broadly as an effort to *match* social institutions with the people whom they are meant to serve. This address is especially important to our concern here as it represents the first real explication of the ecological approach to work with troubled children.

Designed for children who are having serious difficulty in school, Project Re-Ed began with a residential school program (but only during the week—youngsters always went home on weekends). The intent of the program was to prevent hospitalization by providing both a temporary buffer between home and school as well as a rest from the stress and anxiety of each child's current situation. Children resumed living at home on a full-time basis as soon as possible and planning for that objective was always begun at the time of admission.

At the school, teacher-counselors helped youngsters with the usual learning tasks, but also, and of equal importance, with learning what was necessary for successful reentry into their home systems. As youngsters progressed, the liaison teachers (a new role for educators developed in the Re-Ed project) helped youngsters and the significant others in their systems prepare for reentry; they provided the link between the project and the child's home school. Liaison teachers continued their coordinating and mediating efforts through the youngsters' return to home and to the home school and beyond (in an effort to maintain the necessary level of intervention until a youngster's system could work successfully on its own again).

The liaison-teacher role is a critical ecological development of the Re-Ed project. The need for coordination of efforts in programs for troubled children has been discussed at length here and elsewhere. The creation of a staff role designed to focus on that task by linking various aspects of a given child's system stands as a major innovation and contribution of Project Reeducation.

In order to serve as the link between child, school, home, and community, the liaison-teacher must develop some understanding of each of those systems. In addition, in order to facilitate productive educational planning, liaison-teachers must understand and be able to design and implement individualized curricula.

Newcomer (1980) provides the following guidelines for curriculum development and implementation. They are applicable to a variety of school roles as well as to the work of liaison teachers:

1. *It must be relevant* and have meaning to the daily life of the child. It must be functional, taking into account the competencies a child needs to function in his or her own world.
2. *It must be appropriate*, considering the individual's strengths and weaknesses, conceptual level, physical development, age, interests and so on. It must have both behavioral and academic objectives.

3. *It must be well organized.* Appropriate sequence and continuity must be present and the child's prior learning must form a base for new skills and concepts.
4. *It should be reinforcing.* If a child's learning experiences are too abstract, too far removed from real life, the child will tend to lose interest. Far more motivating are experiences that satisfy and reinforce the child's natural curiosity.
5. *It should include naturalized teaching.* Either planned or spontaneously, a teacher can *use experiences outside the classroom* for instruction. For example, a walk through a littered playground can lead to a discussion of ecology and a sudden thunderstorm can become a lesson on the weather.
6. *It must include actualized teaching. A child needs to use the learned skills for practical reasons.* Motivation, which often is a great problem, becomes less of a problem when the child feels that what is being learned has a real purpose.
7. *It must include direct and immediate feedback and evaluation.* For disturbed children, feedback must immediately follow behavior. If the child is ever to monitor his or her performance, he or she must be informed immediately about the level of performance. Immediate feedback is made easier by the use of programmed, individualized instructional materials, rather than by the usual method of collecting, correcting, and returning a child's paper two or three days later.
8. *It must be directed toward the total child.* The curriculum must be directed not only to the child's academic needs, but also to his or her social and emotional needs. Goals in behavioral areas need to go hand in hand with academic goals. The needs of the total child have to be met [pp. 341–42].

Liaison-teachers must also demonstrate an ability to coordinate educational planning efforts. In order to do this, liaison-teachers must be skilled communicators, able to work together productively with colleagues, administrators, parents, social agency personnel, in addition to the youngsters themselves. Finally, it should be noted that all of these skills are also needed by persons acting in other school-based roles (resource teacher, school psychologist, etc.) in order for an ecological approach to impact on a given school.

The Re-Ed model proved successful in reaching its goal of making small social systems work by finding new ways to involve home, school, neighborhood, and community. It has been replicated and adopted in whole or in part at a number of additional sites and stands as perhaps the most comprehensive, best-documented example of ecological intervention with troubled youngsters and their systems.

BRIDGE Program Family Advocates. Another example of an ecological intervention with emotionally troubled children may be seen in the role of family advocate, developed in the BRIDGE program, a comprehensive psychoeducational program for troubled children and families. In their effort to meet the needs of a variety of youngsters within the context of each of their systems, family advocates assumed the following responsibilities:

1. They tried to teach problem-solving skills by working with families to identify the source of current difficulties, develop plans with realistic possibilities for success, and follow through to a positive resolution.
2. They supervised all other program staff working with, for, or on behalf of any family member.
3. They always focused on the coordination of services as an important task. Often advocates were able to serve as "links" binding the many and varied agencies that impinge on the lives of children and families labeled emotionally disturbed into a strong and effective chain.
4. They were always involved in both direct and indirect service functions.

By attending to the critical elements listed above and by working from an ecological perspective, family advocates were able to bring effective and efficient service to a number of very troubled children and families. In the model developed by the BRIDGE program (Apter et al., 1979), it was not at all unusual for an advocate to serve eight to ten such families effectively in a quarter-time (ten hours a week) position. The results of a comprehensive program evaluation have documented its effectiveness. One brief case study from that evaluation is presented here in an effort to concretize the family-advocate role.

The Case of NM. NM, a seven-year-old girl, was referred to the BRIDGE Program by her special education classroom teacher. At the time, NM was a suspected child abuse case because of bruises and scratches. The child abuse report made by the school for action against the family had resulted in increased family anger and alienation toward the school, and a general worsening of an already tenuous home-school relationship.

The advocate comes over every Wednesday morning. Right now they are talking about child abuse, for which the mother has been cited twice. The advocate is in the process of setting up therapy through pastoral counseling. The mother looks forward to the advocate's visits, finding them very helpful. There is no one else whom she can talk to about her problems. Her husband shares her feelings about the role and worth of the advocate in their lives.

The advocate has helped her in dealing with other adults. The mother and the teacher used not to be able to communicate, especially since it was the teacher who turned the mother in for child abuse, and the mother felt that the teacher was always accusing her. The worker from Child Abuse also made her defensive. The advocate has also sat in on conferences with that worker, and has changed the attitude of that worker so that they can talk. For the first time, in a few weeks, the mother is going to try to have a school conference without the advocate there.

The fact that both parents regard the advocate as their friend is a significant breakthrough. Letting NM attend camp was a major concession by the family. The camp experience was most effective in getting NM to intrude less on other children, reduce fighting, and be less impulsive, but it was not a steady progression over the three weeks of camp. While NM's problems are far from alleviated, the significant others in her life: parents, teachers, other school personnel are cooperating more than at any other time [after Apter et al., 1979].

We can see that the family advocate model represents one way to intervene in a child's ecosystem without necessarily focusing exclusively on the child. While NM was the identified "problem" here, the most appropriate intervention strategy seemed to place priorities on efforts to work with parents and with school personnel.

The family advocacy approach to NM and her system also exemplifies Swanson and Reinert's (1979) listing of unique aspects of the ecological point of view:

1. *Focus of intervention is on the child's entire community or ecological system.* There is an attempt to understand the impact of the environment from the perspective of the child.
2. *An effort is made to synthesize information from different social situations* in which the child may find himself. This synthesis may include physical, biological, and social variables.
3. *The approach emphasizes individual adaptation, and adjustment.* The child must adapt not only to the physical environment (e.g., classroom, home), but also to the social environment. The child's ability to successfully interrelate with others provides the framework for coping with the physical environment.
4. *The approach assumes that information obtained from various aspects of the child's environment can be used to facilitate a "congruent" environment.* Intervention is designed to provide teachers and children with more accurate and complete information about the existing environment and environmental choices.
5. *A focus is placed on values or a values orientation.* Although the child's response is culturally relative, the situation the child finds himself in reflects the internalized community values. The ecological habitats are connected with the child and each system so that modification in any one area causes a shift in values for the whole of the child's ecology [pp. 149–50, emphasis added].

CONCLUSIONS

In conclusion, here are some more specific implications of the ecological orientation for work with troubled children.

1. On the whole, we must realize that the traditional children's mental health programs have not been successful in reducing the numbers or the severity of emotional disturbances in children. The ecological orientation proposes that this failure may be due to the narrowness of previous efforts.
2. A systems viewpoint seems to be essential in examining the problem we call emotional disturbance. Even in the case of severely troubled youngsters, it seems clear from a reading of the current literature that the targeted child is seldom, if ever, the *whole* problem.
3. In order to be effective, diagnosis and treatment of troubled children must be much more comprehensive and functional than it has been in the past. It seems clear that we can benefit by gathering data from as many sources as possible; that is, we need to be inclusive instead of exclusive in what information we utilize in our thinking about the youngsters we attempt to serve. New strategies such as ecological mapping, profile systems, comprehensive case reports, and the like are important additions to ecological understanding.
4. Everyone has needs and we must pay attention to them. The ecological orientation stresses the importance of looking at the entire system surrounding each child. Our own experiences and the documentation of efforts by many others indicates the importance of understanding and responding to the needs and concerns of significant others (parents, teachers, friends, etc.) in each child's environment.
5. Objective reality may be less important than perspective. From all that's gone above, it seems clear that the viewpoint of participants in each system actually defines the problem that we call emotional disturbance.
6. Coordination is the key. The efforts of such people as the liaison-teacher developed in Project Re-Education, or the family advocate developed in the BRIDGE program are examples of the newly developing need to focus on a critical aspect of work with troubled children, the coordination of the many people concerned.
7. Building strong ecosystems should be the ultimate goal of intervention with troubled children. Linkages between various aspects of each child's world are seen as critical elements (not "fringe extras" that are only to be considered if time allows) in the development of successful programs.
8. Ecological interventions can use numerous resources ignored by other approaches. Children live and learn within the context of their own environments. Parents, siblings, neighborhood peer groups, church, school, playground are all potential elements of a particular child's world. Each element has an impact on the child and through the child on each other; a youngster's difficulty in one part of his or her system

(e.g., home) can have serious repercussions in another part (e.g., school). Concern is with the whole child.

9. Ecological interventions can have a broad positive impact which will benefit others as well as the "target" child. The implications of an ecological perspective for the *prevention* of emotional disturbances are enormous.

10. Ecological assessment strategies represent efforts to utilize more information in the development of effective programs for troubled children. Hobbs (1975) has clearly documented the inadequacy of our current categorization system and the limited diagnosis-intervention, child-only focus on which it is based. Focusing all our attention on the child while ignoring the family, school, and community that surround him or her can make the identification and remediation of difficulties almost impossible.

11. Educators of troubled children must accept responsibility for alleviating conditions that have created troubled children in the past. For example, Hobbs (1975) discussed turnstile children whose case histories are filled with neglect, abuse, school problems, run-ins with the law, and recommendations for treatment, placement, and education that never came about. The lack of coordination of services for these children results in their continual deterioration, and it is imperative that special educators define their jobs in ways that will allow them to fill these unmet needs.

12. Preparation of teachers to work with troubled children must change to reflect the ecological community model. There are two major directions which this effort may take. First, the curriculum for teacher training should be modified to include instruction in the development, implementation, and management of ecosystems. Second, there should be, as Hobbs (1975) has suggested, experimental training programs for new kinds of roles (liaison-teacher-counselor, child advocate, etc.). If educators believe that disturbance resides in the interaction between people at a particular time, then training must enable teachers to operate on this systems level.

Such training now involves a number of varying educational roles. Morse, Bruno, and Morgan (1975) have pointed out that

> It would seem that training of special teachers for the disturbed child has come to mean several things: the training of all regular teachers since they are all likely to meet such children in their classes; the training of all special education teachers since all (mentally retarded, learning disabilities, etc.) have this as a significant component in their work; the training of "specialist" emotionally disturbed teachers for work with the very seriously socially and emotionally handicapped [p. 254].

The recent report, *Challenges for Children's Mental Health Services* (April 1977), prepared by the MITRE Corporation in collaboration with the Mental Health Service Development Branch of the National Institute of Mental Health provides some insight into the effectiveness of ecological approaches to service delivery. That report, which represents the surveyed opinions of a diverse group of 50 experts in the area of children's mental health, identifies some specific mental health needs of children, services that must be developed or improved in order to meet those needs, and barriers that currently impede the delivery of those services.

It is striking to note that of the ten services selected as the most important in that survey, an ecological approach like the BRIDGE program's family advocacy model has been directly providing eight. That is to say, family advocates have been involved in (1) training and counseling parents to foster healthy mental development in children; (2) providing early detection and referral for appropriate intervention; (3) educating all children in life-management skills; (4) training educators through a developmental and humanistic approach; (5) strengthening and supporting families; (6) improving service coordination and accessibility; (7) providing community-based outpatient treatment; (8) and training teachers about the needs of handicapped children. Also, while family advocates have not typically been involved directly in the provision of the two remaining needed services (comprehensive health care and community-based residential treatment in nonhospital settings), they certainly have acted as facilitators for the provision of those services.

It is also important to realize the impact that an ecological service-delivery approach could have on the ten barriers which survey participants identified as presenting the biggest impediments to the development and/or implementation of needed services. In each case a comprehensive, coordinated systems-oriented approach might be expected to carry more than the usual clout to bear against the following major obstacles:

1. Services not tailored to needs of individuals.
2. Poor working relationships among service providers and agencies.
3. Decision makers who do not perceive the need for services.
4. Inappropriate input to planning for services.
5. Prohibitive cost of mental health services.
6. Political/social resistance to change.
7. Lack of ability to reach potential clients.
8. Medical model which impedes the provision of preventive services.
9. Lack of definition of mental health.
10. Services which dehumanize and frustrate clients.

The ecological viewpoint has had a major impact on the development of effective psychoeducational programs for troubled children. Project Re-Ed, the BRIDGE program, and other "systems"-oriented examples cited above have documented the importance of adopting an ecological perspective to such efforts. Despite the efforts of the variety of people committed to the systems approach cited in this chapter, however, it should be noted that to date, the promise of the ecological viewpoint remains largely unfulfilled. For a variety of reasons, ecologists have not been very successful either in specifying the applications of ecological theory for work with troubled children or in training prospective educators, psychologists, and other human-service workers in the possibilities of this new approach. Perhaps the problem is best articulated by Swap (1978):

> In the final analysis, the ecological model represents a method of analysis, a "tolerance for diversity" of multiple interacting variables in multiple sites at multiple levels. Conveying this notion to others in a way that is clear, acceptable, and ultimately useful represents a major challenge to ecologists [p. 195].

5
Comprehensive Programs: Total Schools and Total Teachers

The ecological perspective described in Chapter 4 stresses the need for comprehensive approaches to the problems of troubled children and troubled systems. In addition, the enormous scope of the troubled systems problem magnifies the need for increased efforts to prevent emotional disturbances from occuring in the first place. We need both: comprehensive programming efforts for youngsters who have already been identified as troubled and solid preventive activities designed to reduce the numbers of youngsters who might be identified in the future.

This chapter focuses on a discussion of the need for our educational programs to provide comprehensive services for some children while attempting to prevent emotional disturbances in others. Said another way, this chapter centers on the concept of a "total school" and the roles staff members might play in such a setting. In so doing, we hope to apply what we know about ecological theory to our program planning efforts in an attempt to bring theory closer to real-life situations and ultimately to increase our impact on troubled systems.

We can begin by examining some recent changes in educational and special educational programming strategies. According to Magne (1977), the basis of the Swedish education system changed in the early 1970s from a narrow- to a broad-front strategy:

Until the last [few] years, the usual strategy of public schooling was the narrow-front strategy. This means that you plan to influence the young people mainly inside the school buildings. You don't bother very much [with] what happens outside the class and hope for a positive transfer from the formal or informal lessons you arrange in your classrooms or otherwise in connection with your specified school curriculum.

The alternative is a broad-front strategy. You organize the influences in many ways. You write and combine activities of several public services, not only inside the school system, but also with the help of social welfare, health service, and non-governmental activities of various kinds. It is the latter type of strategy which is now being introduced in the Scandinavian countries [pp. 8, 9].

This shift to a "broad-front" strategy might also be defined as a more comprehensive approach to programming and has been much discussed in the United States as well as in Scandinavia. Morse (1977), for example, stated one dimension of the need for comprehensive services quite clearly:

I do not see enough examples where the community mental health people and the school are working together with the problems of the family and the child and are trying to deal realistically with the total life dilemma that many of the youngsters have [p. 160].

In that same interview (November 1977), Morse draws the connection between the need for more comprehensive approaches to the education of troubled children and the ecological perspective:

I would say that the biggest thing that has happened is the broadening of the concepts of intervention, that is, basically moving from a rather restrictive dynamic point of view to an inclusion of behavioristic and other learning approaches and to a greater appreciation of the ecological factors that tell us why some of the interventions that we try do not have long-term permanence [p. 158].

Apter et al. (1979) noted that for seriously troubled children enmeshed in a context of multiple and longstanding problems, it may be unrealistic to expect narrow, short-term interventions to have long-range, lasting effects. Comprehensive approaches to programming are needed for the typically complicated situations of troubled children and such strategies are very compatible with the ecological orientation discussed in Chapter 4.

As stated earlier, an ecological orientation to program development is needed because:

1. Traditional programs for troubled children have not been very successful in impacting on the total problem of emotional disturbance.
2. The targeted child is seldom, if ever, the whole problem.

3. The documented inadequacies of our current categorization systems point to the need for more comprehensive diagnostic and treatment plans.
4. In order to intervene effectively with children, it is necessary to understand and respond to the needs of significant others in each youngster's environment.
5. In all cases, coordination of efforts is critical.
6. Building strong ecosystems should be the ultimate objective of our intervention efforts.
7. Ecological efforts can utilize a variety of resources that are ignored by other approaches.
8. Ecological interventions can have a broader positive impact, benefitting others as well as the "target" child.
9. Systems-oriented programs respond to the need to alleviate conditions that have created troubled children in the past.

In discussing the weaknesses of our current categorization system, Hobbs (1975) pointed out that focusing all attention on a child while ignoring his family, school, and community (i.e., the rest of the ecosystem) makes the identification and remediation of difficulties almost completely impossible. In fact, we must recognize by now that there are no absolutely right teachers, methods, or environments. Instead, we need to strive for harmonious ecosystems in which the potential for meeting all human needs is maximized. Swap (1974) described a developmental and ecological view of disturbing classroom behavior and concluded that classrooms are in need of creative and flexible individual-needs-based programming. More specifically, she suggested that each class be planned for maximal teacher-student fit; that every physical environment could accommodate a wide range of programs; that teachers and students should engage in a continuous process of specific goal setting and follow-up; and finally, that the end product of education should be increased strength and competence for teacher and student based on a recognition and valuing of individual differences.

Perhaps most importantly, use of an ecological model implies that educators and others who work with troubled children must accept responsibility for alleviating conditions that have created troubled children in the past. As an example, Hobbs (1975) discussed turnstile children whose case histories are filled with neglect, abuse, school problems, run-ins with the law, and recommendations for treatment, placement, and education that never came about. The lack of coordination of services for these children results in their continual deterioration, and it is imperative that special educators, psychologists, social workers, and the like define their jobs in ways that will allow them to fill these unmet needs.

Adoption of an ecologically oriented model may also require the development of an extended role for the public schools. Stickney (1968) suggested that schools might actually be regarded as community mental health centers because of the many opportunities for crisis intervention with some troubled youngsters and for prevention of emotional disturbances in other children. Consequently, Stickney advocated an ecological model of diagnosis as the only practical way to begin programming for troubled or potentially troubled children.

Hobbs (1975) suggested that public schools accept responsibility for ensuring the coordinated delivery of comprehensive services to *all* children with special needs. Hobbs listed seven elements of the reasoning behind his suggestion:

1. The school is the one public agency normally responsible for helping families to socialize children. In terms of normalization, the school is the most appropriate place.
2. Schools are already responsible for providing educational services to exceptional children.
3. Once special disabilities are attended to, most children's needs are educational and schools are the most competent educational agency.
4. Schools are geographically dispersed to serve the total population, which is an absolute necessity for a comprehensive service program.
5. Available space in school buildings is increasing as the birth rate declines. The use of schools would erase the need for huge capital expenditures.
6. Parents and children are already familiar with schools. The concept of community school is in harmony with the service needs of exceptional children.
7. Schools have a state and local tax base that can provide funds to add to federal or private support in the service of exceptional children.

If we were to accept Hobbs' suggestion, schools might come to resemble what Apter (1977) has termed the "Total School." The total school philosophy, graphically depicted in Figure 5.1, represents one vision of a model for public schools as the locus of comprehensive and coordinated services for *all* children. In addition, a total school could be conceptualized as a comprehensive educational resource for all the children and adults of the community in which it was located.

Based on an ecological viewpoint, the total school philosophy assumes that children live and learn within the context of their own environments. Parents, siblings, neighborhood peer groups, church, school, and playground are all potentially elements of a particular child's world. Each element has an impact on a child and, through the child, on each other; a

Fig. 5.1. The total school.

Total School assumes:
1. Children live and learn in context of own environments.
2. Parents, siblings, neighborhood peer groups, church, school, playground, etc., are all potential elements of each child's world.
3. Each element has impact on child and through the child on each other.
4. Youngster's difficulty in one part of his or her system (e.g., home) can have serious repercussions in another part (e.g., school).

Total School objectives:
1. To focus on important elements of child's system as well as on child.
2. For teachers to see themselves as problem solvers who work together with children to develop solutions to disturbing classroom situations.
3. To provide appropriate educational programs for all children, including those with special needs, in least restrictive setting possible.
4. A commitment to preventing emotional disturbances through efforts to understand better and accept more actively a wider range of individual differences in children.

youngster's difficulty in one part of his or her system (e.g., home) can have serious repercussions in another part (e.g., school).

This kind of a systems orientation necessitates the development of educational programs that focus on the important elements of a child's system as well as on the child. In a total school, for example, adults would attempt to work with families, coordinate efforts, even change their own behavior when appropriate, in addition to helping children develop more effective control of their actions. Teachers could see themselves as problem solvers and work together with children to find solutions to disturbing classroom situations.

There are two major objectives underlying the total school philosophy: the provision of comprehensive, coordinated children's services, and the prevention of emotional disturbances in children.

Comprehensive and Coordinated Children's Services

The concern in a total school is with the whole child. School staff members are committed to providing appropriate educational programs for all children, including those with special needs, in the least restrictive setting possible. In order to maximize the impact of the program for children, a total school might offer continuing educational programs for parents and other local adults, could serve as a central meeting place for neighborhood groups, and would provide a supportive atmosphere in which staff (as well as children) can live and grow.

The concern is also with the provision of timely services that are appropriate to each child's developmental needs and that are based on a thorough and workable planning process that lends itself to continuous evaluation and replanning efforts. Finally, comprehensive and coordinated children's services can be most effectively provided by a careful matching of individual children's needs and available human and material resources.

Prevention of Emotional Disturbance

The systems orientation that underlies the total school philosophy stresses the importance of examining a child's entire "life space" for the sources of disturbance. Disturbance is seen as a mismatch between a child's abilities and the demands of his or her environment. Consequently, either an increase in a child's skills or a decrease in environmental pressures can prevent the occurrence of school situations that produce or exacerbate disturbance.

A total school is committed to preventing emotional disturbance through efforts to understand better, accept actively, and more successfully develop and implement educational programs that can include children with a wide range of abilities and interests. The acceptance of individual differences, along with the ability to utilize approaches to learning, like affective education, that can work to help children improve self-understanding and self-control are important elements in the prevention of emotional disturbance.

A more detailed description of the concept of prevention and specific preventive programs and activities may be found in Chapter 11.

While most communities may be far from able to adopt a total school model, it does seem clear that at the very least the individual-centered deficit model from which special education has grown has not been a very effective basis for efforts with troubled children. The implications of the traditional special education model are not sufficient in terms of understanding the causes of disturbed behavior, developing treatment programs for the remediation of deviant behavior, or preventing the occurrence of troubling behavior in children today. In fact, the increasing complexity in efforts to serve troubled children make the need for a special education model based on ecological theory greater today than ever before.

Efforts to provide appropriate educational programs for emotionally disturbed children, like efforts with other groups of handicapped youngsters, have been changing dramatically over the past few years. Public Law 94:142 and the implications of its entry into program development efforts in local districts are combining to create a variety of new alternatives for the education of troubled children. The effects have been essentially twofold: we are beginning to see more seriously disturbed children in public school settings and we are also seeing the rapid development of new models for the delivery of services to such youngsters.

Unfortunately, in the rush to provide service to more youngsters, many of the models being utilized for educational programs for disturbed children are failing to make use of the experience of earlier programs targeted at this population. For example, though a number of psychoeducational programs have documented the importance of a family orientation to work with disturbed children, great numbers of self-contained classroom teachers, resource teachers, consulting teachers, and the like are prevented from working with families because of the specific demands of particular job descriptions. More generally, despite the strong movement in recent years toward an "ecological" viewpoint that stresses the perspective of emotional disturbance as a mismatch between individual and environment and emphasizes the importance of working with the "whole child," many teachers of troubled children are not allowed to take even one step outside the more limited direct-service-only model developed in an earlier time.

This raises a problem that may be defined by the need to develop new models of school-based service delivery (to children labeled emotionally disturbed/behaviorally disordered) that are: more comprehensive in scope, more consistent with previous efforts to achieve change with troubled children, more oriented toward the developing ecological viewpoint, and more practically implementable in public schools today. The total school model is one example of the type of service delivery format needed for effective intervention into troubled systems, and may be seen as representative of a class of models that share the following characteristics:

1. A focus on ecosystems instead of individuals and a corresponding target population that is not limited to identified children.
2. An effort to utilize a wide array of community resources in program plans.
3. A continuing commitment to the coordination of services and the cooperation needed to attain that goal.
4. An attempt to operate in truly interdisciplinary ways and to overcome difficulties presented by issues of territoriality and professional preciousness.
5. A view of education as a lifelong round-the-clock enterprise.
6. The inclusion of activities aimed at prevention in addition to remediation.

To summarize, a total school model represents a strategy to apply the principles of an ecological approach to the dilemmas presented by troubled children and the troubled systems that surround them. Such models can respond to the need for comprehensive and coordinated programs by offering new ideas and directions for intervening in difficult situations. In addition, a total school model incorporates movement from a narrow- to a broadfront strategy discussed earlier and can be used as the basis for public school programs as well as more clinically oriented facilities.

A total school model can be best explained by focusing on the specifics of role descriptions for staff members who work in such programs. As an example, we can focus here on the development of an ecological or "systems"-oriented model for the resource teacher's role with disturbed children. Ultimately, of course, it is important to recognize that comparable efforts must also be aimed at developing more effective models for the variety of other teacher roles (self-contained classroom teachers, regular classroom teachers involved in mainstreaming, consulting teachers, etc.) involved in the education of children who are labeled emotionally disturbed. It is equally important to focus similar efforts on the roles of other professionals with troubled children.

RESOURCE TEACHER

An increasingly important staff role for the provision of educational services to disturbed children is that of the resource teacher. The resource teacher can provide direct services to children, both individually and in groups of various sizes, and also may provide assistance to the other adults who work with children with special needs. Further, resource teachers often occupy central positions in schools, with lots of opportunities for interactions with children, teachers, administrators, and community members.

Weiderholt, Hammill, and Brown (1978) define resource programs as follows:

> Basically, a resource program is any school operation in which a person (usually the resource teacher) has the responsibility of providing supportive educationally related services to children and/or to their teachers. The resource teacher may provide the student with direct services in the form of analytic, remedial, developmental, or compensatory teaching and/or behavioral management. Such services may be conducted either in the regular classroom or in a room designated for that purpose, such as the resource room or center. The services offered to the regular or special teachers may include, but are not limited to, helping them either to adjust or to select curricula to meet the unique needs of some children and to manage the classroom behavior of disruptive students. In addition, the resource teacher also discusses with parents the problems evidenced by their children [p. 4].

Weiderholt, Hamill, and Brown point out that resource rooms should not be viewed as part-time self-contained special education classrooms, and that resource teachers should be seen as support persons for whole schools (not just for the few youngsters who receive direct services). The Council for Exceptional Children (1976) also emphasizes the importance of cooperation between classroom teachers and resource teachers in the success of resource programs.

If viewed from an ecological perspective, the role of resource teacher carries great potential both for delivering appropriate direct services to disturbed children and for effecting necessary system changes through a variety of more indirect service functions (consultation, in-service education, working with families, etc.). Such a viewpoint is based on the belief that a good resource teacher must be an effective problem solver, skillful at helping both children and adults.

Unfortunately, the often overwhelming need for service and the frustration produced in classroom teachers, administrators, and special educators who deal with disturbed children, combine to create a "clinical press" that strives to find solutions to the complicated problems of troubled youngsters by offering more and more direct services. Frequently, this turns out to be a self-defeating process for the reasons outlined below.

1. The *overemphasis on direct service* to the exclusion of more ecological systems—focused roles can be short-sighted, i.e., more services to

children might be provided today, but there's little evidence to indicate that children served in this limited way will be much better off tomorrow.

2. Equally important is the evidence that indicates *there will never be enough trained personnel to meet the needs* of the number of disturbed youngsters in our society. In other words, no matter how much direct service is provided to troubled children by resource teachers, there will always be more youngsters waiting in line for their opportunity.

3. A direct-service-only model makes it impossible for resource personnel to become involved in what may turn out to be the most critical professional activity related to emotional disturbance in youngsters: *prevention*. This is especially frustrating because of the critical position of resource teachers at the interface of so many of the systems that impinge on the lives of disturbed children.

4. It must also be recognized that the problems enumerated above are magnified by the *ineffectiveness of our typical direct-services-only approach*. In fact, the provision of effective service to troubled children is a very difficult enterprise that hardly guarantees success. As more and more seriously impaired youngsters move into public school programs, we can only expect the task to become even more difficult.

5. The direct-service-only model increases the likelihood that resource teachers will fall into the *"expert trap"* and the corresponding expectations to be able to provide magical cures to very difficult problems. While not diminishing the need for expert services, an ecological perspective to resource teaching emphasizes the importance of coordination and linking functions in the effective implementation of programs for troubled children.

6. An ecological model of service delivery is also more in keeping with the *"least restrictive setting"* philosophy. Such a perspective focuses on the whole child in the context of the systems in which he or she lives, in school and out, strengths as well as weaknesses, affective as well as cognitive domains, prevention before the fact in addition to treatment later on, coordinated with instead of separate from regular education, comprehensive assessment rather than narrow diagnosis, etc.

7. The push toward *mainstreaming* really *demands* that a *coordination* function become a central aspect of the resource teacher role. As Meisgeier (1976) has stated:

If our expectation is that 1-hour daily sessions in the resource rooms will magically or pervasively eliminate children's learning problems without concomitant efforts to teach children in a healthy learning environment the other four hours of each day, we are surely going to be disappointed. The process must be a cooperative effort between regular, alternative and special education to be called a mainstreaming effort [p. 259].

SYSTEMS-ORIENTED RESOURCE TEACHER

Clearly, a direct-service-only model is not the most effective basis for a resource program or for the job description of a resource teacher. The systems-oriented resource teacher's role is not focused exclusively on direct services. Instead, such a role mandates an emphasis on indirect services such as consultation, in-service education, and coordination in addition to the more typical resource teacher responsibilities.

Figure 5.2 depicts the range of potential activities that may fall into the resource teacher's domain. While the constraints of time may make it unlikely that most resource teachers will be able to perform productively in all of these areas, it is essential for each resource teacher to define at least part of the role in terms of the indirect, preventive, and linking services in addition to direct-service responsibilities.

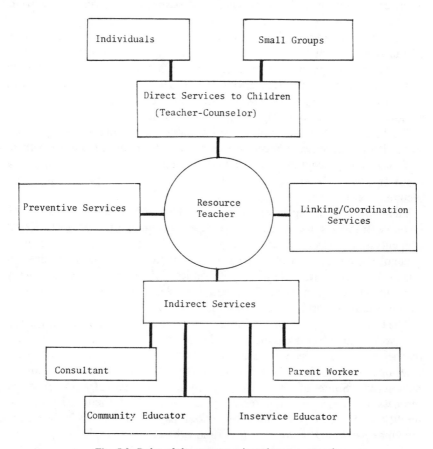

Fig. 5.2. Roles of the systems-oriented resource teacher.

Figure 5.2 depicts a model of resource teaching that includes a variety of direct- and indirect-service functions. In the systems-oriented resource teacher model, teachers are expected to be prepared to spend varying portions of their time, depending upon the needs of the children and the schools in which they work, providing direct services to individuals or small groups of children, consulting with other school members, working with parents, developing and/or delivering formal or informal in-service education programs, serving as liaisons with community services and programs, initiating preventive programs, and serving as the coordinator of services to particular youngsters and families.

Clearly, the model presented in Figure 5.2 is much broader than a direct-service-only format. Consequently, the adoption of this kind of model can be an effective response to many of the problems associated with narrower models discussed earlier. Table 5.1 lists some of the major problems in resource teaching and the reactions of a systems-oriented resource teacher model.

The problems presented in Table 5.1 are divided into five areas: the role of the resource teacher, the model of teaching, the context of resource teaching, the focus of the resource teacher's efforts, and the delivery system. In each of those categories, a number of specific problems have been identified and in every case, the adoption of an ecological approach to resource teaching would help resolve the problem.

For example, the inclusion of both direct- and indirect-service roles would help to decrease the role confusion and role conflicts that stem from differing role perceptions of the resource teacher position. Similarly, a focus on children's strengths as well as weaknesses could provide more effective program ideas than a focus on deficiencies only.

The ecological perspective should also be integrated into each of the resource teacher's roles. Table 5.2 describes some of the most critical elements in the direct-service or teacher-counselor role. Table 5.3 focuses on some of the most important aspects of one of the indirect-service roles: in-service education. Inspection of both tables will reveal some of the many ways in which resource teachers can provide comprehensive services to troubled children and troubled systems.

The brief listing (in Tables 5.2 and 5.3) of critical elements in the teacher-counselor and in-service-educator roles of the systems-oriented-resource-teacher may be seen as guidelines for functioning in just two of the many roles open to school staff members who view their jobs from an ecological perspective. Some of the additional indirect-service roles for resource teachers are described in later chapters, and all of these roles can be modified to fit the situations of school psychologists, social workers, guidance personnel, administrators, and others.

An example of an effort to adapt the systems-oriented resource teacher

Table 5.1. Composite Listing of Problems in Resource Teaching and The Systems-Oriented Resource Teacher (SORT) Model's Reaction.

Area	Problem	ORT Model Reaction
I. Role of Resource Teacher	a. Role Confusion (Direct or Indirect Service)	a, b, c. Inclusion of Direct and Indirect Service Roles:
	b. Differing Role Perceptions (Lack of Common Language)	Teacher Counselor Consultant Inservice Educator Community Educator
	c. Role Conflicts	Parent Worker Coordinator Prevention Worker
	d. Expert/Specialist Trap	d. Generalist/Facilitator/ Coordinator
	e. Rescue Expectations	e, f. Member of a Work and Support Team
	f. Danger of Isolation and burnout	
	g. Serve identified Special Education kids only	g. Serve typical children as well as Special Education Children
II. Model of Teaching	a. Rigid Orientation to task (One right answer)	a. Eclectic, Ecological, Integrating Matching Model
	b. Individualistic	b. Social Systems Perspective
	c. Static Categorization (as in Classical Prescriptive)	c. Dynamic Problem Solving Process
	d. Acceptance of Status Quo	d. Creation of Alternatives
III. Context of Resource Teaching	a. Special Education as it exists	a. Changing Special and Regular Education — Attitudes — Behavior
	b. "My own little world"	b. Culture of School and Community
	c. Confined to School	c. Use of community resources, interagency coordination
	d. No necessary relationship between school and home	d. Demands Coordinated Home/ School Programs
IV. Focus of Resource Teacher Efforts	a. Children in school	a. Whole Child
	b. Children Only	b. Children and adults
	c. Children's deficiencies	c. Children's strengths as well as weaknesses

Table 5.1. (Cont.)

Area	Problem	ORT Model Reaction
	d. Children's cognitive skills	d. The affective as well as cognitive domain
V. Delivery System	a. Segregated Programs	a. Least Restrictive Setting Philosophy
	b. Resident or Itinerant	b. Appropriate Elements of both
	c. Focus on Casualties	c. Prevention as well as Treatment or Remediation
	d. Programs and Placements based on Financial Realities	d. Programs based on Individual Needs
	e. Categorical Programs	e. Noncategorical interrelated programs
	f. Direct Service Only	f. Emphasis on Indirect Service as well
	g. Concurrent with Regular Education (separate tracks)	g. Coordinated with Regular Education
	h. Children must be labeled to be served	h. All kids can receive special services without stigma
	i Diagnosis (medical model)	i. Assessment (ecological model)
	j. Resource Program as Dumping Ground	j. Resource Program as Valued Setting

model for the situation in one suburban school district may be a useful way to summarize this discussion. Table 5.4 describes the resource program developed in the Jamesville-Dewitt (N.Y.) school district.

The program described in Table 5.4 is one example of the way in which an ecological perspective can be utilized to provide a comprehensive base for a newly developing service-delivery system. The resource teacher who works in this program will not be confined to a direct-service-only role, will understand that consultation and in-service education are also important aspects of the resource teacher role, and will function as part of a team. Working in the context of such a comprehensive program would certainly enhance the resource teacher's effectiveness.

Clearly, the resource teacher is in a critical position, able to both provide necessary skills and supports to a range of youngsters as well as to serve a leadership role, coordinating the service provision efforts of others. By

Table 5.2. System-Oriented Resource Teacher: Critical Elements in the Direct-Service
(Teacher-Counselor) Role.

1. Be interested in and skillful at *child-study* (observation skills).
2. Be able to utilize a variety of *comprehensive, nonbiased assessment strategies* (especially in natural environments).
3. Be able to prepare and provide one-to-one and small-group *instruction* in a *variety* of academic areas with a wide range of children.
4. Be willing and able to *listen* to children.
5. Be a *support person/advocate* for all children.
6. Demonstrate mastery at matching *psychoeducational interventions* with particular youngsters.
7. Refuse to let *method* predominate over children's needs.
8. Get *help* when needed and have knowledge of local/national specialists.
9. Be a *creative* and *energetic problem solver*.
10. Be able to *organize* (and help others organize) and manage a variety of learning environments.
11. Be aware of *current resources* and educational approaches which will enhance the overall program.
12. Be able to *adapt teaching style* to match individual learning styles.
13. *Provide opportunities* for students to have meaningful input into their overall programs including participation in establishing goals for the IEP, where appropriate.
14. Be skillful at utilizing *peer counselors* and volunteers of all ages to fortify the program.
15. Provide the learning experiences in a *variety of physical environments*.

focusing on indirect-service roles such as the in-service educator described in Table 5.3 and by becoming skilled in content areas such as comprehensive psychoeducational planning, affective education, the identification and utilization of community resources, teaming or multidisciplinary efforts, and interpersonal communication, resource teachers should not only improve their effectiveness with identified youngsters, but also prevent many additional children from reaching the point where they too would be referred for direct-service help. That is to say, if resource teachers could assist school staff members in their efforts to understand better, accept actively, and more successfully develop and implement educational programs for youngsters with a wide range of abilities and interests, they would surely prevent the occurrence of a number of emotional disturbances. The acceptance of individual differences and the ability to implement programs that can help all children increase self-understanding and self-control are important aspects of both the systems-oriented resource teacher role and the prevention of emotional disturbance.

While there are undoubtedly countless ways in which the resource teacher might pursue his or her goal of providing comprehensive services to troubled youngsters, the use of an ecological basis for such efforts provides a productive starting point. As described above, such a model puts special emphasis on viewing each child in the context of a small social system (in-

Table 5.3. System-Oriented Resource Teacher: Critical Elements in the
In-Service-Educator Role.

A. *Formal*

1. Be prepared to develop and conduct a needs assessment to learn: what current in-service needs exist, what previous efforts (and outcomes) have been, and what formats and resources might be most appropriate.
2. Facilitate the development of objectives that: reflect the needs identified in 1., specify activities and expectations for the upcoming program, result from the efforts of a multidisciplinary planning team, and are realistic in terms of time and resources.
3. Be able to develop a comprehensive plan that attends to the following elements:

   (a) content (areas to be covered).
   (b) type of activity proposed (lecture, "hands on," small group).
   (c) teaching style to be used (informal, formal, etc.).
   (d) length of training (how many sessions?).
   (e) number of participants.
   (f) qualifications of participants.
   (g) voluntary or involuntary participation.
   (h) time arrangements (schedule which matches those of participants, time estimate for each activity, each session).
   (i) release time (substitutes arranged if necessary).
   (j) qualified personnel to conduct the inservice training.
   (k) necessary materials (handouts, equipment, facilities, announcement flyers, etc., packets to be made up to disseminate prior to workshop, during or post workshop).
   (l) evaluation mechanisms.
   (m) follow-up activities.

B. *Informal*

1. Keep staff up to date on current mandates, programs, procedures.
2. Offer to assist classroom teachers, other special education personnel, administrators, parents, students, etc. on a frequent informal basis.
3. Utilize opportunities such as the teacher's lounge, department meetings, etc. to exchange information.
4. Develop a group of staff who are willing to serve as resources to other staff, assisting in efforts to provide more individualized learning environments.

---

cluding the variety of service providers typically involved with disturbed children and families); the coordination of the efforts of the variety of persons involved; the provision of skills and supports to both children and adults; the productive utilization of existing resource networks; and the importance of incorporating indirect-service functions into a variety of human-service role descriptions.

Resource teachers serve in important new roles both for children identified as emotionally disturbed and also for a variety of nonidentified but potentially troubled typical children. Unless we can act quickly to bring an ecological systems orientation to the work of resource personnel, we may well run the risk of re-creating the same kind of narrow, segregated, direct-service-only model that has failed so many troubled children and shortened the professional careers of so many special educators in the past.

Table 5.4. Jamesville-Dewitt School District: Resource Teacher Program.

Rationale

The Jamesville-Dewitt school district seeks to provide a comprehensive program of educational services for all children. Emphasis is placed on prevention of disabilities, and early intervention activities with children exhibiting learning problems and handicapping conditions. Resource programs are established to assist the school staff in considering the uniqueness, diversity, and range of learning needs presented by pupils. Some children exhibit significant deficits in the essential learning processes involved in using spoken or written language. The resource program supports the child who demonstrates a severe discrepancy between intellectual ability and basic educational performance in listening, thinking, writing, spelling, or arithmetic.

Resource Teacher

The resource teacher provides supportive educationally related services to pupils and their teachers. Direct services, provided either in the regular classroom or within the resource room, include assessment, teaching, and consultation specifically related to the child's developmental needs. The duties of the resource teacher are to:

1. Assess individual pupil needs. Critical areas to be evaluated include developmental levels, achievement, learning styles, attitudes toward self and others, and elements of the learning environment.
2. Facilitate preparation and implementation of individualized instructional programs. Individual and small-group instruction programs shall be developed for referred pupils, with special consideration given to the child's specific learning strengths and the regular classroom program in which the child is enrolled.
3. Consult with the school staff. The resource teacher supports the activities of the classroom teacher through consultation about the pupil's specific educational needs, resource room program, regular classroom program, and coordination of all related services being provided to the child and teacher.
4. Participate in planning and conducting districtwide inservice activities as appropriate.

Resource Room

The resource program shall include a room specially equipped and operated under the direction of the resource teacher. Space and equipment provisions shall be made in the resource room for individual and small-group instruction, teacher and parent conferences, and storage of supplies and equipment for the resource program. The room should be centrally located in close proximity to classrooms.

Resource Team

Each building housing a resource program shall maintain an active resource team including membership as follows:

- Elementary School – Principal (Chairperson), Psychologist, Reading Specialist, Resource Teacher, Social Worker, Teacher of child being evaluated, Director of Pupil Personnel Services as appropriate.

- Middle School and High School – Principal (Chairperson), Counselors, Reading Specialist, Resource Teacher, Team Representative for each child being evaluated, Director of Pupil Personnel Services as appropriate.

Responsibilities of the Resource Team are to:

1. Develop a form to be used for written referrals for resource program placement.
2. Review all written referrals for placement of pupils in the resource program.

Table 5.4. (Cont.)

3. Determine priorities and recommend placements in the program.
4. Monitor progress of pupils.
5. Recommend changes in or termination of resource program placements.
6. Assure compliance of resource program with school district guidelines.
7. Communicate resource program guidelines and activities to total building staff and assure that pupils requiring services are appropriately referred.
8. Assure that a staff member is designated to contact parents regarding referral to the resource program if appropriate.

Source: After Jamesville-Dewitt School District, Resource Teacher Program, 2nd Draft, Winter 1978.

CONCLUSIONS

Finally, it may be useful to step back from our discussion of comprehensive programming and from the total school model and resource teacher example in order to look once again at the larger picture. According to the Bureau of Education for the Handicapped (BEH—now the Office of Special Education—OSE):

> In order for an emotionally disturbed child to receive a free appropriate education a number of service providers are going to have to work collaboratively together. Among these service providers are education, mental health, vocational rehabilitation and social services [CCBD Newsletter, 1979, pp. 1–2].

At the present time, many of the services that might be offered to a troubled child and family are provided on a fragmented and disconnected basis. Such a failure to coordinate efforts often magnifies the family disturbance instead of preventing its further deterioration. Clearly, the need for comprehensive programs means a need for coordinated programs. Efforts to coordinate the work of service providers from a variety of disciplines can be optimized through adoption of an ecological perspective and will be discussed in Chapter 7.

It is also important for program planners to know where they fit into the overall service-delivery scheme. Rhodes and Gibbins (1972) have described a naturally occurring threat-recoil cycle with the following sequence of actions:

1. A pattern of threatening behavior occurs (children are acting violently in schools).
2. The behavior attains some public image (these children are emotionally disturbed).
3. The community recoils or reacts (these children are dangerous, something must be done).

4. Spokesmen appear in the community (the children must be treated, punished, etc.).
5. The distress widens (this is not just a classroom problem—our schools are being threatened).
6. The distress becomes a political/power issue (why doesn't somebody do something?).
7. Political action is taken (legislation is passed, priorities are established, funds are allocated, etc.).
8. Program planners are involved (let's set up the program for disturbed children). (After Rhodes & Gibbins, 1972, pp. 364–65.)

Rhodes and Gibbins point out that it is often not until Step #8 in the sequence outlined above that professionals even enter into the programming cycle. So much has preceded their entry that professionals must be aware of in order to be effective:

> The professional person interested in programming for deviant children must, then, have some understanding of the live context created by the structure and dynamics of behavioral threat, power, collective anxiety, and the culture of the geographical area in which he is functioning. He must know, too, that such a context is a shifting one and needs to be assayed from year to year [Rhodes & Gibbins, 1972, p. 356].

Planning effective comprehensive programs requires much more than knowledge of the dynamics of disturbed children. In order to maximize their impact, teachers, psychologists, social workers, and others who work with troubled youngsters must understand and be prepared to intervene on a systems level. Again, according to Rhodes and Gibbins (1972):

> To have an influence the professional must attempt to enter into and become a part of the "intrinsic" associational dynamics in communities that contribute to that cycle. He must understand that his entry does not create the necessary associational dynamics, but rather, that the dynamics are always there, and unless he realizes and makes use of them, he is very likely to be extruded along with his ideas, or have himself and his ideas well encapsulated and neutralized by elements and systems that are already an integral part of the community [p. 364].

In the next chapter, we will examine some techniques for educational planning based on an ecological perspective. Comprehensive as those strategies may be, it is important to remember, as Rhodes and Gibbins have so well described, that they still represent just one piece of the overall service-delivery system.

6
Educational Planning

Discussions of educational planning processes are not new but continue to be essential to our work with troubled children. Now, perhaps more than ever, in an era dominated by individualized instruction, school psychologist as psychological test-administrator, and IEPs (individualized educational programs required by recent federal legislation), it is imperative that we pay careful attention to the ways in which we attempt to understand and remediate the psychological and educational problems presented by troubled children.

While ecological theory may sometimes seem too complex for productive use in program planning, the adoption of such a perspective may be critical to the success of our efforts to educate troubled children. In this chapter, we apply principles of the ecological model to the educational planning process in a most tangible and specific way. In particular, we discuss the educational planning process as a form of problem solving comprised of a logical and comprehensive series of steps. Each of the steps in the process will be described and special attention is paid to the critical first step—assessment.

Further, our discussion in this chapter is guided by two important practical questions: (1) What can teachers, psychologists, and others who work with troubled children do to increase the effectiveness of their planning efforts despite whatever restrictions may exist in their particular settings or job descriptions? and (2) What kinds of changes in role models or environments might lead to more effective planning and service delivery models in the future? We begin with a brief discussion of a critical development in special education program planning, the individualized educational program.

INDIVIDUALIZED EDUCATIONAL PROGRAMS (IEPs)

Since Public Law 94:142 (The Education of all Handicapped Children Act of 1975) has been in effect, individualized educational programs, or IEPs as they're commonly called, have become central to the special education planning process. According to the law, every child receiving a special education because of a handicapping condition must have an IEP on record which includes the following elements:

a) A statement of the child's present level of educational performance;
b) A statement of annual goals, including short term instructionl objectives;
c) A statement of the specific special education and related services to be provided to the child and the extent to which the child will be able to participate in regular education programs;
d) The projected dates for initiation of services and the anticipated duration of services; and
e) Appropriate objective criteria and evaluation procedures and schedule for determining, on at least an annual basis, whether the short term instructional objectives are being achieved [Public Law 94:142, p. 42491].

In the few years that have passed since IEPs first became part of special education procedure, districts have developed a variety of formats for creating, implementing, and evaluating these individualized plans. While some IEPs are clearly much more comprehensive and useful than others, many IEPs still do not represent sound instructional programs. According to Ballard and Zettel (1977), IEPs are not instructional plans but rather:

> The IEP is a management tool that is designed to assure that, when a child requires special education, the special education designed for that child is appropriate to his or her special learning needs and that the special education designed is actually delivered and monitored. An instructional plan reflects good educational practice by outlining the specifics necessary to effectively intervene in instruction. Documenting instructional plans is not mandated as part of the IEP requirements [p. 182].

The following sections of this chapter provide overviews of educational planning strategies and focus especially on an ecological planning process. To the extent that IEPs are built on the principles and techniques to be described, they may be seen as more representative of comprehensive and coordinated educational planning efforts.

OVERVIEW OF EDUCATIONAL PLANNING

Swanson and Reinert (1979) have identified the following sequence of activities as being essential to any educational planning process:

1) determining major goals of the educational system;
2) developing instructional objectives for a particular course of action;

3) determining methods for meeting objectives;
4) determining materials appropriate for meeting objectives;
5) determining optimal conditions for behavior control and learning;
6) evaluating the child's performance related to educational objectives for quality control; and
7) monitoring and modifying the program process [p. 285].

Goals, of course, vary with students. For some youngsters, goals may focus on skill achievement in particular academic areas. For other students, goals may be more oriented toward personality development, improving self-concept, and the like. As Swanson and Reinert (1979) point out, special attention must be paid to meeting the needs of the *whole* child, to working on all appropriate aspects (social, behavioral, academic, emotional, etc.) of an individual youngster's functioning.

It is necessary but not sufficient to know what the major goals might be for each child. General ideas about goals must be translated into specific *instructional objectives*. This may take the written form suggested by Mager (1972) which consists of a statement of expected terminal behavior (what the child will be able to do when the objective has been reached), the situation in which the designated behavior will occur, and the criteria for acceptable performance. Swanson and Reinert (1979) offer the following as a sample instructional objective:

Given the Sullivan Programmed Mathematics Division (Behavioral Research Laboratories) Book Number 27 (one digit quotients, no remainders), the student will write the correct answers in five minutes at thirty digits per minute with no errors [p. 287].

Once the specific instructional objectives have been determined, the methods by which those objectives will be attained must be identified. Methods may include a variety of modalities (visual, auditory), contexts (classrooms, cubicles, outdoors), population sizes (small group, large group, individuals), and teacher roles (direct instruction, consultant, discussant).

Methods lead directly to the next step in Swanson and Reinert's planning process, the selection of materials. Planners must choose materials that match the needs and interests of individual children and that maximize the possibility of attaining the already specified objectives. Materials available vary widely and include printed words and/or pictures, audio tapes and records, video tapes, films and television programs, computerized individualized programs, and so on.

Planners must also focus on choosing optimal settings or conditions for implementation of educational plans. A variety of settings are in use for troubled children, ranging from totally institutionalized programs to completely integrated participation in regular classrooms.

No planning process would prove very useful without an evaluation component. It is imperative that planners develop a systematic process for the documentation of the effectiveness (or lack of effectiveness) of the programs they develop. This may be done through an analysis of selected products (tests, papers, etc.) completed by the child, a series of observations and recordings of child behavior, or some combination of the two.

Evaluation is especially important because it serves as the basis for the final planning phase, program modification. Most plans don't work perfectly and all plans can be improved. The purpose of the planning process is to meet the educational and psychological needs of troubled children. If prepared thoroughly and comprehensively in the first place, a good educational plan will provide continual information for use in ongoing modification and revision of educational goals and objectives, methods, materials, and the like.

To summarize:

> Most theories follow a common approach or educational plan in several areas. Most evaluate before beginning programming to determine the information or behavior level of each child. Once data are gathered most theories emphasize goal setting for each individual as well as the group. Next, the approaches to be used to change behaviors are selected, which includes the selection of appropriate materials as well as techniques. In most theories consideration of motivational factors or arranging consequences is the next step. Finally, the program is evaluated to see if progress has been made or if changes in strategy are in order [Swanson & Reinert, 1979, p. 303].

ECOLOGICAL PLANNING

The ecological perspective mandates a comprehensive approach to planning programs for troubled children. While the outline for an ecological planning process might well resemble the structure recommended by Swanson and Reinert (1979) above, it would also include the following especially critical elements:

1. The need to develop an all-inclusive information-gathering process in an attempt to collect pertinent data from as many aspects of a youngster's world as possible.
2. The need to focus on relationships between adults as a means to improve specific aspects of a youngster's functioning.
3. The need to view case management and coordination functions as critical—not fringe extras—to the success of the planning process.

4. The need to formalize linkages between educational program planners and nonschool elements of each troubled child's "system."

Program planning for troubled children must focus on the important aspects of the systems that surround identified youngsters if the plans developed are to succeed.

As Reynolds (1977a) has said:

> To put the problem in the language that is now emerging in education, the problem is to provide a "match" of the child's characteristics and the features of the instructional program in such a way that it yields the best outcomes for the child.

> An obvious implication of these considerations is that children need to be studied in their school and life settings. Planning for them, the making of an appropriate "match," requires study of both child and situation. Special education teachers, psychologists, and other specialists who join with regular teachers to make educational plans for a pupil must be ecologically oriented in that they always look at the child in relation to a setting, school, home, and playground, for example, and in terms of how the setting, environment, or treatment might be changed. The problems of children are not understood if one looks only at the children and labels them as defective, or looks only at teachers and blames their interactions for children's failures; pupils, teachers, and their interactions in a complex setting as well as family life must be understood if the most promising plans for children are to be devised.

> The test of a classification scheme, for educators, is its educational outcome. Does a scheme permit the allocation of each child to a school situation that is most productive for that child? Obviously, the simple traditional classifications and grouping systems of special education do not supply positive answers. Simple psychometric formulations followed by classification, labels and special placements are often a serious disservice to children [pp. 42–43].

Ecological planning then involves the development and *matching of a program plan to a troubled system*. It is not appropriate or desirable or ultimately effective to engage in program planning that does not consider the variety of contexts in which youngsters spend their time. Sometimes this extended study of systems can increase our understanding of children and help us develop more effective child-centered interventions. At other times, the study of children-in-setting can help us realize that interventions need to focus on persons or situations other than the identified child. In either case, the ecological perpective can only improve the effectiveness of our planning efforts.

In addition, an ecological planning format emphasizes the importance of matching our diagnostic and classification efforts to our service-delivery systems. In other words, the results of our comprehensive assessments should relate directly to the interventions we develop for troubled children and troubled systems. As Reynolds (1977) noted, previous classification efforts have often created more problems than they have resolved. New models, however, may be more successful.

For example, Hobbs (1978) has developed an ecologically based system for the classification of children that is both pragmatic and rational. Contrary to previous classification schemes which have separated classification from treatment, the new plan is designed to improve the efficiency of service delivery by looking at "children-in-settings." Instead of viewing children in isolation from their surroundings, Hobb's model would attempt to classify the mini-social-systems that surround each youngster on the basis of what services need to be performed and/or what actions need to be taken to make those systems work.

Hobbs has proposed an eight-column format that might be used both as a mechanism to keep track of planning efforts and as the basis for the development of classification code. The columns would have the following headings:

1. The child's needs
2. Service requirements
3. Person(s) responsible for seeing that service is provided
4. Person(s) who will actually provide the service
5. Date by which service will be provided
6. Cost of the service and arrangements for payment
7. Criteria for termination of service
8. Follow-up plans

While it seems likely that such a format would improve the efficiency of service-delivery efforts by its careful attention to coordination and the clear determination of responsibilities, the system depends on a complete understanding of the needs of children-in-setting. The next section of this chapter describes one method for developing that kind of comprehensive understanding of troubled systems.

PROFILE SYSTEMS

One especially useful format for ecological planning is known as a profile system. Profiles have the dual advantage of providing the kind of management system called for by Hobbs and demanded by the IEP requirement, and also serving as the basis for sound educational planning efforts.

Described first by Hobbs (1975), the rationale for using a profile system as the basis for educational program planning stems from the following statement:

> Each child is unique, the center of a unique life space. To design a plan to help him grow and learn requires much specific information about him and about his immediate world. The best way we have discovered to get the information needed for good program planning is to construct a profile of assets and liabilities of the child in a particular setting and at a particular time. The profile should describe physical attributes, including salient features of a medical, psychological, and educational evaluation. It should specify what the child can do and what he cannot do, what he can be taught to do, and what is expected of him. It should include people important in his life: parents, brothers and sisters, teachers, a social worker, perhaps, or a physician, other children, other significant adults, and also the people who make the profile and plan and carry out a program to help him. Settings are important, too; the neighborhood, community center, church, the child's school, sometimes an institution. In effect, a profile of assets and liabilities describes the transactions between the child and people significant in his life, always in particular settings and at particular times [Hobbs, 1975, pp. 104–105].

Table 6.1 depicts a general outline for a profile format. A quick review of the table indicates that a profile system is one way to organize the wide assortment of data collected in an ecological planning process. Step I, the listing of strengths and weaknesses is a critical dimension of ecological planning as it responds to the *whole* child and sets a tone for comprehensive assessment of troubled systems. Step II emphasizes the notion that disturbance is equivalent to discordance in the system. Consequently, it is a critical dimension of planning to understand when problems do (and do not) occur. Step III also highlights another important system element: how does the youngster respond to particular kinds of interventions?

Steps IV through VII represent a sequence in the ecological planning procedure: what are the identified needs, how can they be translated into long-term goals, concretized into short-term objectives, and operationalized into specific methods and materials.

Step VIII represents the critical management check by requiring a listing of involved persons and responsibilities. Step IX is the development of an evaluation plan that can provide feedback useful to redeveloping intervention plans for this system.

Table 6.2, Ecological Profile of a Behaviorally Disordered Elementary School Student, describes in summary form the efforts of one resource teacher to develop a comprehensive service plan for a youngster in the midst of a crisis situation in his school.

The profile of John described in Table 6.2 is representative of the manner in which an ecological perspective can bring considerable information into a

Table 6.1. Outline for a Profile System.

I. *Listing of Assets* (strengths) *and Liabilities* (weaknesses)
(academic, behavioral, social—in, after, and out of school)
II. *Points of Discordance* (description of particularly difficult times)
(e.g., in a certain class, in the hall, in the lunchroom, when unable to do seat work, etc.)
III. *Reactions to Teacher Interventions*
(what works and what doesn't work under which circumstances)
IV. *Specific Needs*
(i.e., a clearer understanding of exactly what's expected, daily assistance with a particular subject, more involvement with peers, etc.)
V. *Long-Range Goals*
(what you would like to see happen by the end of this academic year and in future years)
VI. *Short-Term Objectives*
(very specific, observable goals for particular aspects of daily school life—"In the next two weeks . . .")
VII. *Methods and Materials*
(means by which you plan to attain the short- and long-term goals listed above.)
VIII. *List of Persons Involved and Specific Responsibilities*
(who will do what by when?)
IX. *Evaluation Process*
(how will you know you've accomplished your goals?)

comprehensive planning process. While there is much for the teacher to work with in this profile, it is important to point out that the entire process of collecting information, integrating the diverse data into this document, presenting the information to the local school pupil-personnel team, and agreeing on a plan of action for John took less than a week to complete.

Two additional points related to the profile system need to be discussed. First of all, a profile is a dynamic ever-changing entity. The construction of a profile of John done a month or two earlier (or later) would undoubtedly have produced a somewhat different document from that which we see in Table 6.2. Also, the exact format for a profile should be determined with regard to the context in which it is being developed and will be used. The general outline described in Table 6.1 and the example in Table 6.2 represent a base from which a variety of profile formats might be appropriately developed.

Finally, it should be emphasized that at the time that the profile in Table 6.2 was being developed, John was very close to being excluded from public school and referred to an institutional setting for troubled youngsters. Many of the adults who knew John also knew that his two older siblings had been institutionalized for some years and there was considerable feeling that John would inevitably end up in the same place. The rapid development of this profile began a process that balanced John's school system sufficiently to enable him to function satisfactorily in school for at least six years (the time of the last follow-up) and perhaps longer.

Table 6.2. Ecological Profile of a Behaviorally Disordered Elementary School Student.

Introduction:

During the past week I have been working both in and out of the classroom with John. Through interaction and observation and through discussions and input received from his classroom teacher and other interested parties I have attempted to draw up a list of John's strengths and weaknesses and a list of strategies which may be of use in planning for John here at (school). It is my desire to be in a supportive role of teachers and specialists in their dealings with John and I am willing to spend whatever time is necessary to fulfill that need.

I. *Assets*

1. Strong in Academic areas; Math, reading. Enjoys active learning experiences.

2. Enjoys helping others.

3. Responds well to positive reinforcers.

4. Would appear to respond best in situations where limits are well defined and understood.

5. Appears to grasp ideas of consequences and fair play.

Liabilities

1. Lack of self-control in classroom situations (passive learning situations).

2. Constantly running out into halls and disturbing other classrooms.

3. Nonresponsive when discussing his own actions.

4. Lack of response to certain adult controls.

5. Easily bored and distracted in the classroom.

6. In situations where there is already a high degree of peer activity, John's self-control weakens and he will usually add to the chaos.

II. *Points of Discordance*: when does inappropriate behavior occur.

1. In classroom situations (most notably in the afternoon).

2. Lunchtimes.

3. At times when he receives a high degree of peer support (for inappropriate behavior).

III. *Reactions to Teacher Interventions*

1. Seems to respond well to "immediate positive reinforcers" but the power of the reinforcer seems to decrease as the length of time increases.

2. Reprimands — a signaling-out of his behavior at point of occurrence seems to increase acting out behavior. However, he understands the concepts of consequences when presented at a later time.

3. Ignoring — has a major effect on his behavior especially in the instance of his running-out, "come-and-get-me" game. Also his desire to run out and bother other classrooms decreases markedly when he doesn't receive peer support or attention.

4. Acting out behaviors appear to decrease in situations where activities focus on John's strengths.

Table 6.2 (Con't)

IV. *Specific Needs*

  1. A school schedule structured to increase opportunities for success experiences and decrease punitive responses.

  2. More coordinated and consistent school reactions to John's inappropriate behavior.

V. *Long-Range Goals*

  1. John will remain in the regular classroom and, with support from the resource teacher, participate satisfactorily in that setting for the remainder of the academic year.

  2. John will be able to function effectively in the next grade-level classroom, with less resource assistance, in the next academic year.

VI. *Short-Term Objectives*

Within the next two weeks:

  1. John's school schedule will be revised to include breakpoints, i.e., after 45 minutes of appropriate behavior in the regular classroom, John will be able to spend 15 minutes with the resource teacher.

  2. The resource teacher, in consultation with the classroom teacher, will develop more active learning experiences to complement John's classroom reading and math lessons.

  3. John's inappropriate out-of-classroom behavior will be decreased.

  4. John's inappropriate lunchtime behavior will be reduced.

VII. *Methods*

  1. The resource teacher will coordinate the development of a contract between John and all the school personnel involved in John's program. All parties will participate in the process and expected behavior, limits, and consequences will all be carefully described.

  2. When John's behavior falters, it will be the responsibility of one person to work the situation through with John. This will add some stability and consistency to the process and will increase the probability that John will have to deal with the consequences of his inappropriate behavior.

  3. A volunteer will be enlisted to help John through the lunch period. This is a very chaotic time in the building and it may be unrealistic to expect John (and the many other children who have difficulty at this time) to "handle" this period without support.

  4. Increased support will be provided to John's family through the community program into which John has just recently been accepted.

  5. Efforts will be made to improve communication between home and school by sending home regular notes about John's progress, involving John's parents in the development of his contract, working with staff of the community program involved with the family.

VIII. *Persons Involved/Specific Responsibilities*

  1. Resource Teacher   • Supervise contract development

Table 6.2 (Con't)

	• Communicate with family
	• Supplement classroom instruction
	• Deal with John's behavior
2. Classroom Teacher	• Monitor John's classroom behavior and academics
	• Provide curriculum information to resource teacher
	• Write weekly progress notes
3. Principal	• Select volunteer for lunch period
	• Keep school pupil-personnel committee up-to-date on John's progress

IX. *Evaluation*

    1. Provide time at the end of the morning and afternoon sessions for John to evaluate his own behavior.

    2. Provide for periodic meetings between all those working with John. The purpose of these meetings would be to evaluate progress and maintain consistency between all those involved.

Over the past week I have received a great deal of input on John from the people who work most directly with him. Among the suggestions I received were a cooling-off center within the classroom, a reward system whereby if John would get a certain amount of points by the end of the week he could go on some sort of field trip, a card sent home to John's family every day to reward good behavior, and numerous other ideas. The most urgent need expressed to me was the need for everyone to work together in a consistent manner in planning for John. It was the purpose of this writing to tie together various ideas and to present possibilities for implementing those ideas in a consistent program that would be most beneficial to John.

Results (completed at a later date):
At the time this profile was developed (November 1975), John was on the verge of being removed from public school and institutionalized as had been the case with his older siblings. At the current time (May 1981), John is performing satisfactorily in a regular junior high school program. At least some of the results must be attributed to the process begun by the development of this profile.

Perhaps the most important point to be made here is that despite the knowledge of John's siblings' emotional and behavioral problems and their placement in a local institutional program, none of the systems (education, mental health, social services) involved with John and his family seemed able to prevent John from following the same path. Without the kind of ecological plan described in Table 6.2, then, it seems quite likely that John would have been institutionalized as the result of the failure of previous interventions with family members to focus on systems instead of individuals. Once again we can see that in order to deal effectively with troubled children, we must develop our plans for them in the context of the systems in which they live.

To summarize, a profile system is one format for an ecological planning process. More generally, ecological planning might take the form of providing comprehensive responses to the following sequence of questions. Each question might also be seen as corresponding to a particular phase in the overall planning process:

1. What is the problem? (Assessment)
2. What can we do? (Plan Development)
3. Exactly what should we do and when? (Specification and prioritization)
4. Who's in charge here? (Implementation and Coordination)
5. How will we know what we've done? (Evaluation)
6. Can we do it better? (Modification)

As we can see, the ecological planning process begins with a comprehensive assessment phase during which time all possible sources of information should be utilized to gather data and ultimately to use that information to write a statement of the problem. Such a statement would typically focus on who's having the problem and would include information on where, when, and under what conditions the problem occurs.

Once the comprehensive assessment phase is completed, the remaining questions can usually be answered with relative ease. In the second phase, a plan is developed that includes both long-range goals and short-term objectives and that takes into account the particular driving forces (assets) and restraining forces (liabilities) in the situation. In the next phase, methods and materials are specified to match objectives and goals are listed in order of priority. Phase 4 describes the plan of action and lists specific responsibilities (including coordination) for the persons involved. Phase 5 represents the creation of an evaluation procedure and Phase 6 includes efforts to utilize evaluation results in the modification of the overall plan. The process operates in a cyclical fashion: information derived from Phase 6 feeds back into Phase 1, the problem is redefined, and so on.

The assessment phase in which efforts must be made to develop as comprehensive a picture as possible of the troubled system is clearly the base for all ecological planning. The remainder of this chapter will be devoted to a discussion of the developing area of ecological assessment.

ASSESSMENT

Eaves and McLaughlin (1977) have described seven essential methods that can be used by educators and psychologists to collect relevant information about a child. These methods are listed below:

1. Inspection of previously collected data.
2. Informal consultation.
3. Structured interviews.
4. Screening devices.
5. Standardized tests.
6. Nonstandardized tests.
7. Observation systems.

In addition to the variety of ways in which information can be gathered, Eaves and McLaughlin noted that assessment activities are typically conducted according to the following three-phase sequence: screening (development of tentative hypotheses for further investigation); clinical assessment (critical listing of strengths and weaknesses); and follow-up assessment (the final result—a comprehensive profile—to be used as the basis of educational planning).

While the sequential assessment strategy described above might be a good basis for educational planning, the process often fails to operate in that comprehensive fashion. Instead, the situation may be more similar to that described by Blau (1979):

> Children are probably overtested in educational settings and undertested in clinical situations. The ritualistic assessments done in all school systems are of limited value in helping the child [p. 969].

In fact, there are a number of critical problems in the assessment of troubled (or more acccurately, potentially troubled) children. In 1974, for example, Jane Mercer concluded that current psychological assessment procedures violated the following rights of children:

1. The right to evaluation within a culturally appropriate, normative framework.
2. The right to be assessed as multidimensional human beings.
3. The right to a complete education.
4. The right to be free of stigmatizing labels.
5. The right to cultural identity and respect.

Since that time, Mercer has developed the SOMPA (System of Multicultural Pluralistic Assessment) system in an effort to provide an assessment strategy that would allow youngsters to maintain their rights.

Blau (1979) has also provided documentation for his assertion that our tests for appropriate diagnosis of disturbed children are not as good as they should be. He derides the tendency of recent years to "short-cut" the assessment process (i.e., using only one or two subscales of the WISC because they correlate highly with the full-scale score) and concludes:

> Where disturbed children are concerned, quicker or shorter has not proven to be better. Before we can develop cost-effective screening devices for diagnosing disturbed children, much more clinical experience and evaluation of more carefully developed diagnostic systems is required [p. 970].

Instead, Blau called for more comprehensive assessment procedures which would include some specific focus on environmental presses and opportunities in addition to careful assessment of youngsters' psychological and educational needs. Finally, Blau noted that a true cost-benefit analysis must incorporate the tremendous future cost to child, family, and community owing to inadequate "short-cut" assessment strategies today.

Such "short-cut" measures become even more inappropriate when we view assessment from the ecological perpective. The problem of understanding troubled systems is even more complex than assessing one troubled youngster, a very difficult enterprise itself.

Koppitz (1977) has reviewed diagnostic strategies in use with children who have behavioral and learning problems and noted the complexity of "typical" situations:

> Children with behavior and learning problems tend to show a combination of different symptoms and difficulties rather than any single difficulty. The youngsters' symptoms change as they get older. Furthermore the most obvious symptom is not necessarily the most serious problem a pupil has. Most children with behavior problems also have some learning difficulties and vice versa. The diagnostic label a child receives often depends on the person who evaluates the youngster. Diagnostic labels are often of limited usefulness when designing a meaningful educational or therapeutic program for children. A description of the pupil's functioning in different areas is of greater value [p. 139].

Indeed, the classification scheme referred to by Koppitz creates a number of additional problems for our assessment efforts. For example, Nathan (1979) recently reported on an analysis of the latest draft of the developing *Diagnostic and Statistical Manual* (DSM-III) by Norman Garmezy, president of the Division of Clinical Psychology of the American Psychological Association. According to Nathan, Garmezy (1978) questioned the expanded list of disorders, specific to children, being included in the manual. Syndromes such as Specific Reading Disorder, Developmental Articulation Disorder, Academic Underachievement Disorder, and others represent an "over-reaching effort by the creators of the children's section to bring under psychiatry's wing deficits and disabilities that are not mental disorders'' (p. 968).

Garmezy's view is that such an effort makes the entire taxonomy of DSM-III vulnerable, and a vulnerable classification system can have devastating effects on assessment procedures. Hobbs (1975, 1978) has already documented the obstacles to service-delivery efforts presented by earlier versions of that same classification system.

If traditional diagnostic classifications and assessment procedures have been inadequate for purposes of developing appropriate psychological and educational plans for troubled youngsters, what are the alternatives? Oftentimes, there haven't been any, as Wade and Baker (1977) have stated:

> Finally, a lack of practical alternative assessment procedures may lead to the use of psychological tests even by clinicians who are skeptical of their value. . . . many clinicians spend considerable time in assessment. . . . answering assessment needs was rated as a very important factor in clinicians' decisions to use tests. In the face of such needs, *some clinicians may use tests solely because they feel there are no practical alternatives.* For instance, although behavioral observation was suggested as a possible alternative to traditional assessment by many respondents, it was actually used by relatively few [p. 880, emphasis added].

If there are no alternatives, the decision reached by those charged with the responsibility for doing assessment, that critical first step in the planning process, is obvious—continue to use the same tools that have proven so inadequate in the past. Recently, however, there has been increasing attention to the development of more comprehensive alternative assessment strategies and the next section will describe some of the most promising developments in "Ecological Assessment." Table 6.3 provides some descriptions and definitions of ecological assessment.

A review of Table 6.3 indicates that ecological assessment includes the following elements:

- Information about a child is sought from all the environments in which the child spends time.

- The information is utilized to develop a picture of the entire system defined by the existence of the child.

- An effort is made to pinpoint points of discordance as well as points of accord (or agreement).

Newbrough, Walker, and Abril (1978) have reviewed the topic of ecological assessment and described six major principles for that process. Those principles appear in Table 6.4.

Table 6.3. Ecological Assessment: Some Definitions and Descriptions

1. Ecological assessment is a procedure that is gaining popularity. It assesses the child's status in the various "ecologies" or environments in which he functions. Within the school setting, the teacher can assume that children change ecologies each time they change classrooms, teachers, or even specific areas within the same classroom (e.g. when children move from a supervised reading group to an art interest center). On a few occasions, the teacher may also examine non-school ecologies such as home, church, and various clubs [Hammill & Bartell, 1978, p. 233].

2. Once an individual child's ecological system is identified, the next step is to go beyond the information gathered in order to evaluate or assess it. To pull together all that the parents, teachers, agencies, and others have said about the child's behavior, the community or about themselves. . . . On the basis of the information gleaned from this assessment, then, interventions must be planned that take into consideration the ecological system as a whole. If, for example, a child's behavior in physical education is his number one behavior problem, to look *only* at the classroom interactions would be inadequate. However, it is foolishly presumptive to rule out classroom interactions as having no relationship to his physical education behavior until a careful analysis has been made.

   The most useful interventions then, are those that look at the whole ecological system and do several things at once. This means mobilizing and coordinating efforts which focus not merely on helping the child alter his behavior patterns but also modifying the demands and expectations of the people with whom he interacts [MacKay, 1978].

3. If we look at a child's ecology, for example, we might illustrate it by showing first the child as a complete entity. But in order to better understand him, we add to his ecology those areas where he spends significant periods of time such as his home, his school, his church, his boy scout troop, his neighborhood. It is easy to see that just as no two people are ever identical, no two ecologies are ever identical and in our search for problem solutions, we must look at a child's total ecology to seek out the points of discordance as well as the points of accord. By dealing directly with the significant people in a child's ecological system, problem solving becomes much more attainable.

   Where problems exist however, we find that one of two situations usually are occurring: demands far exceed the individual's ability to meet them and steps are too large for the individual to grow to meet the demands, so he fills the gap with inappropriate behavior [or] the skills of the individual exceed the demands placed upon him and he also fills the gap with inappropriate behavior. With careful analysis of the problem and the context in which it occurs, possible solutions are more easily attained [Dokecki & Hutton, Prevention-Intervention Program, Teacher-Training, Mimeo, 1977].

4. Educational assessment of children experiencing failure in school has shown an increasing ecological trend in recent years, typified by the direct examination of the child and the various environments in which the child operates. More specifically, the professional who conducts an ecological assessment attempts to view the child and his or her environment (e.g., the classroom, home, etc.) in its totality rather than as discrete and separately functioning entities. The reasons for this is that an individual does not usually act independently of outside forces in any given situation, but is continually responding to a series of situational factors that may or may not be apparent to the casual observer. Such variables as peer pressure, teacher and parent demands, school climate, and the child's own self-concept all have the potential to either "positively" or "negatively" influence a child's academic and social behavior. It is logical that analysis of an underachieving or misbehaving child in relation to the environment(s) directly affecting this behavior may yield for the teacher considerable data regarding the nature of an observed problem, as well as suggest remedial strategies that may lead to its eventual amelioration [Wallace and Larsen, 1979, p. 99].

As can be seen in Table 6.4, ecological assessment begins with the broad perspective that views problems as being systems-centered instead of individual-centered. Consequently, interventions must be planned to match the varying needs and norms of each system by attending to system strengths and weaknesses and by having the harmonious functioning of the target system as a goal.

Such an approach assumes that there is no single best solution to a problem. Instead, there are at least three categories of intervention plans that might be made:

1. We can try to change the person who is believed to have the problem.
2. We can try to change the people who perceive the existence of the problem.
3. We can try to change the situation.

Consequently, the ecological assessment strategy must maintain a broad and open stance in order to secure the variety of information that may be helpful to such a comprehensive program planning endeavor.

THE PROCESS OF ECOLOGICAL ASSESSMENT

Ecological analysis attempts to assess youngsters' interactions in the many environments that make up a child's ecosystem. Children's behavior does not occur in a vacuum but is influenced by the physical characteristics and human reactions that occur in response to each youngsters' actions. All too often, however, these interactions do not become the object of our assessment efforts.

Wallace and Larsen (1979) noted that:

> Although it is interesting to note the interrelationships between environment and behavior, they are seldom taken into account during consideration of students who are experiencing school failure. In most cases, when a child is observed to be underachieving or acting out in an inappropriate manner, the major area of evaluative focus is only upon the child. Frequently, the identified student will be referred to a specialist within the school for intensive diagnostic efforts that are designed to isolate inherent disorders or deficits existing within the child that are "responsible" for the learning or behavioral difficulty. Seldom does the educational evaluation attempt to probe those situational factors that may, in fact, have initiated or at least maintained the behavioral patterns that are of concern to the teacher [pp. 99–100].

Wallace and Larsen concluded that "at least as much diagnostic and remedial intervention needs to be directed towards school environments as

Table 6.4. Principles of Ecological Assessment.

---

1. Ecological assessment begins with a broad perspective of the problem or situation. The individual is seen in a context. The professional tries to understand the network of interrelationships among various individuals and their environment. Later, when appropriate, the focus may be on the individual, but always keeping in mind that the individual is part of a system and cannot be understood without reference to that system.

2. Problems belong to a system, not an individual. The goal is not to change the individual, but to make the system function in a way that enhances the development and well-being of all of its members.

3. Before intervening in a system it is necessary to evaluate how the intervention will affect the system as a whole, i.e. one should analyze the indirect effects of the intervention.

4. Each system has different norms of conduct. The professional must have a flexible attitude in order to discover these norms and how they are enforced. Questions to ask oneself are:

   • What is it that the person does that causes problems?
   • In what settings does he do it?
   • For whom does it cause problems?

   Problems are often caused by discrepancies between the behavior of an individual and the expectations of significant persons in a particular setting. A behavior may be functional in one setting and dysfunctional in another. Thus it is important to view the problem in the context of the setting.

5. The goal is a system that functions well, using its own resources and energies. Intervention creates an artificial situation in which the system may come to depend on the professional in order to function. While we are intervening, we do not know how well the system can function on its own. For this reason, we try to make the most minimal intervention possible, and to identify and reinforce resources of the system itself.

6. Ecological assessment looks for not only the weaknesses but also the strengths of the system. These strengths represent the most valuable resource for solving problems of the system.

Source: Newbrough, Walker, and Abril, 1978, mimeo, pp. 2–3.

toward the individual child'' (p. 100), and offer the following quotation from Ruben and Balow (1971) as additional documentation:

> schools and teachers are oriented to a narrow band of expected pupil behaviors which are not consistent with typical behavior patterns of young boys; any pupil outside of that narrow range is treated as needing special attention. Clearly, the problem is not with the child alone [p. 298].

Clearly, environmental factors can play an important role in the creation of emotional disturbance in children. Consequently, assessment techniques, at the very minimum, must help us understand critical aspects of child-system interactions.

Again, according to Wallace and Larsen (1979):

> Unless such evaluations are conducted, it is highly likely that whatever diagnostic and remedial efforts are employed with the child in isolation will be largely ineffective. In other words, an ecological assessment should be considered as a vital component of any evaluative effort where the purpose is to delineate those patterns of interaction that may be seriously exacerbating a given school problem [p. 102].

Ecological assessment, then, has the potential to bring new and different information into the planning process. In order for that potential to be maximized, however, there must be a plan by which the assessment process can be conducted. Because the ecological assessment process can be interpreted so broadly, the lack of a management plan might cause those trying to use such techniques to flounder in a never-ending sea of useful and not-so-useful information. Teachers, psychologists, and others initiating ecological assessments should know what kinds of data to search for and to what ends their process is directed.

Consequently, various formats are being developed for the ecological assessment process. Representative of these is the sequence recommended by Newbrough et al. (1978) that includes the following steps:

• Hear the presenting problem or complaint and find out what has happened and how (identify daily rounds and social networks).

• Identify relevant actors and make contact with them.

• Arrange a meeting with these persons (identify perspectives, goals, potential solutions, priorities, timelines).

The information gathered in the three steps listed above is then used as the basis for developing and implementing an agreed-upon effort to resolve the problem.

Wallace and Larsen (1979) offer a similar sequence of activities, beginning with delineating the environments in which problem behavior occurs from those where the behavior does not exist. Second, both kinds of settings are studied to determine expectations, types of interactions, required skills, and the like. Finally, environmental changes are made in an effort to elicit more appropriate student behavior and students are helped to gain skills needed for effective classroom participation.

Finally, Laten and Katz (1975) have provided an example of the use of an ecological assessment technique as applied to the assessment of adolescents. Their technique is divided into the following five phases:

I. Assimilate referral data.
II. Identify ecological expectations.
III. Organize behavioral descriptions.
IV. Summarize data.
V. Establish new goals and expectations.

In the first phase, information is gathered from a broad spectrum of environments by enlisting the support of as many individuals as possible from the child's ecosystem. Next, the expectations each environment holds for the youngster are identified. The goal of this phase should be to learn exactly what the child has to do in order to succeed in each setting.

In the third phase, specific descriptions of the youngster's behavior in each of the identified environments are collected and organized. When possible, the focus should be on behaviors as they relate to the expectations identified in phase II. In addition, the behaviors of adults in identified environments should be described and used to identify particular skills and services available in each setting.

Finally, the data are summarized (in phase IV) and used as the basis for the development of goals and expectations (phase V) for both children and adults in the identified settings.

An example of the use of the Laten and Katz format is provided by Wiederholt, Hammill, and Brown (1978) and reproduced in Figure 6.1.

The presenting problem has been defined as Phyllis's disrespectful behavior toward the classroom teacher. The broken line in Figure 6.1 represents the existence of a problem in the regular classroom only—the results of the ecological assessment revealed no problem in any other aspect of the system that surrounds Phyllis. The information gathered in the first three phases of the Laten and Katz format indicate that while expectations are too high for Phyllis in the regular classroom, they are more realistic (and hence her behavior is more appropriate) in the other school environments. After summarizing the data in phase IV, the plan of action developed in phase V would have the dual focus of lowering the classroom teacher's expectations of Phyllis while the resource teacher worked to reduce the deficits Phyllis demonstrates in specific areas. In this way, the problem of Phyllis's "disrespectful behavior" might be reduced.

Wiederholt et al. (1978) have noted that resource teachers can profit greatly from data produced by ecological investigations. Though it might be possible to study a number of outside-school environments (home, community, etc.), Wiederholt et al. suggest that resource teachers limit their investigations to the variety of settings that exist within each school building.

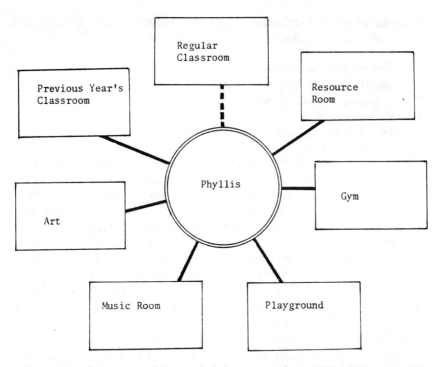

Fig. 6.1. Use of the Laten and Katz ecological assessment format (Wiederholt et al., 1978, p. 208).

In this manner, resource teachers can gather considerable information about the match between a particular child and a broad diversity of school environments—regular classroom, resource room, playground, gym, etc.—without consuming too much time.

Wiederholt et al. state:

> The concept of in-school ecological assessment is relevant to the resource teacher. First, it gives the teacher the opportunity to observe a referred child in several environments. This analysis may yield significant information regarding the pervasiveness of the child's behavior problems. For example, a child may present problems in only one environment in the school, such as the regular classroom, but may perform adequately in other settings, such as the gym, the playground, the lunchroom, the resource room, and the music room.
>
> Ecological assessment also yields information on both the positive and negative factors in the child's environment. The resource teacher may isolate particular aspects that appear to facilitate adequate conforming behavior (he/she is allowed movement, can work with his/her peers, appears to enjoy what he/she is doing, attends a highly structured class), or that appear to

thwart good behavior (the child is required to remain seated for extended periods of time, is not allowed to interact with his/her peers, does not act as if he/she enjoys doing specific tasks, appears to dislike the teacher, only misbehaves in environments that are loosely structured).

Ecological assessment relates directly to situational variables and to the child's interactions with these variables in different environments. The resource teacher must analyze the child, especially if he/she is evidencing any type of behavior problem, in different environments in the school and make adjustments in the environments in which the child is having difficulty, adjustments with the child, or adjustments in both [p. 208].

ECOMAPPING

Figure 6.1 above demonstrates the use of an increasingly popular aspect of ecological assessment, ecological mapping or ecomapping, as it is sometimes called. Ecomapping is based on the premise that each child is part of a mini-social-system *and* that it is possible to represent that ecosystem graphically. The resulting schematic representation of a youngster's ecosystem is termed an ecomap. The process by which the ecomap is produced is known as ecomapping.

The simplest kind of ecomap might look like this:

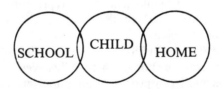

Note that the child is at the center of his own system and that home and school environments overlap with different parts of the child (and elicit different behaviors from the child).

Before the simple ecomap above can be extended to include more information, it is necessary, as MacKay (1978) says, "to do some detective work." By visiting and observing the child in a variety of settings and talking with the adults who interact with the youngster, a teacher or psychologist might be able to determine exactly where the disturbance in the system occurs.

Figure 6.2 represents the ecosystem of a seventh-grade boy (MacKay, 1978) whose problems seem to center on math class (observations indicate no problems in other settings). Further, it has been determined that the issue in math class is that the material is too difficult for the youngster and new

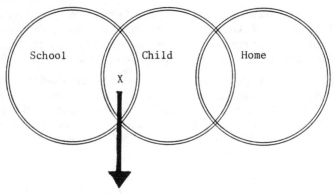

Math Skills below grade level

```
┌─────────────────────────────────────────────────┐
│                                                   │
│     Provide math teacher with Stern Materials     │
│                                                   │
└─────────────────────────────────────────────────┘
```

Fig. 6.2. Ecomap of the troubled math-class system of a seventh-grade boy (After MacKay, 1978).

or different materials must be provided in order for the math class system to become balanced again.

The X in the overlapping child-school area represents the disturbed math class system for our "troubled" child. The box at the bottom of Figure 6.2 outlines the remediation plan.

Should time and the specifics of your job description allow, you might next decide to investigate the home sphere. Whenever this is possible, it is a good idea, as it certainly can provide more important information for the ecomap (and for your planning efforts) and can also often be a first step in developing better home-school relationships.

Figure 6.3 represents a series of more elaborate ecomaps of MacKay's seventh-grade boy. The uppermost map (Figure 6.3a) represents the two major findings of the analysis of the seventh-grader's home system: the boy has essentially no outside activities and the home atmosphere is marked by the parents continual fighting. At this point in the ecomapping proccess, some new system disturbances have been identified, but remediation plans have not yet been developed (hence the two empty boxes in Figure 6.3a).

MacKay suggests looking for obvious solutions first. In this case, it is her belief that the obvious solution to finding outside activities for a seventh-grade boy is to check at his school. Should that prove unproductive (the bus schedule may prohibit his staying after school hours), it would make sense to check on neighborhood facilities near the youngster's home. If we assume that our seventh-grader cannot stay at school and needs to find outside-the-home activities in his neighborhood, the remediation might be involvement in a nearby youth program and the ecomap might now look as it does in Figure 6.3b.

The final discordance in our seventh-grader's troubled system might require the services of another agency. In this case, it might be appropriate for one or both parents to receive assistance from the community family and

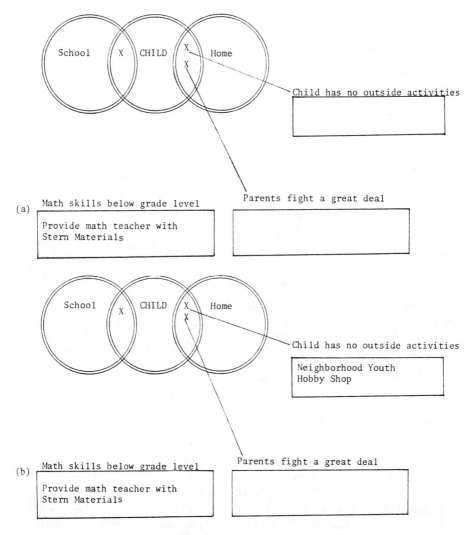

Fig. 6.3. Progression of eco-maps in planning for a seventh-grade boy (After MacKay, 1978).

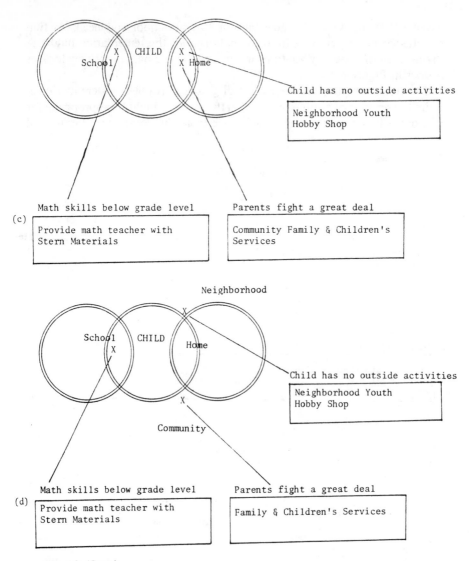

Fig. 6.3. (Cont.)

children's service, and now the ecomap would be depicted by Figure 6.3c. Incidentally, MacKay points out the need for ecological assessors to serve as facilitators in the service-delivery process. For example, it may be extremely helpful for the teacher, psychologist, social worker, or other professional involved in this example to accompany the parent(s) on the first trip to the family and children's service agency.

MacKay also points out that the use of an ecomapping technique can not only help in the development of appropriate intervention plans but may also revitalize aspects of a youngster's system that can become very productive assets for the future:

> Although we have identified and provided a solution for every need that seems to be the most serious for this child and our ecological map looks complete, we have actually changed the ecological map of this child by the nature of our interventions. We have added two components to his ecology that were dormant as far as his life was concerned: neighborhood (through the Youth Hobby Shop) and Community (through the Family and Children's Service). We cannot know how involved these two components will become in the life of this child and his family but the chemistry of the interaction will have an effect on both and hopefully, the experiences in both components will give the child and the family more alternatives for success and joy in life [p. 11].

Figure 6.3d shows the completed ecomap, and indicates how neighborhood and community components of our seventh-grader's system have been brought to life and integrated into remediation plans for one youngster's troubled system.

The ecomap technique has been utilized in a variety of settings. Hartman (1978) for example, provides some description of ecological assessment for social workers:

> Social workers have recently attempted to use the ecological metaphor to provide a new way of thinking about and understanding what has always been the central focus of social work, "person-in-situation." Such a stance appears to be useful in assessment and in devising ways of being helpful.
>
> . . . Utilizing the ecological model for assessment in social work leads us to focus on the complex ecological system which includes the individual or family and the total environment and the transactional relationships between that individual or family and the environment.
>
> . . . An ecological assessment which focuses on the transactions between human beings and the complex of systems which compose their environments leads naturally to a model of social work practice which focuses interventions on these transactions and to particular reliance on such social work practitioner roles as mediator, enabler, social broker, and advocate. The goals of such ecologically oriented practice is the enhancement of the quality of life.
>
> . . . An ecological assessment requires the visualizing of a highly complex system with many variables acting simultaneously. . . . One picture however, is worth a thousand words and thus, through drawing a rather simple map of the person or family in the life space, many of the complexities and interrelationships can be captured [p. 18].

Hartman (1978) also suggests four ways to utilize the ecomap and the ecological mapping process:

1) *A "thinking tool" for the worker*—The worker may simply want to think about a family situation, organize data, discover areas where more information is needed, and begin to locate possible areas for intervention. Sketching out the map may enable the worker to "see" the situation in a new way and out of this enhanced understanding may come meaning by creative problem solving.

2) *An assessment tool to be used jointly by worker and client(s)*—Doing the Eco-map together moves both worker and client to a view of the total situation. The construction of the map gives the information gathering some pattern and structure. Following completion of the map, the worker and client(s) can examine it together and reach a joint assessment of the situation and a plan for change.

3) *A recording tool*—Some agencies have found the map to be a useful recording and communication tool. The presence of an Eco-map in a case record can give another staff member or a supervisor a quick sense of the situation and communicate considerable information.

4) *A measure of change*—Some agencies have experimented with drawing the Eco-map at intake and again at termination. A comparison of the two will demonstrate what change has taken place [p. 20].

An ecomap is one especially ecological assessment method. In addition, a variety of more traditional assessment tools can also be utilized within the context of an ecological orientation. For example, systematic observations can be made of youngsters in as many components as possible of a particular child's system.

More specifically, formal or informal observations might focus on the interactions between teachers (or other adults) and identified troubled children. Instruments for classroom observation, for example, are available and have been used for a variety of research and program planning efforts in the past. To be useful, of course, such instruments must be both valid and practical (appropriate to the situation at hand).

Checklists and rating scales are additional measures that may prove useful in ecological assessment practices. Checklists can be formal or informal and can be utilized best as a means by which youngsters' or environments' strengths and weaknesses can be assessed and described. Oftentimes, checklists can be devised by teachers for particular situations. Ecologically, however, teachers or others who devise such instruments must be careful to be comprehensive in scope, to look for positive as well as negative characteristics, and to develop tools that can be useful in a variety of settings.

Rating scales are somewhat more sophisticated than checklists; they can describe the *degree* to which particular characteristics exist in the situation which is being examined. Rating scales may also be devised for specific situations so long as scale developers pay careful attention to validity as well as practicality concerns.

Finally, sociometric techniques can also be a useful addition to the ecological assessment process. Sociograms enable assessors to understand the web of relationships within any particular behavior setting more clearly. They are particularly helpful in our efforts to understand the place of troubled children in classrooms.

CONCLUSIONS

It is essential that the assessment process which forms the initial and critical first step of any problem-solving or planning process have an ecological basis if we expect to develop programs with the potential to effect troubled systems. While we have discussed a number of specific strategies for ecological assessment, it is most important to recall that however it is done, assessment must be of the system, not simply of the child in isolation from the contexts that surround him or her.

While techniques for ecological assessment are still developing, we are beginning to understand some critical aspects of this process. For example, the importance of considering strengths is emphasized by Koppitz (1977), especially in relation to work with older children (though the point holds equally well for young children):

> When older children are seen for evaluation it is just as important to determine what they are good at than what their problems are. Even though every effort should be made to remediate specific learning difficulties most children learn best and are taught most successfully by building on their areas of strength [p. 137].

Wiederholt et al. (1978) have suggested that resource teachers follow the following guidelines adopted from Wright (1967). At this phase in the development of ecological assessment techniques, we believe it would be appropriate for other teachers, psychologists, social workers, and other workers to use the following as the basis for their own assessment activities:

1. The resource teacher should focus on both the child and the environment during data gathering.
2. The teacher should report on these two variables in as much detail as possible.

3. The resource teacher should objectively record data and avoid making his/her own personal interpretations of the information.
4. Whenever possible, the information should be stated positively rather than negatively; for example, the statement "Phyllis can attend to an academic task for a short period" is better than "Phyllis doesn't attend to an academic task for very long."
5. The resource teacher should try to be as specific as possible in describing the child and the environments [p. 210].

Finally, the purpose of ecological assessment and planning strategies is to develop effective interventions for troubled systems. In the next chapter, we focus on a variety of techniques for ecological interventions.

7

Ecological Interventions

As we noted in Chapter 5, Rhodes (1967, 1970) has discussed the phenomenon of emotional disturbance as a reciprocal interchange between child and environment. More specifically, Rhodes described the child in such interactions as the "excitor" who elicits reactions from school, family, and community representatives, or "responders." Children whose behavior does not match the expectations of a given setting or environment may be seen as threats which require immediate reaction (sometimes called "recoil" by Rhodes) from the community. One typical reaction has been to label the youngster and remove him from the mainstream of community life, a sequence of events that Rhodes terms the "threat-recoil cycle." The ways in which professional educators, psychologists, social workers, and the like inject themselves into this cycle may be combined under the heading of ecological interventions.

Swanson and Reinert (1979) remind us that the ultimate goal of ecological assessment, of course, is to develop a basis for effective ecological interventions. Such interventions, according to Swanson and Reinert, must be implemented in the context of a "feedback relationship" with the community as depicted below;

Table 7.1 depicts some of the advantages of ecological intervention strategies as compared to nonecological efforts. Examination of Table 7.1

reveals the comprehensive and coordinated nature of ecological intervention formats.

In this chapter, we try to provide an ecological framework for interventions with troubled children and to discuss the ways in which specific intervention strategies can be woven into an ecological orientation. Two assumptions form the basis for this point of view. First, we believe that a child's actions have an impact on his or her environment and that environmental characteristics influence children's behavior. Second, we contend that although research may present us with seemingly unrelated, if not contradictory findings about the respective contributions of individual characteristics and environmental conditions to emotional disturbance, the ecological approach has the potential to integrate such data into a cohesive point of view. As Swanson and Reinert (1979) noted:

> [The Ecological viewpoint] chooses not to disentangle these variables but places emphasis on both the child and the community in remediating emotional behavioral difficulties [p. 135].

Hobbs (1975) emphasizes the importance of conceptualizing interventions in ecological terms. Reminding us that points of discordance in troubled systems—discrepancies between the way the identified "troubled child" is acting and the way important other(s) in the system expect him or her to act—represent targets for ecological intervention, Hobbs notes:

Table 7.1. Comparison of Ecological and Nonecological Intervention Strategies.

Nonecological strategies	Ecological strategies
Responsive only to child crisis.	Responsive to child, is adaptive to classroom context.
Deals in specific assessment measures.	Concern with comprehensive assessment and individually adapted measures.
Requires consent from social system for intervention.	Requires participation from child's social system.
Alleviates conflict in classroom.	Confronts conflict of child in all natural settings.
Short-range classroom planning.	Long-range community planning.
Standardized and formalized classroom procedures of intervention.	Innovative classroom intervention.
Separate services provided child and community.	Coordinated services for child and parent.

Source: Swanson and Reinert, 1979, p. 151.

Discordance is always defined in behavioral terms. Exactly what is person A doing or failing to do that is causing problems? In what setting does he do it or not do it? Specifically what does person B expect him to be doing instead? Behavior is discordant only if it violates the expectations of important others in one's environment; points of discordance cannot be defined unless the unmet expectations are specified. Of course, some discordance is ever present and constructive, leading to adaptation and achievement. We speak here of discordances that result in the disruption of the system, at home, in school, in the community [Hobbs, 1975, p. 120].

Table 7.2 lists some of the ecological intervention targets proposed by Hobbs and demonstrates the systemwide applicability of an ecological intervention approach. Note that all elements of troubled systems are seen as potential targets for intervention. Children, the adults who surround them, environmental conditions, and specific interpersonal relationships are all equally likely to become the focus of an ecological intervention.

Ecological intervention then might include the direct teaching of constructive social behavior to children; efforts to change the nature of social interactions in natural settings; helping children gain competence in relevant areas of their daily lives; modifying environmental elements of a youngster's system; working to change the attitudes or behavior of the adults and children in an identified youngster's system; and, in general, any

Table 7.2. Ecological Intervention Targets.

1. Provide ways for the child to build on his present competencies and to attain new ones.

2. Provide ways for other individuals in the ecosystem (mother, father, teacher, grandparent) to revise their perceptions or to attain new competencies.

3. Change the child's priorities by giving him new ways of understanding his situation (reading lessons may be unpleasant, but they are helping him reach a desired goal such as learning how to read about things that interest him).

4. Change the priorities or expectations of individuals significant to the child by increasing their understanding of the problem (help a father see how important it is to spend more time with his child; help a parent or teacher adjust the discrepancy between a child's tasks or responsibilities and his current abilities).

5. Acquire needed resources for any individual in the system (glasses or a hearing aid for the child, an activity outside the home for the mother, psychotherapy for the father).

6. Restructure the ways that the child and others interact, so that there are more opportunities for all to be rewarded and fewer instances of anyone's being punished.

7. Remove the child from the discordant situation.

8. Intervene through some combination of the above strategies.

Source: Hobbs, 1975, p. 120.

action designed to increase the goodness of fit between a child and his or her usual environments.

For purposes of our discussion, we can divide interventions into two major categories: direct and indirect service. In the direct-service aspect, we describe a variety of interventions that can be utilized directly with children. We also discuss a group of interventions that teachers and others at work in programs for troubled youngsters can apply directly to themselves.

Indirect services include a variety of roles, some of which are discussed elsewhere in this book (working with families in Chapter 8; prevention in Chapter 10). Here we focus our discussion primarily on two critical roles: coordinator and consultant.

DIRECT SERVICES

Intervention with Children

There are two major areas of direct service to children: the teaching of skills or the provision of competencies to youngsters and the management or modification of inappropriate behavior. Both elements are especially important in educational settings. Youngsters who act inappropriately are frequently seen by the adults in schools as "disturbing" and often become labeled as emotionally disturbed or behavior disordered. Children who fail to demonstrate competence at required and/or expected tasks may often become the individual focus of remediation for a troubled-system problem.

The interventions suggested for both of these critical areas are not uniquely ecological. They represent, instead, a wide range of strategies developed from a variety of theoretical perspectives. The key to ecological intervention may be the broader, more systems-focused context in which interventions may be applied. Even when intervention is directed specifically at an identified child, it is never applied in isolation from the surrounding context. Indeed, whenever possible, interventions are aimed specifically at the disruptive child-adult interactions.

In their work on Project Re-Ed, Hobbs (1966) and his colleagues described 12 concepts that formed the basis for their ecological intervention efforts. Those concepts, described below, remain useful for developing an understanding of the ecological context in which direct service to children can be provided:

1. *Life is to be lived now.* Every minute of every day is important. If children are continually challenged to live constructively, they usually will. Each day should be planned to maximize the probability of success experience.

2. *Time is an ally.* For a variety of reasons, troubled children are frequently kept in special programs for too long a time. Many youngsters and families function better with the passage of time—long stays in special programs get in the way of this process and should be avoided.
3. *Trust is essential.* The first step in the reeducation process is the development of trust. Many youngsters are unable to learn from adults owing to bad experiences with adults in the past.
4. *Competence makes a difference.* Being able to do something well brings confidence and self-respect to children as well as increased acceptance by others. This is especially important with regard to school skills—the usual measurement standard for school-age children.
5. *Symptoms can and should be controlled.* Symptoms that stand in the way of normal development and that alienate the child from other children and adults should be altered or removed whenever possible.
6. *Cognitive control can be taught.* Children can learn to manage their own behavior and think through their own problems. They can also acquire the habit of talking things over as a way to gain more control over life events.
7. *Feelings should be nurtured.* Children should have the opportunity to know all of themselves—anger, fear, resentment, joy. Activities can be planned to encourage appropriate expression of feelings.
8. *The group is important to children.* The group can be a source of motivation, instruction, and control. It can also be a forum for constructive discussion of conflict and friction.
9. *Ceremony and ritual give order, stability and confidence.* Many troubled youngsters have lived in very chaotic systems. Regular routines and rituals help reduce interpersonal disarray.
10. *The body is the armature of the self.* Clearer experiencing of the boundaries and potential of the body may lead to clearer psychological definition of the self. Activities that challenge the body may result in increased psychosocial functioning.
11. *Communities are important.* Many youngsters live in families that are isolated from community life. Activities can be planned to help youngsters learn that community services and facilities exist for their benefit and that each of us can find a way to contribute to community life.
12. *Finally, a child should know joy.* We do not focus sufficiently on psychological well-being. Activities should be planned to help children feel joy each day and look forward to joy-giving events in the future.

Rhodes (1970) has identified four critical areas of direct service to troubled children: behavior intervention, group dynamics, curriculum as planned environment, and behavior training. We shall examine some specific suggestions in each area.

Beginning with the area of behavior intervention, there are times when youngsters' specific surface behaviors get in the way of more effective comprehensive planning. A variety of techniques for handling such behaviors has been suggested by Redl and Wineman (1951) and many of their suggestions have been used profitably by teachers for many years. When surface behaviors are appropriately modified, the agitated exchange described earlier may lessen in intensity, allowing more thorough efforts to begin. Redl and Wineman's interventions are described in Table 7.3.

As can be seen in Table 7.3, Redl and Wineman's techniques cover a broad range of actions from "planned ignoring" to "hurdle help" to "antiseptic bouncing." The important thing is to match the intervention with the needs of the child and the context in which the intervention is being applied.

Another area for intervention with children has to do with group dynamics or the study of interpersonal relationships within ecosystems. Barker (1968) has studied the "circuits" that exist in the behavior settings that youngsters inhabit and concluded that four major kinds of circuits exist:

1. *Goal circuits* that involve all of a child's attitudes and actions related to goals and how to achieve them.

Table 7.3. Techniques for the Antiseptic Manipulations of Surface Behavior.

1. Planned Ignoring—Don't attend to behaviors that will extinguish themselves in a short time.
2. Signal Interference—Use nonverbal techniques to communicate your control.
3. Proximity and Touch Control—Suppress inappropriate behavior by moving closer to identified youngsters.
4. Involvement in Interest Relationship—Use child's interests to increase attention.
5. Hypodermic Affection—A "shot" of love.
6. Tension Decontamination through Humor—Relieve building anxiety with laughter.
7. Hurdle Help—Assist child in jumping first barrier, before tension builds.
8. Interpretation as Interference—Let child know you understand his or her feeling, even if inappropriately expressed.
9. Regrouping—Change interpersonal match-ups.
10. Restructuring—Use different format to reach your goals.
11. Direct Appeal—Ask child to stop.
12. Limitation of Space and Tools—Cut down on potential disorganization.
13. Antiseptic Bouncing—Remove child from situation in nonpunitive fashion.
14. Physical Restraint—Help child regain control and prevent injury to self or others.
15. Permission and "Authoritative Verbot"—Let child know what's OK and what isn't.

Source: After Redl and Wineman, 1951.

2. *Program circuits* that delineate the essentials of how a setting such as a classroom operates.
3. *Deviation-countering circuits* which focus on ways that the setting overcomes the obstacles to carrying out its programs.
4. *Vetoing circuits* that involve the ways in which settings remove deviant aspects.

According to Swanson and Reinert (1979), analyses of Barker's circuits can help explain why some youngsters' systems appear congruent or balanced while others' are filled with discordance. For example, when the program circuit is "reading" and Johnny does not demonstrate reading behavior; "An incongruence or aggravated exchange can occur when a systematic program or structure is unclear from the child's perspective" (Swanson & Reinert, 1979, p. 140).

Specific interventions with children, then, must take such circuits into account by helping youngsters understand how to perceive accurately and act appropriately in the context of their ecosystems. For example, youngsters could learn about their own needs for physical space and their reactions when "their space" is violated. If that reaction has a tendency to intensify the aggravated exchange, youngsters could be helped to develop alternative responses that are designed to lead to more positive outcomes.

Curriculum as planned environment has to do with the creative and therapeutic use of program planning for troubled children. Teachers, psychologists, social workers, and others who work in troubled systems should know how to use a variety of content areas and materials to increase youngsters social learning and skill development. Rhodes (1970) has suggested that there are four major areas of curriculum planning to be considered: enterprises; arts and crafts/drama; physical education/recreation and play; and group interaction.

Enterprises centers on the use of units as flexible cores for individual learning. Swanson and Reinert (1979) have provided the following guidelines for the enterprise approach.

1. Providing children with several materials, objects, or mechanical devices to stimulate attention, questions, and generalizations.
2. Providing information on units that can be gathered from many sources (field trip, resource people, various materials, etc.).
3. Providing guidance in inquiry through discussion and repeated questions.
4. Providing each child with encouragement to summarize his or her own findings as well as allowing for teacher-monitored group comparison [p. 144].

Arts and crafts and drama have been utilized as formats for expression of feelings in productive but nonverbal ways. In addition to their potential for helping youngsters release tensions, these kinds of activities can give youngsters a sense of control over themselves and their environments; provide greatly needed success experiences; help youngsters begin to relate socially to peers and to adults; and assist children in the development of skills, competencies, and interests that may last long into the future. Newcomer (1980) has provided extensive discussion of the use of art, music, drama, and play in therapy for troubled children.

Physical education, recreation, and play offer many of the same advantages to troubled children. It has been said that the work of children is play, and many youngsters identified as disturbed may have limited or nonexistent play skills. Activities in this area can help children learn how to play in addition to helping them become more aware and more comfortable with their own bodies.

Group interaction may provide a number of spontaneous opportunities for children to learn social skills and gain awareness and confidence in their abilities to contribute to the life of the group. Such opportunities may also be programmed more formally through techniques such as Glasser's (1971) classroom meetings.

Finally, behavior training involves the learning of new interpersonal and social skills through any of a variety of techniques. Behavioral approaches such as contingency contracting, token economies, and other positive reinforcement systems discussed earlier are all applicable to this area.

Child Development Contracts

Hobbs (1975) points out that:

> The goal of ecological planning and programming is to restore the system to productive equilibrium. This is done by providing the critical amount of assistance for the child and for the important people in his environment, so that the system functions on its own in a way that keeps discordance at an optimal level and maximizes opportunities for growth and gratification [p. 120].

One comprehensive strategy for intervening in troubled systems is what Hobbs has called the "child-development contract"—a "detailed analysis of the child-in-setting, from which is derived a list of specific, realistic objectives for the child and for the significant people in his life" (p. 121).

Although Hobbs believes it may be unnecessary to develop an actual formal written contract, others, including Gallagher (1972) and Abeson et al. (1975) have discussed the usefulness of a written document. Gallagher (1972), for example, describes his notion of a special education contract this way:

> The essence of a special education contract would be as follows. Placement of primary school age mildly retarded or disturbed or learning disabled children

in a special education unit would require a contract signed between parents and educators, with specific goals and a clear time limit. . . .

The contract, composed after a careful educational diagnosis, would commit the special educational personnel to measurable objectives that would be upgraded on a 6 month interval. Ideally, it should start at age 3 or as early as possible so that maximum results can be obtained with minimum effort. . . .

The advantages of such a contract would be obvious from the standpoint of the parents, but it would have clear advantages for the special educators as well. First, it would give them a clear set of objectives around which they could mold their own program. Second, it would give them a bargaining point within the educational system for more resources of personnel or equipment, if the existing ones were clearly inadequate to carry out reasonable objectives p. [111].

There is a clear similarity between these ideas for a child development contract and the Individualized Educational Program (IEP) mandated by Public Law 94:142. A variety of formats have now been developed for IEPs but all of them contain elements of the contractual agreements described above. Gallagher noted that the use of such a contract would ensure parents' involvement in the decision to place a child in special education; specify the objectives for the youngster's special educational plan; put a time limit on the youngsters segregation from the regular classroom and clarify the role of both special educator and classroom teacher in the youngster's educational program. Each of those elements is now part of the usual IEP development process.

Contracts may also be utilized in a less global fashion, as a format for clarifying agreements between teachers and children. Usually, this takes the form of a contingency contract that specifies what the child is expected to do in return for the reward that the teacher is expected to provide.

Table 7.4 depicts a contract form and lists some guidelines for contract development. Table 7.5 is an example of a worksheet for contract developers that can serve as a useful step-by-step checklist for contract development.

Interventions with Adults

Every child is an inseparable part of a complex web of interrelated systems. For "normal" children, these mini-social-systems function appropriately and may be defined as congruent or balanced. When the systems break down, we term them incongruent or unbalanced. We also tend to place the blame for such incongruence on the child, rationalize our action by labeling the child as emotionally disturbed, and plan our interventions to focus on remediating the identified child's emotional disturbance while neglecting the other aspects of the system.

Table 7.4. Example of Contract Format and Guidelines.

Date _____

CONTRACT

This is an agreement between _____
CHILD'S NAME

and _____. The contract begins on _____
TEACHER'S NAME   DATE

and ends on _____. It will be reviewed on _____
DATE   DATE

The terms of the agreement are:

Child will _____

_____

Teacher will _____

_____

_____

If the child fulfills his part of the contract, he will receive the agreed-on reward_____ from the teacher. However, if the child fails to fulfill his part of the contract, the rewards will be witheld.

Child's signature _____

Teacher's signature _____

1. The contract must be negotiated and freely agreed on by both the child and the teacher.
2. The contract must include the desired achievement or production level.
3. The reinforcer must be consistently delivered in accordance with the terms of the contract.
4. The contract must include the date for review and renegotiation.
5. The performance should be rewarded after it occurs.
6. The contract must be fair to both parties.
7. The terms of the contract must be clear.
8. The contract must be honest.
9. The contract must be positive.
10. Contracting must be used systematically.

Table 7.5. Worksheet for Contract Developers.

(X)	Tasks	Comments
( )	1. Establish and maintain rapport.	
( )	2. Explain the purpose of the meeting.	
( )	3. Explain a contract.	
(	4. Give an example of a contract.	
( )	5. Ask the child to give an example of a contract; if there is no response, give another example.	
( )	6. Discuss possible tasks.	
( )	7. Child-suggested tasks:	
( )	8. Teacher-suggested tasks:	
( )	9. Agree on the task.	
( )	10. Ask the child what activities he enjoys and what items he wishes to possess.	
( )	11. Record child-suggested reinforcers.	
( )	12. Negotiate the ratio of the task to the reinforcer.	
( )	13. Identify the time allotted for the task.	
( )	14. Identify the criterion or achievement level.	
( )	15. Discuss methods of evaluation.	
( )	16. Agree on the method of evaluation.	
( )	17. Restate and clarify the method of evaluation.	
( )	18. Negotiate the delivery of the reinforcer.	
( )	19. Set the date for renegotiation.	

to modify such behaviors, the chances for a balanced classroom ecology are remote [p. 57].

When classroom systems become disruptive, our tendency has been to "blame" youngsters whom we can identify as emotionally disturbed. If, on

Frequently those other system components turn out to be the adults who impact on the lives of children identified as emotionally disturbed. Parents, teachers, support personnel, agency staff members, neighbors, and friends are all intertwined in a given youngster's ecosystem. If not neglected, such persons can be critical in the remediation of troubled systems.

Unfortunately, our attention has been so intensively focused on the children that we have frequently failed to develop effective formats for working with adults. Ecological theory emphasizes the essential need to increase our ability to work effectively with the adults who populate the systems of troubled children. While much of that work comes under the heading of indirect services—intervening with others with the ultimate goal of improving the identified child's situation—the ecological perspective points out that some efforts with adults should stand as direct service interventions on their own. As Mour (1977) has noted:

> If one assumes that in order to maintain a balanced classroom ecology, children must behave in ways that are in harmony with teacher expectations, then it is consistent to assume that the teacher should exhibit behaviors which permit the children to discern those expectations, and in ways that do not create negative or disruptive behaviors in the children. In addition, teachers must understand themselves and realize that how the teacher relates to the children significantly influences the reciprocal behavior of the children [p. 56].

Mour divides teacher behaviors into two types: those behaviors that promote learning (productive behaviors), and those that inhibit learning (counterproductive behaviors). He suggests that teachers have overlooked their own behavior as a critical factor in the classroom ecology and proposes that:

> Teachers need to focus upon their own positive behaviors as a way of creating a classroom environment where learning can flourish. For example, when children know the teacher genuinely likes them, they are less likely to engage in behaviors which will upset or disappoint the teacher. When the teacher trusts the students, and they are aware of that trust, they will be reluctant to break that trust. And even the most academically demanding teacher will be respected if he/she is fair. Finally, when one respects others, the respect is returned in kind [p. 57].

Mour hopes that an increased focus on teacher behaviors will help move the onus for change from the child to the teacher—child interaction, a more appropriate focus for intervening in troubled systems. He concludes that

> Until teachers are willing to examine their own behaviors as the possible causes/sources of unacceptable behaviors on the part of children, and attempt

the other hand, we adopt an ecological perspective, we must examine the entire classroom system for points of discordance. Oftentimes such an examination might demonstrate that particular dimensions of the classroom environment or structure are proving problematic for particular children. In ecological terms, the expectations of the classroom environment are not a good match for the capabilities of particular class members. While one solution might be to remove the identified student or otherwise remediate said youngster's deficiencies, ecological theory points out that *other solutions may be equally viable.* Changes in classroom structure or teacher actions might be sufficient, for example, to bring the system back into balance or congruence.

Most of us are not especially open to others' ideas on how to perform our jobs (this may be one reason for our continual assumption that the child owns the problem—he or she has less power to resist our efforts to change his or her behavior than have adults). Teachers are no exception to this rule. It is critical, however, for teachers to study their own classrooms and one way to do this without raising counterproductive defenses is for teachers to engage in anonymous self-study. Table 7.6 represents one example of a checklist for self-study of classrooms. As can be seen in the table, teachers are asked first to indicate which of the items they believe to be important in the education process, and second, to assess their own performance in those selected areas. The list of items can be modified to make it more applicable to particular groups of teachers (early childhood, secondary school, etc.) and the format is a useful way to incorporate teachers' input into the classroom-study process.

It is hoped that the results of such a self-study would lead to appropriate changes in teacher behavior. If, for example, a teacher views item #8 in Table 7.6, "provide immediate verbal feedback" as important and also believes that he or she could perform that behavior more effectively, then it may be reasonable to assume that the teacher would attempt to find help (books to read, people to talk with, a course to enroll in, a colleague to observe, etc.) in that area.

Fox et al. (1975) point out that a balanced evaluation of one's own role activities seems to be most conducive to effective role performance. In other words, teachers who view themselves neither as completely negative nor as totally effective may be most likely to function successfully. It might be useful, in this regard, for teachers to consider constructing profiles of their own performance, outlining their own strengths and weaknesses, just as they might do for a child (see Chapter 6).

To summarize, perhaps the most effective direct-service interventions focused on teacher behavior are self-administered and based on a teacher's own proactive understanding of his or her role functions. Fox et al. (1975) have provided a format that may be helpful to teachers attempting to con-

Table 7.6. A Checklist for Teachers' Self-Study of Classrooms.

Here is a list of activities, attitudes, and concepts that some people feel apply to teachers.

Please read each item and check in the appropriate space whether you think it is important for a teacher or not.

If you do feel that an item is important, then also mark in the appropriate space whether you see yourself as doing okay on that item or would like yourself to be better on it.

Please write in additional items which are not on the list, but which you feel are important.

Items	Important	Not Important	I'm doing okay	I'd like to do better	
1. Involve students in lesson.	_____	_____	_____	_____	1
2. Stimulate class participation.	_____	_____	_____	_____	2
3. Present information.	_____	_____	_____	_____	3
4. Repeat important points.	_____	_____	_____	_____	4
5. Use examples and illustrations.	_____	_____	_____	_____	5
6. Ask questions that stimulate discussion.	_____	_____	_____	_____	6
7. Use group techniques in class.	_____	_____	_____	_____	7
8. Provide immediate verbal feedback.	_____	_____	_____	_____	8
9. Solicit feedback from class.	_____	_____	_____	_____	9
10. Serve as resource for students.	_____	_____	_____	_____	10
11. Use verbal praise.	_____	_____	_____	_____	11
12. Use nonverbal rewards.	_____	_____	_____	_____	12
13. Use punishment.	_____	_____	_____	_____	13
14. Be accepting of ideas students express.	_____	_____	_____	_____	14
15. Try new approaches.	_____	_____	_____	_____	15
16. Assess worth of innovations.	_____	_____	_____	_____	16
17. Assign grades to students.	_____	_____	_____	_____	17
18. Set standards for class.	_____	_____	_____	_____	18
19. Set limits for class members.	_____	_____	_____	_____	19
20. Enforce limits.	_____	_____	_____	_____	20
21. Let others know when I do not understand something they have said.	_____	_____	_____	_____	21
22. Let others know when I like something they have said.	_____	_____	_____	_____	22

Table 7.6. (Cont.)

Items	Important	Not Important	I'm doing okay	I'd like to do better	
23. Let others know when I disagree with them.	_____	_____	_____	_____	23
24. Let others know when I think they have changed the subject or become irrelevant.	_____	_____	_____	_____	24
25. Let others know when I'm getting irritated.	_____	_____	_____	_____	25
26. Let others know when I feel hurt or embarrassed, or put down by something they have said or done.	_____	_____	_____	_____	26
27. Listening to understand rather than preparing my next remark.	_____	_____	_____	_____	27
28. Before agreeing or disagreeing, checking to make sure I do understand what others mean.	_____	_____	_____	_____	28
29. Checking out with others what I think they are feeling rather than assuming I know.	_____	_____	_____	_____	29
30. Talking in group discussions.	_____	_____	_____	_____	30
31. Being able to stand tension and conflict.	_____	_____	_____	_____	31
32. Accepting help from others.	_____	_____	_____	_____	32
33. Offering help to others.	_____	_____	_____	_____	33
34. Standing up for myself among peers.	_____	_____	_____	_____	34
35. Giving in to others.	_____	_____	_____	_____	35
36. Feeling positively about being a teacher.	_____	_____	_____	_____	36
37. Being optimistic about education in our system.	_____	_____	_____	_____	37
38. Understanding thoroughly materials I teach.	_____	_____	_____	_____	38
39. Knowing about resources available in my district.	_____	_____	_____	_____	39
40. Monitoring nonverbal cues of students and others.	_____	_____	_____	_____	40
41. Being assertive with administrators and parents.	_____	_____	_____	_____	41
42. Being a model for students to admire and emulate.	_____	_____	_____	_____	42

Table 7.6. (Cont.)

Items	Important	Not Important	I'm doing okay	I'd like to do better	
43. Spend time alone with individual students.	_____	_____	_____	_____	43
44. Consoling children who express fears and problems.	_____	_____	_____	_____	44
45. Playing with students in and outside class.	_____	_____	_____	_____	45
46. Talk informally to students.	_____	_____	_____	_____	46

Additional Items

ceptualize their roles. The Self-Conception of Own Role Performance and directions for its use may be seen in Table 7.7.

Fox et al. point out that this instrument might be used both to list a teacher's actual behaviors and/or a teacher's expected behaviors. If teachers complete the report twice, once for actual behaviors and once for behaviors they believe to be expected of them, the resulting contrasts might become the basis for productive consideration of potential role change.

One way in which teacher roles might change is for teachers to incorporate more of an advocacy orientation into their work. Barnes, Eyman, and Bragar (1977) note that advocacy involves efforts to change policies that have led to a particular problem, in addition to acting on behalf of someone who has the identified problems. They also note the critical relationship between the ecological model and the role of advocate:

> To be an advocate, one must see behavior as a product of the interaction between a person and their environment (the ecological model) rather than as located within a person (the medical model). So no child is a "behavior problem" in a vacuum; rather, he or she is disturbing to a particular person in a particular situation. The remedy then relates to the situation and the interaction between the child and the situation, not just to changing the child.
>
> To advocate for one person to change his/her situation may help that particular person. But often others are in the same or similar situations: what seems like a private or personal problem is often a "public" one. An advocate will try to change the policies that create the public problem, not just find a solution for one particular case [p. 166].

The move toward an advocacy role for teachers is one important way in which teacher behavior can be changed directly. Teachers might also define their roles more in terms of community education, or parent education, or prevention, each of which would broaden the notion of teaching and increase the likelihood of harmonious student-teacher ecosystems. Perhaps most important, teachers and other adults who work with youngsters regarded as emotionally disturbed or behavior disordered must examine their attitudes and the impact of those attitudes on the lives of the children they serve.

Rubin and Balow (1978) conducted a longitudinal study of teacher identified behavior problems and noted that "behavior that at least one teacher is willing to classify as a problem is the norm rather than the exception for elementary school children" (p. 102).

Rubin and Balow went on to provide a detailed discussion of their findings and concluded:

> The commonness of the belief by teachers that children are problems may partially account for Morse's (1964) finding that children's self esteem drops markedly from grade 3 to grade 11. This is a particularly troublesome matter that clearly requires further investigation of the nature and dimensions of the problem as well as means of separating out whatever portion of problem behavior in schools may be in the eye of the beholder. Once that is accomplished, correction can proceed to deal with the school and its representatives as well as with the children [p. 110].

This finding, while dramatically presented, is just one of many results that demonstrate the critical importance of teacher attitudes and teacher behavior for student behavior. The teacher remains the most essential resource in the educational process and it is of the utmost importance that teachers understand their own motivations and perceptions and contributions to the problems of troubled systems.

INDIRECT SERVICES

The first part of this chapter focused on direct-service efforts—interventions that center directly on youngsters or on adults. This section will address the ways in which we can intervene in troubled systems without necessarily focusing on the identified troubled child or attempting to change a particular adult's behavior in a problem situation. Such interventions are known as indirect services and in this chapter we will pay special attention to two indirect-service roles: coordinator and consultant. Later chapters describe other indirect-service functions such as working with parents (Chapter 8) and prevention (Chapter 10).

Coordination

It should be quite apparent by now that the ecological perspective views each child as an inseparable part of a unique social system. Further,

Table 7.7. Self-Conception of Own Role Performance.

All of us have certain things about our own role performance which we think are important. There are ten numbered blanks on the page below. In the blanks, please write ten adjectives or short descriptive phrases, each referring to the simple statement, "As a teacher, I do the following things." Answer as if you were giving the answers to yourself, not to somebody else. Write the answers in the order that they occur to you. We are interested in both positive and negative aspects. Do not worry about logic but try to be as clear as possible. Write each descriptive word or phrase as rapidly as possible. Your first impressions are good enough.

AS A TEACHER, I DO THE FOLLOWING THINGS:

1.
2.
3.
4.
5.
6.
7.
8.
9.
10.

Now go back and evaluate each of these things according to how positive or negative you see it. In order to represent a range, place double plus (+ +) if you feel the characteristic is quite positive, a (+) single plus if you see it as somewhat positive, a single minus (−) if you see it as somewhat negative, and a double minus (− −) if you see the thing as quite negative. Be sure to evaluate each descriptive word or phrase by placing one of these sign configurations on the small line to the right of each. Remember there are four such signs, (+ +), (+), (−), and (− −). Work rapidly.

Source: Fox et al., 1975, p. 39.

youngsters who are identified as emotionally disturbed or behavior disordered are usually part of many separate but somehow related systems. Even within a school, such youngsters are often involved with educators, social service workers, mental health people, and the like.

In order for even the best-developed educational plans to succeed, the efforts of persons from this range of systems must somehow be coordinated. The ecological perspective points out that even very highly trained specialists need to bring some generic skills to their work with troubled systems. Psychologists, social workers, special educators, and others must all see the importance of coordination and must be prepared to take on the coordinator's role.

The need for better coordination of services for troubled youngsters has been described in a variety of sources. The President's Commission on Mental Health (1978) noted that mental health services needed to be coordinated more closely with each other and with other community and neighborhood support systems. *Challenges for Children's Mental Health*

Services (1977) identified the poor working relationships among service providers as a barrier to the provision of coordinated services to youngsters.

Finally, the President's Commission report (1978) also noted that the demand for better coordination requires new roles for service providers. They described one increasingly popular staff function in mental health systems: case manager.

> Strategies focused solely on organizations are not enough. A human link is required. A case manager can provide this link and assist in assuring continuity of care and a coordinated program of services. Case management is an expediting service. The case manager should be sensitive to the disabled person's needs, knowledgeable about government and private agencies that provide housing, income maintenance, mental health, and social services, and should be in close touch with the community's formal and informal support systems [p. 24].

In a particular program, a case manager might fulfill the role of "Childrens Service Coordinator" and perform the following functions: develop an initial service plan for the child; expedite the child's entry into the various service settings; monitor the child's progress; continue serving as coordinator or liaison for the various system components actively involved in the provision of service to the identified child and family; see to the provision of additional services when appropriate; provide support to the youngster and important others in the system while service is being delivered; and follow up on the child's progress after service has been terminated.

Whether the role is called case manager or coordinator or liaison or by some other term, there are really two essential qualities that such a person must have. First, a coordinator should know what resources a community has to offer and how to secure them in the most efficient manner. Second, a coordinator should be skilled at the group problem-solving process. This includes the ability to bring relevant parties together and to guide the group's planning process in a direction that maximizes the likelihood that troubled systems will be restored to ecological balance. These skills are especially critical to the educational planning process, especially when it involves the kind of group process described below.

Committee on the Handicapped Meetings

Teachers of troubled children, psychologists and social workers involved with troubled children, administrators of buildings in which troubled children are educated, and others all have a variety of responsibilities to the youngsters they serve. In recent years, one common responsibility for all these persons, an aspect of their jobs for which they have typically been unprepared, is participation in the interdisciplinary group charged with planning educational programs for children with special educational needs. Usually such groups are now called committees on the handicapped, although different titles (Pupil Personnel Committee, Pupil Services Team) are used in different locations.

New York State Guidelines (1978) for Committees on the Handicapped are based on one overriding purpose, "to find out what each handicapped child in the district needs and to recommend to the Board of Education the appropriate educational services and programs to meet the child's needs" (p. 2). To fulfill that function, each committee in New York state has six major responsibilities:

1. To make recommendations on classification, evaluation, and educational programs for children who require special education.
2. To make recommendations on the frequency and nature of appropriate re-evaluations of handicapped children by appropriate specialists.
3. To insure that the adequacy of existing special education services and programs is evaluated.
4. To inform the Board of Education about the adequacy of existing special education services and programs and to advise them about the unmet needs of handicapped children in the district.
5. To report annually to the Board of Education the status of each handicapped child and each child thought to be handicapped in the district.
6. To maintain the census of all handicapped children annually [p. 2].

While the guidelines described above are most relevant for district-level committees on the handicapped, they also pertain to local- or building-level committees. At the building level, committees on the handicapped are charged with the first part of the IEP development: determining the child's current level of educational performance, describing the child's specific educational needs, recommending an appropriate classification for the child, and determining if the child should be referred for placement in a special education program. Building-level committees are also often involved in the reintegration of youngsters from special education into regular classrooms.

Whatever their job description and regardless of the name of the planning group, participants need to be "coordination wise" in order to be productive contributors to these committees. From an ecological perspective, it is the failure of building-level committees to coordinate their efforts that causes even very good educational plans to fail and systems to remain troubled. The "blame" for such coordination failures typically falls on the identified child—"He was so disturbed that our plan didn't work." Unfortunately, it might often be more accurate to say, "Our committee process was so lacking in coordination that our plan was never really implemented."

In order to be effective coordinators, adults who work with troubled children must first be effective communicators with their colleagues.

Communicating with others is a skill and like other skills, some adults have learned it and can display it more effectively than others. Persons interested in assessing their own roles on planning committees might start by asking themselves to complete the Personal Role Checklist found in Table 7.8.

Examination of the results of such a checklist might yield two important bits of information. First, it would help participants understand that there are a variety of roles to be played in groups and that some of those roles might be more helpful than others, depending on the specific circumstances. Second, it would demonstrate to participants the nature of their own role in the group's process. The results might be surprising and lead to efforts to change roles or they might be useful as checks to ensure that participants are functioning as they would like to in the group's deliberations. In any case, new information is useful, if participants can incorporate it into their own future actions and thinking.

Finally, participants in educational planning groups must focus more actively on the need for coordination in their group's process. Since coordina-

Table 7.8. Personal Role Checklist for Planning Committee Participants.

PERSONAL ROLE CHECKLIST	NAME:
	DATE:

What behaviors (no more than three) do you see yourself having engaged in most today? (Rank 1, 2, and 3.)

——— Initiating. Trying to start some action.
——— Asking others for information or opinions.
——— Giving information or opinions.
——— Summarizing or elaborating on the ideas of others.
——— Trying to coordinate the activities of others.
——— Evaluating the group accomplishments or individuals' contributions.
——— Encouraging other members.
——— Being the object of attacks.
——— Trying to bring harmony to the group.
——— Aiding in the communications process.
——— Helping the group set standards for itself.
——— Loyally following the lead of others.
——— Avoiding involvement.
——— Listening attentively.
——— Dominating by trying to coerce or manipulate other members' behavior.
——— Playing around, joking, etc.
——— Other (describe below.)

tion is typically not the province of any one professional area, any participant (teacher, psychologist, social worker, administrator) could be coordinator for a particular child's "case." In some schools committees rotate the responsibility for coordination and each committee member takes a turn.

Often this takes the form of the committee's providing an advocate for each referred child. Advocates are responsible for the overall coordination of the process, gathering data from important members of the child's system as well as from other professionals in contact with the child, leading the committee's discussion of the child, checking on possible placements if appropriate, clarifying plans and checking to see that plans are actually implemented, following up on the child after the committee has completed its work, and so on. School psychologists, social workers, teachers, or administrators who find themselves in this kind of role might want to develop a format similar to the one proposed by Hobbs (see Chapter 6) in order to keep actively "on top of" the complex planning and implementation process.

Consultation

According to Caplan (1970), perhaps the most prominent writer on the subject of mental health consultation, the following defines the consultation process:

> a process of interaction between two professional persons—the consultant, who is a specialist, and the consultee, who invokes the consultants' help in regard to a current work problem with which he is having some difficulty [p. 19].

Conoley, Apter, and Conoley (1981) point out, however, that the consultation process may be much more problematic and not readily resolvable by simple referral to an "expert." They conclude:

> Consultation should be seen, therefore, not as the more knowledgeable consultant giving answers to a puzzled consultee. Rather, it must be viewed as a collaborative problem solving process during which the consultant facilitates the creative, coping skills of the consultee *and* learns from the consultee about the unique aspects of the problem and the consultee's situation. [p. 113]

Gallessich (1972) has noted that Caplan's consultation model can be integrated into a systems approach to consultation with schools. The primary assumption behind such an effort according to Gallessich:

> is that the system, whether it is a small unit, such as a team of two or three

teachers or a larger unit, for example, a school district, contains the basic resources for effective problem-solving; the consultant enters the system with the goal of facilitating organizational growth through more effective use of indigenous resources [p. 13].

The need for consultation efforts stems primarily from the inadequacy of a direct-service-only approach to the problems of troubled children. It has become quite clear that there will never be enough trained personnel to meet the needs of the millions of children suffering from some degree of emotional stress. Consequently, if we ever hope to have an impact on the problem of emotional disturbance in our society, it is essential that we develop and utilize techniques that enable us to "spread the effect" of our efforts more widely. That is to say, if a resource teacher or a school psychologist or a social worker can provide effective consultation to a classroom teacher, a double positive effect may result. First, the classroom teacher may be enabled, by the consultant's support, to develop a better approach to the child (client) in question and consequently that youngster may receive better, more effective service. Second, the classroom teacher may develop a better understanding of how to work with similar youngsters in the future and so the effects of consultation around one child may have positive impact on countless other children in years to come.

From an ecological perspective, consultation is an essential aspect of intervention into troubled systems. While it is important to support adults' efforts to meet the needs of particular identified troubled youngsters better, it is equally critical that we assist those same adults in their efforts to change their own behaviors, attitudes, and expectations.

While consultation has become a standard tool in many school psychologists' arsenals, it often takes a back seat to diagnostic testing. For special education teachers, consultation techniques have typically not been included in training programs as exemplified by the following quotation from Brown and Palmer (1977):

With Public Law 94-142, most special class teachers will be confronted with a greatly changed teaching situation. Most mildly to moderately emotionally disturbed pupils now in special classes will in all likelihood be mainstreamed, while more severely disturbed pupils will be placed in public school special classes. However, most special class teachers of emotionally disturbed children have little or no experience with the most severely disturbed population. *Special educators also are likely to assume more of a consulting role with regular class teachers who have exceptional pupils mainstreamed into their classrooms. Yet, there are few inservice training programs to help special educators develop the necessary consulting skills for this new role* [p. 174, emphasis added].

Speaking about the importance of incorporating consultation into the resource teacher role, Wiederholt, Hammill, and Brown (1978) note

> The emphasis that we give to the consulting role in the resource program model is long overdue in special education. Most teacher-training institutions have been slow to include such skills among their competencies; until the advent of the resource programs, public schools had no practical instructionally oriented arrangement that lent itself conveniently to providing consulting services to teachers. In any event, the schools in which the resource teachers are permitted to perform only two duties (to assess and to remediate children's problems) are overlooking a profitable avenue for improving the education of both students and teachers. In fact, in selecting resource teachers, one primary consideration might be their ability to implement tactfully the consulting aspects of the resource program [pp. 32-3].

In an interview (*Exceptional Children*, November 1977) in which he discussed both the move to an ecological point of view in work with disturbed children and the role of the resource or helping teacher, Bill Morse said that resource teachers for troubled children "need a lot more training in consultation and working with both teachers and systems to figure out how they can change some of these fundamental elements that cause or accelerate problems" (p. 163).

Resource teachers themselves have expressed their needs in this area, 76 percent of the participants in a Syracuse, New York survey (Apter, 1978, unpublished) emphasized a desire to incorporate more indirect service (defined primarily as consultation) into their roles. Evans (1980) reached similar conclusions; resource teachers, classroom teachers, and principals in her study agreed that resource teachers could productively double the amount of time they spent doing consultation.

There may even be some evidence that consultation can improve the likelihood of successful integration for a seriously troubled child. Wixson (1980) found that while 30 percent of a sample of disturbed pupils receiving direct services from the resource teacher were able to return to regular classrooms, 57 percent of the youngsters receiving indirect services (defined as resource teacher consultation and classroom teacher implementation) made successful returns to full and unaided classroom participation.

Table 7.9 summarizes some critical aspects of consultation for resource teachers. Most if not all of the points described in Table 7.9 are also applicable to persons working with troubled children from a variety of job descriptions.

Perhaps the most important element described in Table 7.9 is the sequence of stages in the consultation process: establishing the relationship, exploring and defining the problem, considering alternative solutions, planning the chosen intervention, evaluation, and termination. The first stage,

Table 7.9. Summary of Consultant Role Information for Systems-Oriented Resource Teachers.

1. One thing we know about resource teacher positions is that the responsibility for providing direct service (as opposed to consultation, in-service, community education, etc.) prevails.
2. Consequently, much of the consulting many resource teachers do must be done "on the run" — a condition which is not conducive to good consultation.
3. There are many models of consultation stemming from a variety of theoretical and role perspectives (mental health, behavioral, organizational development, etc.). In all cases we can look at consultation as a problem-solving process that occurs in the context of a helper (consultant)–helpee (consultee) relationship.
4. The consultation process may be characterized as having the following essential stages:
   a. establishing the relationship,
   b. exploration and definition of problem,
   c. exploration of alternative solutions,
   d. planning the chosen intervention,
   e. evaluation, and
   f. termination,
5. Despite the fact that consultation begins as a helper-helpee relationship, it should be looked upon as a *mutual problem-solving effort by peers*. It is not usually productive for either party to expect the consultant to have the one right answer for the problem under investigation.
6. Consultants should be experts in conceptualizing and facilitating the problem-solving process.
7. The goal of consultation is to help others find more effective ways to help themselves; both in the immediate situations as well as over a longer period.

establishing the relationship, is essential if the consultation process is to begin at all. Following are some guidelines that may be helpful in the building of consultation relationships:

1. *Establish proximity.* Hang around, appear approachable.
2. *Participate in scheduled meetings.* Conform to the regularities of your setting.
3. *"Sit beside the consultee."* Ask enriching questions, get the whole story.
4. *Foster consultee's self-respect.* Don't make snap judgments; respect consultee's fear of looking foolish.
5. *Deal with consultee's anxiety.* Model calm, concerned problem solving.
6. *Be a role model.* Demonstrate three "Human Service Universals," empathy, tolerance of feelings, belief that (with enough information,) all human behavior is understandable.
7. *Maintain confidentiality.*

Once the consultation process begins, the consultant's responsibilities primarily involve facilitation of the mutual problem-solving process as it moves through a logical sequence of steps: defining the problem, exploring alternative solutions, planning the agreed-upon intervention, evaluating the effectiveness of your efforts, altering your plan, and so on. Much of the work in each of these phases involves interviewing skills. Table 7.10 lists some dos and don'ts for consultants.

Montgomery (1978) has offered special educators the following five tips that may serve as useful guidelines for effective consultation:

1) *Being an expert is not so smart.*
   Don't assume that you are the only one who really understands Johnny's problem. Curb your tendency to offer pat answers to complex issues. Few people like or are able to utilize unsolicited advice.
2) *It's what you don't say that counts.*
   Listen! Consultees may need to "blow off steam" and you can serve as an understanding audience. Also, it's consultees who have the information needed to understand and remediate the troubling situation. If you don't listen, you'll never hear it.
3) *If everybody likes what you're doing, you're probably doing it wrong.*
   Consultation is a change process and change is never easy; it usually hurts. There will undoubtedly be discomfort, efforts will be misunderstood, errors are inevitable. Systems resist change and consultants must be wary of being co-opted.

Table 7.10. Some Dos and Don'ts for Consultants.

I. *Techniques which generally have a favorable effect*:
1. Redirection for elaboration
2. Reflect feelings in empathic way
3. Clarify expectations for interview and for the consultation contract
4. Active listening
5. Nonverbal attending behaviors (eye contact, nodding in agreement, etc.)
6. Ask pertinent specific questions
7. Being Tentative with suggestions ("do you think"; it sounds like")
8. Supportive Comments
9. End with concrete plan (even if only for the next meeting)
10. Admit nonexpertise
11. Give several options on observation arrangement
12. Let consultees vent their problems
13. Pauses may generate more data
14. Be natural

II. *Techniques which generally have an unfavorable effect*:
1. Excessive redirection of questions (leads to frustration)
2. Shifting, fiddling, excessive movements (communicates boredom)
3. Asking defensive questions ("what do you want me to do?")
4. Abrupt changes of subject (communicates lack of interest)
5. Distracting behaviors (doodling, staring out the window)
6. Pursuing irrelevant or confusing issues
7. Focusing interview on self
8. Setting self up as expert
9. Overuse of technical language or jargon
10. Providing false solutions or premature closure

4) *A teacher's classroom is her castle.*

  Everyone gets anxious when someone peers over their shoulder. Teachers are no exception. Be sensitive to teachers perceptions; don't be an evaluator, give positive feedback, be as unobtrusive as possible. After a while, your visits will be less threatening.

5) *Everything broken doesn't have to be fixed.*

  Don't create problems through a preoccupation with "normality". All youngsters are not the same and being different does not necessarily require intervention. Don't fixate on the child, when the problem may reside elsewhere in the system [Montgomery, 1978, pp. 110–12].

Consultants must prepare themselves to deal with commonly found issues in the consultation process. Adequate communication among adults involved in the system(s) seldom exists, consultees may resist the entire consultation process for fear of appearing incompetent (if I need consultation, I must not be doing my job well), every system has "regularities" that consultants must respect and work within (i.e. no business talk in the teachers' room), etc.

Levine (1973) has developed five postulates that are useful additions to this discussion:

1. The setting is always part of the problem.
2. Some obstacle blocks effective problem-solving behaviors.
3. Help must be located near the setting.
4. Goals and values of consultant must be consistent with goals and values of setting.
5. Form of help should have potential for being established on a systematic basis using the natural resources of the setting.

If consultants keep these postulates in mind, always think about "person-in-setting" as the unit of analysis, and see themselves as problem-solving catalysts, their job will be eased.

Consultation is a mutual problem-solving process, however, and it is equally important for consultees to be prepared for their role in these efforts. For example, Reynolds (1979) suggests that:

It is essential now that all teachers have opportunities to master the knowledge and practices involved in effective consultation and other forms of professional communication. Every teacher should have instruction and practicum experience leading to assured capability in these areas as part of preservice preparation [p. 14].

Table 7.11 presents some guidelines for classroom teacher consultees. As can be seen in that list, Reynolds (1977a) is calling for consultees to assert

Table 7.11. Consultation Guidelines for Classroom Teachers.

1) Remember that you "own" the problem, you are in charge of the education of the pupil or the class procedures that are under consideration.
2) Be sure that there is early agreement with the consultant on the nature of the "problem" and on how decisions will be made. Draw up a contract orally or in writing early in the relationship on goals, methods, and responsibilities.
3) Be sure that it is clear that you (the teacher) are the client—that all communication flows to you. The consultant is there to help you structure your work, not somebody else's. This relationship does not preclude some direct assessment of children and observations in the classroom by the consultant if they are agreed upon as part of the contract.
4) Avoid status problems. Consultants and clients are co-equals.
5) Avoid entering personal subjective materials (letting attention shift to your personal needs and problems); instead, keep the content of the relationship centered on the child and the instructional situation.
6) Seek alternative suggestions from the consultant rather than a single or set plan.
7) Try to use each period of consultation as a learning experience to increase effective communication and listening, building trust between professionals, and maximizing instructional effectiveness.
8) Evaluate each consultation experience objectively and share your conclusions with the consultant.

Source: Reynolds, 1977a. p. 32–3

their rights, to maintain their responsibility and to learn how to utilize consultants most productively. The guidelines are useful for anyone who may utilize a consultant's help at some time.

Consultation and coordination are two critical indirect-service roles for professionals involved in work with troubled children. Their importance cannot be overestimated, especially if we hope to have an impact on the far-ranging problems of emotional distress in children. The most important area of intervention in troubled systems, however, may focus on efforts to work with the families of those youngsters who are identified as emotionally disturbed or behaviorally disordered. Families form the first and most intimate microsystems for all children and demand attention in our discussions of troubled systems. We turn our focus to efforts to work with families in the next chapter.

8
Working with Families

In recent years, increasing attention has been paid to the place of parents in programs for troubled children. Contrary to earlier efforts, when parents were often "blamed" for the disturbances presented by their offspring, current strategies focus much more specifically on the development of partnerships between parents and professionals. The ecological perspective stresses the importance of working with the systems that surround each child and emphasizes the critical role families may play in the remediation of troubled systems.

In this chapter, we examine some of the critical issues in modern American family life, discuss parental reactions and concerns about disabled (especially disturbed) children in their families, summarize previous efforts and evaluate the results of a variety of professional interactions with families of disturbed children, offer some guidelines and suggestions for particular programs and activities with relevance for parent-professional relationships, and describe some implications and models for further development in the future.

There has been much discussion of the breakdown in modern family life. According to Bronfenbrenner (1977a):

> The family is falling apart. There is a lot of evidence to substantiate this. Since World War II the extended family of several generations, with all its relatives, has practically disappeared in this country. Even the small nuclear family of mother, father, and the kids is in decline.
>
> . . . Today, more than one-sixth of all children in our country are living in single-parent families. Meanwhile, despite birth control, the number of unwed mothers is skyrocketing.

. . . And there has been a rapid rise in the number of mothers who work. Over 50 percent of women with school age children are now employed. So are over one-third of those with children under six. In fact, one-third of women with children under three are working. We've got a situation in which the father is working and the mother is working, too.

. . . And the question is, who is caring for America's children? The answer is disturbing. Fewer and fewer parents are doing their job of caring for children. Meanwhile, substitute-care facilities are in very low supply, at least in this country. They're expensive for those who can afford them and practically nonexistent for those who can't.

. . . What's destroying the family isn't the family itself but the indifference of the rest of society. The family takes a low priority [Bronfenbrenner, 1977a, p. 41].

In his frightening description, Bronfenbrenner cites all the issues we've come to hear so much about: the need for both parents to work in order to combat inflation, the increasing numbers of mothers in the work force, the paucity of high quality, reasonable-cost day-care arrangements, the dramatic escalation in the number of one-parent (usually mothers, but increasingly fathers as well) families, the decrease in availability of extended family members to provide child care, and so on.

Perhaps most important, however, is Bronfenbrenner's description of the effectiveness of the family structure in providing youngsters with the supports that they need to grow and develop:

Of course, once we do apply our best minds to the problem of caring for children, I think we'll have the deflating experience of rediscovering the wheel. We'll find that families, after all, are really very efficient. We don't need a new social vehicle. All we have to do is to create new conditions to enable families to do what they do better than anybody else. We need to make it possible for children and adults to enter each other's worlds. It will be good for both of them.

. . . The family is also the first sanctuary. If a person gets a good start in the family, he can cope with all sorts of problems in later life. In that primitive Ping-Pong game, that back-and-forth between an infant and its caretaker, a person learns how to get his basic needs satisfied by other human beings. As adults we're not conscious of using these skills in our relationships with our colleagues and friends, but we do [Bronfenbrenner, 1977a, p. 45].

Families are important then, not only because they can supplement the school's educational program or the community mental health center's treatment plan, but also because they are the critical system in which youngsters learn how to satisfy their needs, and how to get along in the world. Better than any other system, families can provide the support and experience necessary for youngsters' psychological growth and development. Consequently, the prospect of working with troubled children without also attempting to intervene on some level with families becomes a self-defeating activity.

While Bronfenbrenner speaks to the universal issues in modern family life and child development, there also exists a more specific area defined by families that include disabled youngsters. MacKeith (1973), for example, describes the role of parents in such families and emphasizes the need for professionals to be prepared to help:

> But the contribution of parents is paramount. Individual parents behave individually to their child according to their physical health, their attitudes and values, their marital feelings, their memories of their parents' behavior towards them as they saw it, and the molding influence their own child has on them.
>
> The presence of a handicapped child in a family is an unusual situation with advantages as well as the disadvantages we tend to emphasize. Most families with handicapped children succeed; but the interactions of parent with child, child with siblings, family with neighbors are sometimes unusual. If such families are to be helped to the maximum, those who are liable to be asked to help them need to give hard thought beforehand so that they are prepared to meet the call for help.
>
> It would be pointless to attempt to play down the importance of the physical or of the larger social environment of the child, *but for many practical purposes, the environment of the child is his family.* This is true whether the family is nuclear or extended, enriched or deprived [pp. 131–132].

MacKeith proceeds to list (on the basis of his own experience with families of disabled children) some of the most frequently encountered feelings and behavior patterns experienced by parents in response to their disabled youngsters.

With regard to feelings, MacKeith notes that there are two common biological reactions: protection of the helpless infant and revulsion at the child's abnormality. Obviously, there are times when these feelings can act in contradictory directions.

Second, parents may feel inadequate at fulfilling their reproductive function and/or in terms of their capacity to raise their disabled youngster (a common fear of parents of "typical" first-born children as well).

Third, parents may feel bereaved of the expected "normal" child and of a youngster through whom they might (vicariously) fulfill their own frustrated ambitions. Such bereavement often carries with it corresponding emotions such as anger (at fate for inflicting this burden), grief (feelings of sadness and hopelessness), and the feelings that accompany adjustment (getting accustomed to the situation).

A fourth feeling may be shock or surprise. This may be expressed as incredulity, the feeling that this can't have really happened, or helplessness, the belief that nothing can be done.

Fifth, an often-cited feeling is guilt, a feeling of somehow being personally responsible for what has gone wrong. Conscience may also be involved as the birth of a disabled child may be interpreted as punishment for earlier moral wrongdoing. Parents may also experience feelings of guilt in response to other feelings about the child (e.g., anger or rejection).

Finally, according to MacKeith, parents may also feel embarrassed, especially if they are people who depend upon the approval of others.

Cohen (1974) has described some of the most common stresses in family life related to the inclusion of a handicapped child. That list is repeated in Table 8.1.

It is valid but perhaps not very compelling to discuss feelings or behaviors of parents of disabled children in general terms. Even the descriptions provided by MacKeith and Cohen above may not convey the essence of parental concerns and reactions.

The following excerpts are taken from a letter written by a father to the teacher of one of his children, Debbie. The content of the letter is real although the names have been changed. While the letter focuses primarily on Debbie, note the sections that focus on Kurt, Debbie's younger brother as well as on each of the parents. Note also that this letter was written before Public Law 94:142 required individualized educational plans. An

Table 8.1. Some Stresses in Family Life.

1. Constant fear that the child will hurt himself because of his limited understanding of danger and of how things work.
2. Necessity of helping the child with all aspects of self-care, including toileting, feeding, dressing, bathing, grooming.
3. Difficulty in getting babysitters or in enlisting relatives to care for the handicapped child so that the mother can get "a break" from time to time.
4. Worry about and anger at child's rejection by other children and adults in the neighborhood.
5. Difficulty in finding a suitable educational program for the child.
6. Difficulty in arranging for transportation for a physically handicapped child, and architectural barriers which prevent this child from access to many public places.
7. Difficulty in finding appropriate recreational programs.
8. Tendency of some professionals and lay people to blame the parents for the child's disability.
9. Difficulty in communicating ideas to the child and in teaching him new things that he needs to know in order to function more independently.
10. Child's great dependence upon the mother, psychological as well as physical, and great fear of separation.
11. Frequent medical care which the child may need.
12. The bizarre behavior of the child which the parents can't understand and which causes them shame and/or grief.

Source: Cohen, 1974, p. 7.

IEP based on the ecological profile system detailed above, might have been very helpful for Debbie and for her family.

Dear Ms. Aronson:

We really haven't had a chance to meet except for a few brief moments at Open House in November. I'm Debbie's father and I write this because we seem to have a common interest in Debbie's development. And, more than just a common interest, we have a stake in each other because I and Deb's mother are "teachers" in her informal education curriculum just as you are her teacher in the formal schooling environment. What you and Debbie do while in school has substantial influence on what we do at home. How we handle the home learning environment, I assume, has some bearing on Deb's development and learning in school. Frankly, I've got a stake in making you the best you can be and I would guess that you have a stake in having Mrs. Donlan and me be the best we can be. And Deb has the most intense stake in our cooperative success.

It is difficult to write this kind of a letter. I guess that not only is Debbie an "exceptional" child but that, in a *similar* sense, we are "exceptional" parents. That is, we have needs as individuals and as a family unit that differ in degree, if not kind, from the so-called nonexceptional family. As parents (and as teachers of our children), we need help in order to provide help. No one likes to admit that they are different, that they face different problems, that they have different needs, that they feel guilty and live under the dread of failure, that they lack knowledge and skills to function satisfactorily and effectively, that they are lonely, and that the mainstream of family life is experienced as spectators and not as participants. . . .

[But] as a family we *are* different and this obviously has some bearing on the learning environment a family provides for its children—and for all its members for that matter.

Why write this to you? Why lay on you that we need help? I suppose that I could say that we write because you have been specifically trained in such matters. But you haven't. You have an excellent background in special education but it is unfair to assume that this provides you with the skill, knowledge, and time to link the various learning environments with which Debbie interacts and from which she learns, let alone the training to facilitate the quality of those environments. I know that teachers are "context" people and that their task is primarily within a place called a school. And I know that the school part of learning doesn't focus on the "total" child (a phrase we hear so often at PTA meetings). It's unfair to expect you to do the impossible. I write to you, then, perhaps to help you understand some dimensions of the "other" learning environment—the one you and Debbie build from and with. And, I trust that understanding may help you in the school part of her education. And there's another reason too, I guess, and that is the dim hope that perhaps teacher training might some day go beyond the school to the "total" child—to go beyond a fragment and a context to an education in a full sense of the word.

. . . But the family environment includes other members of the family. The exceptional family flows into exceptional individuals. Debbie's brother for example. Younger biologically by two years, it is hard for him and for Debbie. Sibling rivalry is always present. Robbie plays the clarinet and the family goes to see him perform in the school orchestra. There is jealousness and some of his toys are deliberately destroyed. He can't understand how two different sets of "norms" are at work in the family and how "discipline" is approached differently depending upon the situation and the child. He claims that we spend more time with Deb and that we love her more. We try to help him understand that which we have a hard time understanding. His friends have been overheard to tease him about his sister and he increasingly shows impatience with her and with us and with the whole situation. Debbie's loneliness leads her to demand that her brother include her in all of his interests and he is robbed (or at least not protected from) having his own friends, his own places to retreat, his own hobbies. Once, when he made a model airplane, Debbie destroyed it . . . "I hate him." And Mrs. Donlan and I worry about Robbie and what his membership in our exceptional family may foster. When Debbie strikes out or is loud in her demands or is physical in response, Robbie follows the same pattern.

And Mrs. Donlan is a member of this exceptional family. Her needs and wants and fulfillment have become sublimated to the maintenance of the family as a unit. The anticipated satisfactions that are supposedly derived from family life are increasingly distant and remote. A sensitive and creative person, she has given her life to the family environment—a psychologically and physically exhausting task.

. . . And, there is the husband and father who constantly courts a "toughness" that the economic responsibilities force and which he doubts his ability to meet—as they must be. His patience is thin, and he too, is exhausted by work and by fears of when he is no longer around to provide. . . ? His concern with the future robs him of the here and now of family membership and keeps him from sharing with his wife. Being the "he," I must admit a constant awareness of failure to my wife, my kids, and to my "exceptional" family and an equally constant rationalizing that some day they may appreciate my efforts. I, too, know the emptiness of this dream and how unfair it is to all. But, what does one do?

So, Ms. Aronson . . . This is the exceptional family. Not different in kind from other families, but different in degree and intensity. One doesn't talk about these things because people get embarrassed or say "you just can't handle it," or think it a sign of weakness. Be that as it may . . . however, Debbie does live in what I call an "educational" environment (and this is the home) while she is also in the "school" environment. The two are not linked and almost adversaries with Debbie caught in the middle between two completely different sets of aspirations and learning experiences.

And just as you, the teacher, need a working environment—support, resources, feedback, satisfactions, and encouragement, so does the exceptional family need support, resources, feedback, satisfactions, and encouragement if we are to provide a sensible and healthy education for our youngsters. There must be a way to link the two. Debbie bridges both worlds. We need help. No question. But, part of our help can come by providing help to Debbie through forming a partnership with you. As I said earlier, I am not faulting you, although I wonder why you don't question some of the things we question—like report cards, and academic goals, and no real home contact. Maybe you do . . . and that's our hope. Maybe you need help too. Criticizing the family as a poor environment is to beg the question. Being professionally righteous and all knowing is kind of a shabby cop out when it comes to helping youngsters like Debbie forge her own world and her joy in living in that world.

I sound bitter. And maybe I am. I know that Debbie wants to learn, can learn, is sensitive, and can accomplish things that are of significance to her. All I ask is that somehow we form a partnership in which youngsters like Debbie no longer have to ask if we're proud but will know it, and that they no longer say "I can't know."

This letter raises a number of critical issues: the strains on parents and siblings, the effort by the child to discover what she can do, the need for assistance to the family, and others. Most of all, the letter represents one parent's plea for understanding and cooperation from another tremendously important person in the child's system—her teacher.

From a teacher's or other professional's perspective, it is important to hear and respond to the request described in this letter. It is more difficult but equally important for school staff members to reach out to parents who are not as able or willing to initiate requests for help. Finally, from our ecological perspective, it is critical for professionals to recognize that families represent the most immediate microsystems of their students or clients. Consequently, it is imperative that professionals incorporate a family systems approach into their efforts on behalf of troubled children.

FAMILY SYSTEMS APPROACHES

An especially critical aspect of the ecological perspective to emotional disturbance is an increased focus on families, an area in which the interest of the general as well as the professional public has recently been reawakened. The literature is filled with references documenting the importance of efforts with families to the ultimate success of the work of psychologists, special educators, and other professionals with troubled children. A few highlights follow with the purpose of demonstrating the strength of the need to adopt a family focus.

Letulle (1979) has discussed the major changes in both the organization of and the treatments offered by residential treatment centers as the result of the move to a family systems theory orientation. Paulson et al. (1978), in a study of suicide potential in children aged four to twelve, discovered that youngsters' disorders were symptomatic of acute family breakdown, often including marital disharmony and verbal and physical violence. Firestone,

Kelly, and Fike (1977) reported on the success of a program in which parents were taught to deal more effectively with the behavior problems of their children (ages three to eleven). Families spent an average of 11.5 hours learning new techniques following which decreases in problem behaviors were noted by both parents and teachers.

Craw's handbook (1976) designed to help teachers deal with the problems of five- to eight-year-old children contains a special emphasis (as do many similar works) on family and environmental factors. Daly et al. (1977) have reported on a successful parent training program developed as an alternative nonresidential program for delinquent youth.

The Pendleton Project (Pooley, 1976) was designed to reeducate children with behavioral problems and their families so that future maladaptive behavior would be less likely to occur, ultimately preventing the necessity for later incarceration.

Lowitt et al. (1975) questioned the traditional unidimensional model of childhood psychopathology. They point out that parents both influence *and are influenced by* their children and go on to document the need for more systematic exploration of family life in order to increase our understanding of family.

Johnson, Bolsted, and Lobitz (1975) investigated the transference of positive interventions with children from one setting to another. They found that unprogrammed positive generalization rarely occurred and concluded that if children were having difficulties in both school and home settings, there probably needs to be simultaneous intervention in both settings. In a related study, Lobitz and Johnson (1974) showed that the parent attitude variable was the most important element in discriminating between children who were or were not referred for help with acting-out behavior. They concluded that child behavior is not always the critical variable in referral and that multiple assessment of child-family problems is therefore critical.

Fowler (1970) described a course for teachers of disturbed children with special emphasis on understanding family systems. Morrison and Smith (1970) point out the importance of family intactness to children's psychiatric emergencies. Brownbridge and Van Fleet (1967) discuss the critical role of families in the prevention of emotional disturbances. Garrigan and Bambrick (1977) demonstrated how family therapy improved the school behavior of children labeled emotionally disturbed. Cherry (1976) found that a family-child-community orientation was one of three critical variables in the success of at least six treatment programs for disturbed children.

Clearly, the research described briefly here demonstrates the relevance of families to interventions with children labeled emotionally disturbed or behaviorally disordered. In addition, conclusions emphasize the need for simultaneous home/school intervention and planning, matching exactly the request of the parent who wrote the letter to Ms. Aronson excerpted above.

There are only a handful of studies which have investigated the relative effectiveness of involving parents in the treatment of troubled children. D'Angelo and Walsh (1967), in a study of a clinical facility in a school setting, compared four groups in treatment: child only in individual psychotherapy; parent only in group psychotherapy; parent seen in group therapy and child seen in individual therapy; and a control group where neither parent nor child was seen. After six months of therapy significant positive changes were observed in the children whose parents were seen while there was a negative trend for children who were seen alone. Results suggested that parents play a significant role in their children's adjustment problems. In addition, the D'Angelo and Walsh study singles out the effectiveness of a community-based clinic which appears to encourage more interest, motivation, and participation on the part of families.

Lessing and Shilling (1966) also concluded that improvement in the child was significantly associated with improvement in the mother. Gluck et al. (1964), in an evaluation of 55 child guidance cases found that more than half of the improvements in children's symptoms were reported by families in which both parents as well as the children were seen in therapy (the father's participation in particular was related to improvement). The importance of the participation of the father was underlined by Cole and Magnussen (1967). They compared remainers in therapy (family stopped therapy only with mutual consent of the therapist) with terminators (family decided to stop against the advice of the therapist). The results indicated that the treatment of remainers involved both mothers and fathers while the treatment of terminators involved only mothers.

Other studies reporting improved results in children when one or both parents received some sort of assistance include Perkins (1970), Dee (1970), and McGowan (1968). We can conclude, on the basis of the studies described above, that the involvement of parents in the treatment programs of their children is crucial for affecting and maintaining changes in both interpersonal and school-related behavior.

There have also been a number of efforts to train parents to become therapists for their own children. For example, Guerney and colleagues (Guerney, 1964; Andornico et al., 1967; Guerney et al., 1967) attempted to train mothers of emotionally disturbed children to utilize techniques of client-centered play therapy with their children at home. Results indicated that filial therapy (their name for this process) reduced children's symptoms and maternal dissatisfaction (Oxman, 1971).

Behaviorists have also attempted to teach parents to be therapists for their children. Recent reviews of this literature have been presented by O'Dell (1974) and Tavormina (1974). Various techniques were employed (programmed teaching, videotaping, etc.) to modify specific behaviors of children who were labeled as brain damaged (Patterson et al., 1965; Salzinger et al., 1970), retarded (Walder et al., 1967), autistic (Mathis, 1971), and school phobic (Patterson et al., 1965).

The training approaches varied from educational groups wherein parents are taught the basic principles and techniques of behavior modifications through lectures, films, and discussions to controlled learning situations in which the experimenter observes parent-child interactions and directs the behavior of the parents. Although most of the research does not allow for an evaluation of the efficacy of parental involvement as therapists as compared to a matched control group, Wiltz (1969) compared a group of parents who were trained in behavioral techniques with another group used as controls. It was reported that the deviant behavior demonstrated by the children of the experimental group decreased by 50 percent whereas the behavior of the other children increased by 30 percent.

The research by Guerney and colleagues as well as the research on parents as behavior modifiers demonstrate the efficacy of including parents in therapeutic intervention strategies with troubled children. Further, the results may be viewed as additional evidence for the effectiveness of intervening in the family system in order to effect changes in the lives of emotionally disturbed children. The diversity of efforts to work effectively with parents emphasizes the need to continue to consider a variety of formats for parent involvement. Some of the most recent work has been focused on the development of an educational model for working with parents.

PARENTS IN EDUCATION

Some models focus on preparing parents for still another role, that of teacher to your own child. For example, Hunt (1971) offered a summary and evaluation of parent-child centers which suggested the efficacy of involving parents in programs geared toward improving the child's development. Gray and Klaus (1963) developed a special summer nursery school for disadvantaged children. Mothers were taught how to improve their children's language skills and how to reinforce them for developing appropriate skills. The parents were also able to discuss their own problems and were helped to find new ways of coping. Results indicated that children of mothers who participated in the program showed (as compared to control groups) improved test performance, as did younger siblings of identified children.

Karnes (1968) trained mothers to be more effective teachers with their own children. The mothers were encouraged to believe that their assistance was highly important for developing educational competence in their children. Post-treatment measures showed gains of 7.46 points in IQ over a 12-week period as well as gains in visual decoding and auditory and verbal associations. In a later study Karnes (1969) compared the same program with regular teachers helping the children, compared with mothers. The results indicate that the children who were taught by their mothers had mean IQ gains of 12.5 points whereas those children taught by professional teachers had mean IQ gains of 14.3 but the difference was not statistically significant. Similar results were obtained by Badger (1973).

In addition to changes noted in the performance of children, Miller (1974) reported that over half of the mothers who participated in the early training programs had gone on to complete their high school degree, enrolled in courses to upgrade their vocational skills and upgraded their employment status as well as demonstrated a greater concern for community affairs. Badger (1973) noted a change in the life styles of the mothers who participated in the program from that of helplessness to enthusiasm and self-determination.

It appears that involving parents in roles which allow them to become important determiners of their children's behavior and learning, can also facilitate changes in parents' behavior. From an ecological perspective, we can see that effecting change in one part of the system (parent-child interaction) can have an impact on another part of the system (parent-community) relationships. In turn, productive changes in parents' life plans can have positive impacts on other aspects of family life, etc. Ultimately, a very troubled system can be returned to balance and harmony as the result of the first intervention, involving the parents of a child who is identified as troubled.

There are a number of ways in which parents can be involved in the education of their children. Kelly (1973) has listed three major formats for parent involvement in special education programming: providing instruction, home-school cooperative interactions, and community participation. For example, Schiff (1963) reported that parent participation and cooperation in school affairs leads to pupil achievement, better school attendance, better study habits, and fewer discipline problems.

More striking is the finding by Brookover et al. (1965) that children whose parents had become more intimately involved with the school showed increased self-concepts and made significant academic progress during the academic year whereas the children who received individual counseling did not. Results of both studies indicate that active participation on the part of the parent in the school environment may be critically related to improved performance in school and the development of a more positive self-image in the children.

Finally, there has been increasing attention to the need to work with families as one implication of the recent move toward educating youngsters with special needs in least restrictive settings. Chinn, Winn, and Walters (1978); Coletta (1977); Miller and Wilmshurst (1975); Bennett and Henson (1977); and Kroth (1975) have all written extensively on the need for special educators, including those who work with troubled youngsters, to become more involved with families.

Clearly, the research summarized above documents the importance of a family systems perspective to work with children labeled emotionally disturbed or behavior disordered. What was presented here represents only a fraction of the work being done in this area. Taken together, the results of the work described in this section present a strong argument for multiple forms of parent involvement.

Lightfoot (1981) has argued that families must be viewed by school personnel as educative environments. Further, Lightfoot notes that instead of asking how parents might become involved in the school curriculum, we should really attempt to build a single educational program that reinforces and expands upon appropriate experiences in both the school and the family spheres. This does not happen very often and Lightfoot believes that the root cause of our inability to work together more productively toward this goal lies in each group's conflicting misperceptions of the other:

> Parents' and teachers' perceptions of each other as uncaring about children and as not valuing the educational process lead to distance and distrust and the need to blame one another. Rather than search for the origins of conflict and finding effective strategies for real (rather than contrived) participation of parents and teachers in a collaborative task, schools develop sophisticated methods of exclusion; parents draw farther and farther away from parental responsibilities in the schooling process; and children fail—often experiencing the failure as their own individual inadequacy, incompetence, and lack of motivation [Lightfoot, 1981, p. 7].

Utilizing our ecological framework again, we can see from the above quotation that much of what we consider "children's failure" may really be due to ineffective school-family interactions. The gap between parents and school staff members can poison the system and may often result in the assignation of blame to a youngster who is caught in the middle.

The first teacher, and the teacher with whom the young handicapped child spends the most time is a parent, usually his mother. Traditionally, as Lightfoot (1981) described, teachers and and psychologists have ignored the parent role or have been critical of parent behavior and actively discouraged parents from involving themselves in their child's education. Recently, a number of factors have combined to change the attitude of many professionals toward parent involvement. These factors include recognition of the critical role of early experience, fiscal limitations which prevent the extension of programs staffed by professionals to preschool handicapped children in any extensive way, and the growth of strong organizations of parents of the handicapped who have demanded input into the educational process. Public Law 94:142 mandates considerable parent involvement and sets standards for the rights of parents to participate in the education of their disabled children. The remainder of this chapter focuses on a variety of formats for working with parents of troubled youngsters.

GUIDELINES FOR WORKING WITH PARENTS

In this section, we explore some specific ways in which special educators and psychologists can increase the effectiveness of their efforts to involve parents of troubled children in their program planning and implementation. We begin by exploring the teacher's role.

According to Cohen (1974), the teacher's responsibility in parent-teacher interactions ought to include the following components.

- To welcome communication with parents about the child.

- To communicate his or her dedication to helping their child learn.

- To communicate his or her desire to work cooperatively with parents toward this end.

- To listen to parental concerns and goals for their child.

- To communicate a willingness to learn about the parent's point of view.

- To communicate an interest in working in a complementary manner with the home.

- To explain the goals and program in the classroom for the child.

- To report on the child's progress.

- To offer ideas for possible use in the home for helping the child learn.

- To make use of information and (selected) ideas obtained from parents.

- To suggest and/or arrange for the parent to see a clinician or other specialist when the parent expresses a need for personal help.

On the other hand, Cohen emphasizes that the teacher's role should not include:

- Probing parents' feelings about themselves or their child.

- Giving advice about personal and interpersonal problems of family members.

- Giving parents "assignments" to carry out in their home which were not mutually conceived and fashioned.

- Criticizing or berating parents for not doing enough.

Cohen points out that parents can be a potent force in shaping educational policies and programs for the benefit of handicapped children in general, as well as in helping their own child's educational achievement. In order for special educators to involve parents in a cooperative venture, they must recognize the following premises:

1. Parents of young handicapped children play a major role, actively or passively, for better or worse, in both the educability and the education of their children.
2. The role of parents in the education of handicapped children is likely to become even more critical in the future, as society moves from institutionalization of severely handicapped children to community based, non-residential programs.
3. Parents have knowledge, insight, and ideas about their children which are needed by the school.
4. Parents very often are willing and eager to help their children's educational development to a greater extent than they are now doing. They need and want aid from the school for this purpose.
5. The school cannot afford to ignore the role and potential contribution of the family in the education of the young handicapped child; nor can it limit itself to complaints and antagonisms about insufficient parental cooperation. Instead, teachers must learn how to plan for and enlist the support of the family in the young handicapped child's education [Cohen, 1974, pp. 7-8].

If the need for working with parents of troubled children has seemed clear, the methods for doing so have been much less obvious. Table 8.2 provides a series of guidelines for teachers on ways to begin working with parents.

Finally, we turn to an example of one teacher's efforts to involve a parent in a specific educational program. The teacher, whom we'll call Ms. Jones, taught a second-grade class in an inner-city school. One day in February, a new child, Bruce, was brought to her class. Bruce was seven and a half years old and although he had never been held back, he had changed schools *nine* times!

Bruce had some assets: interest and some achievement in academic areas, a desire to communicate with others, and a concerned parent. Ms. Jones soon realized that Bruce also had some serious difficulties; his health was poor (as was his mother's), he had few positive peer interactions, and he and his mother were beset by a host of reality concerns and a scarcity of supportive people to help them.

It was Ms. Jones' belief that she could help Bruce develop better peer relationships in school, that Bruce's mother could and would assist in the attainment of that goal, and that if they were successful, Bruce's mother would also be demonstrating her own ability to bring about positive change in her own and her son's lives.

Specifically, Ms. Jones and Bruces' mother agreed that they would try to improve Bruce's ability to relate to his peers on the school bus. Bruce's mother agreed to keep Bruce in the same school until summer vacation and to plan to return him there the following fall. Ms. Jones pointed out Bruce's strengths and decided that her conversations with Bruce's mother would always include some discussion of Bruce's assets. Together Ms. Jones and Bruce's mother agreed to identify and enroll Bruce in an appropriate after-school recreational program and to seek out an appropriate summer camp placement. They also agreed to speak to Bruce's physician and discuss any implications of the doctor's recommendations for this home-school plan.

This plan worked reasonably well to help Bruce get along better on the bus. Ms. Jones discussed the appropriate issues with Bruce and the other youngsters who had been involved in the bus trouble and Bruce's mother checked progress with Bruce each day. Even more importantly, the bus issue turned out to be a model for dealing with other concerns. With the teacher's help, Bruces's mother learned to break down seemingly over-whelming problems into smaller parts that were more amenable to creative parent-teacher problem solving.

The process worked in the other way as well. With help from Bruce's mother, Ms. Jones was able to clarify the urgency and severity of some of Bruce's needs and could then develop more appropriate priorities for her educational planning. Finally, Bruce was able to see quite clearly that both his mother and his teacher cared about him and that his cooperation with that home-school program could have a positive impact on his life.

Nick Hobbs' book, *The Futures of Children* (1975), offers considerable insight into the need for more effective home-school or home-agency plan-ning for troubled youngsters. While the suggestions that follow (taken from Gorham, 1974, and reprinted in Hobbs, 1975) are certainly appropriate for all professionals (including teachers) who work with troubled children, they may be particularly relevant for psychologists who work in or with educa-tional programs.

Table 8.3 points out the value of having parents as real participants in the educational or treatment planning for their youngsters. It is critical for parents to be involved from the beginning in as many aspects of the plan-

Table 8.2. Tips for Teachers on Working with Parents.

1. *Meet parents early.*

   Conferences held with parents before school starts reduce pupil absenteeism, discipline problems, and increase academic growth, etc.

2. *Give parents information.*

   Parents can serve as powerful reinforcers, increasing academic growth and reducing behavioral problems if they have data (daily or weekly reports).

3. *Be positive.*

   Parents need reinforcement (phone calls, notes, special reports, etc.) when their children do well or for working with their children at home.

4. *Think ecologically.*

   Recognize where the problem exists. Children may react differently in different environments. If the problem exists at school, solicit parent expertise. Nothing is gained by "parent blaming"!

5. *Consider parent groups.*

   Parent groups improve parent ability to consider long-term goals, realize they are not alone, help in problem solving, and;
   - a. are usually most effective with from 4 to 12 participants,
   - b. provide valuable opportunities for informal parent-teacher exchange,
   - c. are best scheduled in a series of short (not more than two hours) convenient meetings,
   - d. *should* reflect parents' concerns and interests,
   - e. usually focus on ways to help children learn,
   - f. must be well planned and organized in order to be effective,
   - g. should encourage active parent participation in the meeting and follow-through at home.

6. *Consider individual parent conferences.*

   Individual meetings should be arranged for parents who are not ready or able to participate in group meetings, or when the needs of a particular child are so special that small group meetings are not adequate for parental training, or when it is preferable to include the child in the meeting.
   - a. The time and place of these meetings should be arranged with parent needs uppermost.
   - b. The content of these meetings should match parental concerns about the child as well as teacher concerns.
   - c. The parent-teacher relationship should be focused on mutual interest in helping the child.
   - d. Input from the parent about the child's functioning is solicited.
   - e. Short-term goals are either jointly selected or presented by the teacher as possibilities for parental support. (Don't identify a problem unless you have a solution to propose. It may make the problem more severe.)
   - f. In general, at least one concrete idea for implementation should be decided upon at each meeting. (Parents need specifics if change is desired, not generalities.)
   - g. When possible, each meeting should involve teacher demonstration, parent observation and/or parent practice of the idea(s) to be implemented.

Table 8.2. (Cont.)

---

    h. It may be useful to include the child in part or all of the meeting. Whenever the child is present, care must be taken to include him or her as a participant.

    i . Plans for implementation, record keeping, and follow-up should be worked out before the close of the meeting.

    j . A written sheet which can serve as a guide and reminder to the parent is often a helpful thing to provide at the end of a meeting. Sometimes a teacher leaves some carefully selected instructional materials for use at home.

Source: After Cohen, 1974, and Kroth, 1975.

ning process as possible and not just as token participants. It is equally critical that professionals communicate appropriately with parents, keep informed about available community resources that might be helpful to the family, help parents understand the strengths of their child as well as his or her weaknesses, and try to convey to parents the everchanging dynamic process of planning for troubled children. Professionals need to master the act of being realistic with parents, in developing management plans, in their written and oral communications, and in their efforts to help parents understand the imperfect service-delivery systems with which they're becoming involved.

Table 8.4 lists some suggestions for parents. It emphasizes the need for parents to assume responsibility for their children's educational and treatment planning. If parents view themselves as advocates for their own youngsters, they will find themselves involved in many of the suggested activities—keeping records, gathering comprehensive information, clarifying terminology in reports and records, continuing to initiate discussion with teachers, psychologists, and others involved with your youngster, etc. In other words, parents should more actively follow up on the premise of the first suggestion in Table 8.4: "You are the primary helper, monitor, coordinator, observer, record-keeper and decision-maker for your child. Insist that you be treated as such."

MODELS FOR THE FUTURE

For educators, psychologists, and others who work with troubled children, one viable avenue for developing better working relationships with parents may be to assume the role of child or family advocate. By placing yourself clearly in the corner of the youngster and his family, a professional can utilize his training and experience optimally—in the context of a strong and supportive relationship with a family system.

Table 8.3. Working with Parents: Suggestions for Professionals.

1. Have the parent(s) involved every step of the way. The dialogue established may be the most important thing you accomplish. If the parent's presence is an obstacle to testing because the child will not "cooperate" in his presence, the setup should include a complete review of the testing procedure with the parent. (Remote video viewing or one-way windows are great if you are richly endowed.)

2. Make a realistic management plan part and parcel of the assessment outcome. Give the parents suggestions for how to live with the problem on a day-to-day basis, with the needs of the child, the capacities of the family, and the resources of the community all considered. Let the parents know that you will suggest modifications if any aspect of the management plan does not work.

3. Inform yourself about community resources. Give the parents advice on how to go about getting what they need. Steer them to the local parent organization.

4. Wherever possible, make the parent a team member in the actual diagnostic, treatment, or educational procedures. It will give you a chance to observe how the parent and the child interact.

5. Write your reports in clear, understandable, jargon-free language. Professional terminology is a useful shortcut for your own note-taking; and you can always use it to communicate with others of your discipline. But in situations involving the parent, it operates as an obstacle to understanding. Keep in mind that it is the parent who must live with the child, help him along, shop for services to meet his needs, support his ego, give him guidance. You cannot be there to do it for him, so the parent *must* be as well informed as you can make him. Information that he does not understand is not useful to him. The goal is to "produce" a parent who understands his child well enough to help him handle his problems as he grows up.

6. Give copies of the reports to parents. They will need them to digest and understand the information in them; to share the information with other people close to the child; and to avoid the weeks or months of record-gathering which every application to a new program in the future will otherwise entail.

7. Be sure the parent understands that there is no such thing as a one-shot, final, and unchanging diagnosis. Make sure he understands that whatever label you give his child (if a label must be given) is merely a device for communicating and one which may have all kinds of repercussions, many of them undesirable. Make sure he understands that it says very little about the child at present and even less about the child of the future. Caution him about using that label to "explain" his child's conditions to other people.

8. Help the parent to think of life with this child in the same terms as life with his other children. It is an ongoing, problem-solving process. Assure him that he is capable of that problem solving and that you will be there to help him with it.

9. Be sure that he understands his child's abilities and assets as well as his disabilities and deficiencies. What the child *can* do is far more important than what he cannot do, and the parent's goal thereafter is to look for, anticipate, expect, and welcome new abilities and to welcome them with joy when they appear. Urge him to be honest and plain speaking with his child. Tell him that the most important job he has is to respect his child, as well as love him, and to help him "feel good about himself." Tell him that blame, either self-blame or blame of the child, has no part in the scene. *It is no one's fault.*

Table 8.3. (Cont.)

10. Warn the parent about service insufficiencies. Equip him with advice on how to make his way through the system of "helping" services. Warn him that they are not always helpful. Tell him that his child has a *right* to services. Tell him to insist on being a part of any decision making done about his child.

11. Explain to him that some people with whom he talks (teachers, doctors, professionals of any kind, or other parents) may dwell on negatives. Help train the parent not only to think in positives but to teach the other people important in his child's life to think in positives.

Source: Gorham, K.A., Desjardins, C., Page, R., Pettis, E., and Scheiber, B. Effect on Parents. In N. Hobbs, ed. *Issues in the Classification of Children.* Vol. II. San Francisco: Jossey-Bass, 1975.

A more detailed description of the BRIDGE program family advocate model described in Chapter 4 may serve as an example of a comprehensive systems-oriented approach to families:

> The typical BRIDGE Program parent could be characterized as being out of the mainstream of society, i.e., jobless, with limited providing and coping skills, overwhelmed by the demands of parenting and limited in awareness of community supports or resources. Further, many of these families were beset by chronic medical problems, handicapping conditions, and school problems involving at least one child and often several. Add to this a distrust of "interference" by social service providers and school personnel, and one is struct by the isolation and weight of inertia experienced by these families. . . .

> . . . .[T]he "typical" BRIDGE Program family was also invariably involved with a variety of different social service agencies at the time of BRIDGE Program contact. Because of frequent lack of coordination and conflicts of interest and priorities among agencies, however, most of these families' involvement had been unproductive. In some cases contact with social agencies actually had the opposite effect—had become destructive—with the net effect being a family "turned off" by too much manipulation in their lives [Apter, et al., 1979, pp. 39–40].

Figure 8.1 depicts the role of family advocate. The following quotation provides a comprehensive description of this diagram:

Overview of Family Advocate Role
  The first responsibility for a Family Advocate is the implementation of a comprehensive initial interview process. Each time a child was referred to the BRIDGE Program, the Family Advocate would: read the written referral and discuss it with the person who submitted it; set up an appointment to talk with the child and at least one parent in the family's home; talk on the phone or meet with all other school or agency personnel who are involved with the family; and formulate an assessment of the family's needs at the current time.

Table 8.4. Working with Professionals: Some Suggestions for Parents.

1. *You* are the primary helper, monitor, coordinator, observer, record keeper, and decision maker for your child. Insist that you be treated as such. It is your *right* to understand your child's diagnoses and the reasons for treatment recommendations, and for educational placement. *No* changes in his treatment or educational placement should take place without previous consultation with you.

2. Your success in getting as well informed as you will need to be in order to monitor your child's progress depends on your ability to work with the people who work with your child. You may encounter resistance to the idea of including you in the various diagnostic and decision making processes. The way you handle that resistance is important. Your best tool is not the angry approach. Some of your job will include the gentler art of persuasion. Stay confident and cool about your own abilities and intuitions. You know your child better than anyone else could. You are, obviously, a vital member of the team of experts.

3. Try to find, from among the many people whom you see, a person who can help you coordinate the various diagnostic visits and results. Pick the person with whom you have the best relationship, someone who understands your role as the principal monitor of your child's progress throughout life and who will help you become a good one.

4. Learn to keep records. As soon as you know that you have a child with a problem, start a notebook. Make entries of names, addresses, phone numbers, dates of visits, the persons present during the visits, and as much of what was said as you can remember. Record the questions you asked and the answers you received. Record any recommendations made. Make records of phone calls too; include the dates, the purpose, the result. It is best to make important requests by letter. Keep a copy for your notebook. Such documentation for every step of your efforts to get your child the service he needs can be the evidence which finally persuades a program director to *give* him what he needs. Without concise records of whom you spoke to, when you spoke to him, what he promised, how long you waited between the request and the response, you will be handicapped. No one can ever be held accountable for conversations or meetings with persons whose names and titles you do not remember, on dates you cannot recall, about topics which you cannot clearly discuss.

5. Make sure that you understand the terminology used by the professional. Ask him to translate his terms into lay language. Ask him to give examples of what he means. Do not leave his office until you are sure you understand what he has said so well that you can carry the information to your child's teacher, for instance, and explain it to her in clear, understandable language. (Write down the professional terms too. Knowing them might come in handy some time.)

6. Ask for copies of your child's records. You probably will not get them, but you *could* ask that a tape recording be made of any "interpretive" conference. It is very hard to remember what was said in such conferences.

7. Read. Learn as much as you can about your child's problem. But do not swallow whole what you read. Books are like people. They might be offering only one side of the story.

8. Talk freely and openly with as many professionals as you can bump into. Talk with other parents. Join a parent organization. By talking with people who "have been through it already," you can gain a perspective on your particular problems. Besides, you will receive moral support and will not feel quite so alone. Get information from parent organizations about services available, about their quality. But bear in mind that a particular program might not help your child even though it has proved helpful for another child. Visit programs if you have the time and energy to do so. There is no substitute for firsthand views.

Table 8.4. (Cont.)

9. Stay in close touch with your child's teacher. Make sure you know what she is doing in the classroom so that with her help, you can follow through at home. Share what you have read with her. Ask her for advice and suggestions. Get across the idea that the two of you are a team, working for the same goals. Make your child a part of that team whenever possible. He might have some great ideas.

10. Listen to your child. It is his point of view that he is giving you, and on that he is an expert.

11. Work hard at living the idea that differentness is just fine — not bad. Your child will learn most from your example. Help him to think of problems as things that can be solved if people work at them together.

Source: Gorham, K.A., Desjardins, C., Page, R., Pettis, E., and Scheiber, F. Effect on Parents. In N. Hobbs, ed. *Issues in the Classification of Children.* Vol. II. San Francisco: Jossey-Bass, 1975.

When this has been completed, the advocate attempts to match the family's needs to the resources available through programs in the community, including the BRIDGE Program. Basically, there are three outcomes to each initial interview process:

1. REFERRAL AND FOLLOW-THROUGH TO EXISTING COMMUNITY SERVICES
   When the needed service is being offered in the local comunity, Family Advocates would inform families, assist them in gaining access to the service, and follow-up to be certain the service is actually provided.

2. CHILDREN'S SERVICES
   For many families, the clear and immediate need continued to be service for a specific child. In such cases, Family Advocates were able to offer the summer camp, counseling (not necessarily including camp), etc. A new kind of service through which a BRIDGE Program staff member served as a gatherer of facts and mediator in child-school-family disputes was also included in this category.

3. ADULT SERVICES
   When the adult member of the family seemed to have the greatest needs, Family Advocates would try to provide the needed service. Direct service might take the form of individual counseling or parent education groups. Frequently too, Family Advocates provided the support and assistance necessary for adults to more effectively resolve their own problems.

Education and training is the more system-focused preventive aspect of the Family Advocate role. There are two major elements: (internal training and supervision and community education) [Apter et al., 1979, pp. 14–15].

We can return now to a more extended discussion of the direct-service aspects of the family advocacy role. Frequently, the advocate's entry into a family began with a meeting of family members and soon progressed to

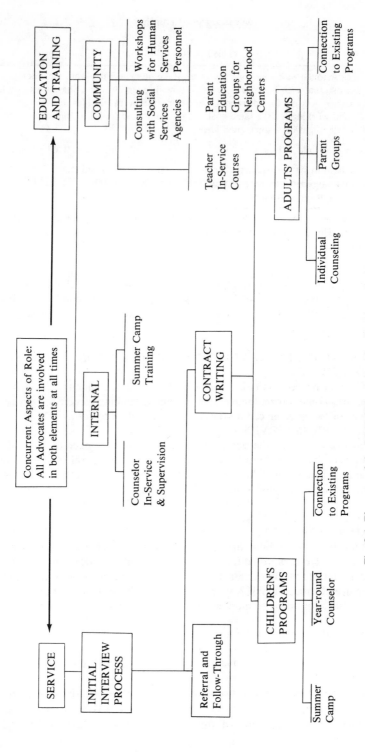

Fig. 8.1. Elements of the BRIDGE program family advocate role.

another meeting to which all support people involved with the family were invited. Such meetings were often unprecedented in a family's history despite the length and breadth of their involvement with social service and educational programs and personnel.

Usually these kinds of meetings resulted in new comprehensive intervention plans for the identified family, including, when appropriate, BRIDGE program and family advocate involvement. One important contribution to these new plans was the advocate's willingness to respond to a broad range of needs not typically accepted as part of the role of a traditional helper, providing a ride to doctor's appointment, setting up a job interview, going out for ice cream, challenging an eviction notice, and the like.

CONTRACTS

While the specific nature of advocate-family relationships varied considerably, it was usually described in a series of short-term contracts. Contracts spelled out goals, expectations, and responsibilities for family members and for family advocates and were continually renegotiated. Whenever possible, school personnel were invited to participate in the contract process. In this way, family-school relationships could be fostered and/or strengthened with the help of the family advocate who served as an intermediary for as long as necessary.

Table 8.5 contains the summary of an early contract between the BRIDGE program's family advocate and Mrs. R., the mother of M.R., a youngster referred to the program.

Family advocates assumed many roles as they intervened. They served as models, teachers, counselors, coordinators, and social workers. But perhaps what stands out as unique in the advocate's relationship to a family is the importance of trust. The families were quick to pick up that the advocates were on their side—without necessarily condoning or excusing all behaviors of family members. With trust as a solid cornerstone, advocates could insist, confront, and, most important, motivate. The following case example illustrates both the range of advocate roles and the trust that developed between Mrs. R. and her advocate.

THE CASE OF M.R.

M.R. is an eight-year-old boy who came into the BRIDGE Program because of the social worker's recommendations. M.R. was engaging in what the school termed as "wild" behavior—spitting, running around, shouting, swearing, and other acting-out behaviors. M.R. attended camp which concentrated on the above behaviors (with some success).

Table 8.5. Summary of Family Advocate's Contract with Mrs. R.

WHAT MRS. R. WILL DO:

1. Meet with the advocate weekly and allow M. to see his counselor weekly.
2. Keep a list of every bad behavior M. does. (This was an attempt to get Mrs. R. to specify what annoyed her instead of thinking of her child as totally "bad.")
3. Begin to explore the possibility of beauty school. (Mrs. R. had reported that if given a choice, she would like to be a hairdresser. Together, the advocate and she got information about schools, funding, etc., and she did enroll.)

WHAT THE ADVOCATE WILL DO:

1. Get a counselor to meet with M. weekly, enroll him in BRIDGE camp, supervise counselors who work with M.
2. Meet with Mrs. R. weekly to help her talk about and deal with her frustration with M. and help her meet some of her own needs.
3. Be available to Mrs. R. in time of emergency or crisis. Be a support person in ways Mrs. R. can define.
4. Coordinate efforts of school and agency personnel working with R. family.

M.R.'s counselor sees him weekly, mostly on Saturdays. She takes him to her sorority house and does crafts with him and allows him to mix with the others there. Her goals for M.R. are to have him be more expressive verbally and more at ease socially.

[According to Mrs. R.] BRIDGE is important because it helps M. to go places; otherwise, he would be confined to the area around home because they have no car. When he comes back from his visits with his counselor, he is a changed child. Once the mother called the counselor when she could not tolerate his behavior any more and needed some relief—the counselor came.

The advocate comes over frequently (the mother could not remember the name of any other adult whom she mentioned with the exception of the advocate—the expression on her face made it clear that the advocate is an extremely significant person in her life). They talk about children, legal crises she is going through, vocational plans. She calls the advocate a lot; and the advocate gives her advice. She trusts the advocate, she says, because the advocate really cares about her and is not there to pry. The mother has been cited for child neglect, which has brought her into contact with Children's Division. The advocate helped her with her contact there; she feels that the advocate does a great deal more with her and for her than her caseworker.

There have been times when she has wanted M.R. placed in an institution. The advocate, however, fights that; and it is only with the support of the advocate that the mother feels that she can continue to keep M.R. at home. She feels that BRIDGE is a good program and something that was needed a long time ago—if there was no BRIDGE, she feels that she would "probably go nuts."

If BRIDGE had been there before, maybe, she feels that M.R. wouldn't be the problem that he is.

BRIDGE's working with M.R. provides support for him that other agencies have been unable to provide. According to the school social worker, M.R. is currently functioning satisfactorily in the school. He is enrolled in a regular class, and teachers no longer have reason to send him out of the class for disruptive behavior. "He was running all over the school when he first came" [Apter et al., 1979, pp. 40–43].

CONCLUSIONS

Research on efforts to involve parents in the educational and psychological programs for their children has demonstrated the need for and the effectiveness of a systems orientation that focuses on families. Until very recently, parents had little say in their children's programs, a situation that undoubtedly caused many parents to feel powerless. Such a condition, however, is not inherent to the parent role but only to the ways in which professionals had perpetuated the myth of powerlessness. One might understand the striking results of the empirical evidence presented in this chapter in terms of the power concept; parents, in a variety of ways, received the message that they were important change agents in the psychological and educational development of their children. Thus, they not only felt more powerful but also were more powerful in effecting changes in their children's lives and in their own lives as well.

From an ecological perspective, partnerships between professionals and parents are critical. If we are serious about seeing troubled children as representatives of troubled systems, we are required to develop home-school programs in order to have real and lasting impact on the youngsters we serve. The question, then, is not whether teachers, psychologists, and other professionals should work with parents of children labeled emotionally disturbed, but rather what form those efforts should take. One hopes that the next few years will see more focus on that question and further development of some of the models and ideas described in this chapter.

9
Mainstreaming

Defined simply, mainstreaming is the conscientious effort to educate handicapped children in the least restrictive setting which is appropriate to their learning needs. For example, some children who have been institutionalized may be moved into community settings (their own homes or foster homes) and then enrolled in appropriate programs, perhaps attending "special" classes in public schools. Other children who had previously been educated in self-contained classes might be integrated into regular classrooms. Both are examples of mainstreaming. Thus, the mainstreaming movement is toward placing all handicapped youngsters in settings which provide as "normal" a learning environment as possible.

The following quotation from Meisels (1977) summarizes:

> The goal of mainstreaming is to provide a favorable and "normalized" learning environment for special needs children, and to provide this experience in the least restrictive environment possible. . . .
> . . . Mainstreaming can be justified legally, morally, socioculturally and educationally. Legally, mainstreaming ensures equality of educational opportunity and equal protection under the law. . . .
> Morally, mainstreaming is regarded as a means for reducing isolation and prejudice while enhancing an understanding and acceptance of differences. . . .
> . . . From a socio-cultural perspective, mainstreaming increases the potential contribution of handicapped individuals to society at large. Children who are segregated at an early age in institutions or special classes frequently spend their youth—if not their entire lives—in these specialized settings. Their ability to function as independent, self-sufficient citizens in the mainstream of society is not developed under such conditions. . . .
> . . . Educationally, mainstreamed classrooms provide handicapped children with positive peer models and reinforcements [Meisels, 1977, pp. 4–5].

There is no one way to mainstream. Rather, the concept can be applied through a spectrum of plans for organizing instruction, space, and facilities to accommodate the educational needs of handicapped pupils. When mainstreaming includes participation in the regular classroom, classroom teachers and special education teachers cooperate to determine each youngster's schedules and assignments. In this process regular classroom teachers broaden and adapt instructional procedures and content so that all children are incorporated into regular programs at levels which are manageable for each child and for the teacher. Special educators provide supplemental instruction to the youngsters and support services to the classroom teacher.

Good mainstreaming practices, while varied, should be based on the principle that disabled children do not necessarily have to be segregated in order to receive the special education to which they are entitled. In fact, most youngsters should be educated in regular classrooms (with supportive services when appropriate) and removed to special classes or special schools only when necessary, and only until their needs can once again be met in the regular program. In ecological terms, educational placements ought to be determined by the match between a youngster's needs and a program's ability to meet those needs, not by an arbitrary label with little if any educational relevance.

Mainstreaming is a term which, despite its popularity in recent years, remains vague in meaning. Because definitions of mainstreaming vary so dramatically and since the word seems to conjure up so many different images (from glowingly positive to damningly negative), the usefulness of the concept has undoubtedly been undermined. Perhaps it is similar reasoning that caused the writers of Public Law 94:142 purposefully to refrain from ever mentioning the word "mainstreaming" in that landmark piece of legislation! Instead, the law describes the rights of children with special needs to receive a free public education in the "least restrictive setting appropriate to their needs."

Nevertheless, Public Law 94:142 is commonly referred to as the "Mainstreaming Law" and it is important for us to consider the various uses and abuses of the mainstreaming concept in some depth. We can begin by examining some of the most critical and controversial elements of the mainstreaming concept. According to Hewett and Taylor (1980), the following are important points to consider when formulating opinions on mainstreaming:

1. Mainstreaming is an approach that has been used successfully with mildly handicapped students in some school districts for many years.
2. Mainstreaming does not mean that special classes and centers will be abolished; these placements will still be provided for students who need

them, but more thought will be given to how they can be made less restrictive.

3. Mainstreaming also means not removing students from the regular program unless it is absolutely necessary.

4. The application of the mainstreaming concept to more severely handicapped
students is relatively new; however, when a given handicapped child stands
to gain from involvement, even for a very short period of time, in a given
regular classroom and does not restrict the other children's learning rights,
the concept should be explored.

5. Students can be "mainstreamed" for a major part of the school day, or
only for certain activities such as physical education, music, and lunch.
The degree of mainstreaming will depend on the student's learning skills
and needs.

6. Integrated school settings allow the exceptional child to be a part of the
real world, to learn to accept limitations, to observe and model appropriate behaviors, and to become more socially acceptable to other
children and adults. They also teach nonexceptional children valuable
lessons regarding individual differences and the fact that there can be different right things rather than the same right things for all.

7. Mainstreaming is most successful when the child, the parents, the teacher,
and the class are prepared in advance [pp. 336–37].

There are many factors behind the move toward mainstreaming in recent
years. Those that seem most important and influential are outlined below.

The effectiveness of conventional special education has been questioned.
There is no consistent, established body of literature indicating that children
with handicapping conditions show more academic or social learning in
segregated special classrooms despite the fact that such settings were
established for that very purpose. All children, but especially handicapped
children, need educational experiences which prepare them to become independent and self-reliant adults, a goal which is difficult to reach in totally
segregated programs. In addition, there is a growing realization that handicapped and nonhandicapped children must have opportunities for long-
term normal interactions if common misconceptions about handicapped
people are ever to be dispelled. Without normal interaction, nonhandicapped
and handicapped children may never learn to interrelate and to accept each
other as persons with common needs and aspirations.

*The fairness and accuracy of psychological and educational testing has
been questioned.* Standardized tests have been shown to be unreliable in
measuring ability of children who are not from the dominant culture. The
overrepresentation of minority group children in special education classes
has resulted in the questioning of the testing process. In addition to concerns over the probable inaccuracy and unreliability of frequently used standardized tests, there has been a growing rejection of the entire labeling process as more attention has been paid to the potential harm associated with

classifying children as disturbed, retarded, delinquent, etc. The inappropriateness of our classification system for children has been well documented elsewhere (see especially Hobbs, 1975).

Parents are becoming more active on behalf of their disabled children.
The inappropriate placement of youngsters in segregated programs, the ineffectiveness of available programs for youngsters in need of a special education, and the failure of local school districts to provide educational programs for a wider range of disabled children has led to a dramatic increase in parental advocacy for their youngsters. In the past ten or fifteen years, more parents have been speaking out as individuals and as members of new coalitions and advocacy groups which formed at a rapid rate in the late 1960s and early 1970s.

Parents who were dissatisfied with the educational system's responsiveness to their youngsters, began asserting their convictions through formal administrative and legal channels. One result has been that changes have been accelerated as courts have affirmed the right of all handicapped children to a free, appropriate public education.

To summarize, mainstreaming really calls for a widening of our tolerance, an increase in acceptance for a greater diversity of children, programs, and delivery systems. As Meisgeier (1976) states:

> Mainstreaming advocates the right of all children to acceptance within school programs regardless of how they may deviate from "norms" in appearance, performance, or behavior. As an educational philosophy, mainstreaming promotes acceptance of all children within the flow of school life. This is accomplished by making the school responsible (accountable) for adapting its programs to meet each child's needs rather than requiring the child to adapt to an inflexible school program designed for a hypothetical "average child" [p. 245].

Mainstreaming encourages us to do away with the idea that the concept of handicap is a completely dichotomous black-and-white notion. It is not necessary to accept the idea that people are either handicapped (disturbed, retarded, blind, deaf) or normal as the basis for educational planning. Instead of what Reynolds (1977a) called the "two-box" model (special education children went into one box, "regular" kids into the other) of education, mainstreaming helps us understand that we need a continuum of services and programs to match the needs of a continuum of children. McDaniels (1978) has noted in his discussion of Public Law 94:142:

> The law encourages us to stop thinking of the handicapped child as a representative from a homogeneous disability group; a homogeneous group for whom a single educational service will be adequate. Professionals are asked to first document the child's needs, then to identity the services which should be pro-

vided to meet these needs. These services may be best provided by the classroom teacher, by scheduled trips to a resource room or teacher or by placement in a specialized classroom. Underlying the successful implementation of this principle is the assumption that the professional talent in this country is sufficient to make decisions regarding the individual service needs of children [p. 2].

ECOLOGICAL PERSPECTIVES ON MAINSTREAMING

While much of the rhetoric surrounding mainstreaming dwells on cooperation and joint efforts by classroom teachers and special educators, carrying such suggestions into action has not been an easy task. Though Reynolds and Birch (1977) have noted that special education ought to be seen as part of general education, this has not really been the dominant conception.

In fact, the two-box model described above has had a very powerful impact not only on the kinds of programs we've developed for youngsters but also on the ways in which we train prospective teachers. Consequently, there are also grave negative implications for attitude development and ultimately for mainstreaming. Classroom teachers in all too many cases have been trained in a box that excluded consideration of youngsters with even mild special needs. Special educators, on the other hand, often learned that since their box was the only place for handicapped children, they themselves would be the only adults who could work with such youngsters.

Consequently, the typical mainstreaming approach has been beset by two standard sources of difficulty: special educators who weren't ready to give up their children and regular educators who weren't quite ready to accept them. The point, however, is that despite this kind of resistance (which is perfectly reasonable given the training and experience of both classroom and special educators), it is not appropriate to push youngsters into special education simply because they don't fit very neatly into regular education. Yet, that is precisely what happened in the two-box model.

Too many of our educational models and programs operate on the assumption that children are always the ones who must change. The ecological perspective points out the importance of studying and focusing change efforts on other elements of the systems defined by each child—the classrooms, the schools, the teachers, the families, etc.

Cantrell and Cantrell (1976) have discussed the tie between mainstreaming and the ecological orientation as follows:

The concept of mainstreaming, simply stated, requires that "exceptional" children be educated in the same environment as all other children wherever possible. Support for the notion of mainstreaming has grown out of earlier concerns over the doubtful efficacy of the traditional approach of separating "exceptional" children from their peers for special educational services. . . .

Conceptual support for mainstreaming can be derived as a logical extension of an idea advanced 12 years ago by Nicholas Hobbs (1963). Project Re-ED, the realization of Hobbs' ideas, has proven to be a successful model for a number of programs for emotionally disturbed children across the country. Essentially the Re-ED approach involves: (a) viewing the child as part of an ecological subsystem, (b) analyzing the discordances in that subsystem which led to labeling the child as "different" or "problematic," and (c) utilizing the best applied knowledge currently available in the fields of education and human behavior to reduce the discordances to such an extent that the child can be maintained within the ecological subsystem. Although the Re-ED approach was implemented within the framework of a short term residential setting, these concepts are certainly applicable to public schools which are the inevitable locus of maintaining efforts [pp. 381–82].

Cantrell and Cantrell's description of the Re-Ed approach brings to life the ecological realities of a system in which discordance can be caused by a variety of factors, but interventions are generally aimed only at an identified child. Theoretically at least, mainstreaming represents an effort to intervene at a systems level by recognizing the failure of some longstanding programs to meet the special educational needs of children. Good mainstreaming practices stem from the belief that it is not only the children who will have to change. Teachers and other professionals *and* their training programs, physical environments, schools and school districts, attitudes and expectations, patterns of service delivery may all require alterations in order to bring troubled systems back to a balanced and harmonious state.

Perhaps the most useful model for applying the ecological approach to mainstreaming in the public school system is the Cascade of Special Education Services (Deno, 1970). One version of the cascade model is described in Figure 9.1.

We can see in Figure 9.1 that the inverted pyramid represents a range of services of varying levels of restrictiveness. The wider the pyramid, the more youngsters should be included at that level. At the very top in this version of the cascade is a level described as "the prevention of handicapping behavior" to indicate the critical importance of efforts to reduce the number of youngsters in need of a special education as a first priority. The next chapter will focus specifically on prevention.

Levels two through eight represent increasingly more restrictive environments and we can see that the number of youngsters ought to decrease as the environments increase in restrictiveness (level 8 is represented as potentially having more youngsters since it includes residential settings associated with all human service systems). The critical feature of the cascade model with regard to mainstreaming has to do with the way youngsters move through these levels of service. As represented by the arrows on the sides of the pyramid, children should move to more restrictive settings only when it is absolutely necessary. Conversely, youngsters should

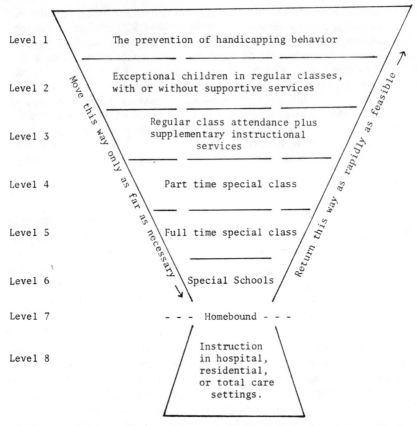

Fig. 9.1. The cascade system of special education service (adapted from E. Deno, 1970).

move to less restrictive settings as soon as it is appropriate for them to do so.

The cascade model demonstrates the broadness of the mainstreaming concept. The notion is not restricted to the wholesale shifting of youngsters from special to regular classes, but is more focused on the rights of individual children to be educated in the least restrictive setting appropriate to their needs. Youngsters should not be segregated into special classes if the provision of support services to the regular classroom would be sufficient to accommodate their educational needs.

The cascade demonstrates the need for a range of services. The "old" special education model was much more restrictive; *either* one was labeled with some sort of handicapping condition (mentally retarded, emotionally disturbed), in which case one was sent off to a special class program where it was hoped that one would receive special education and probably remain for the remainder of one's school experience, *or* one was a "normal" child who received his or her education in the usual public school classroom. The two populations seldom mixed and as a result the model probably exacerbated the problem of negative attitudes about disabled people. In addition, great numbers of children have been mislabeled and inappropriately placed in special education.

The cascade model also points quite clearly to the idea that what we need is a bigger universe of alternatives for the education of children—*all* children. In fact, youngsters are not either "special" or "regular," but spread themselves out over a broad range of individual differences. Our failure to recognize and accept the notion of individual differences may be one of the most critical needs being addressed by the mainstreaming concept.

This is an issue for both special and regular education, for program development as well as teacher training.

In July of 1975, Edwin Martin (1977), then director of the U.S. Bureau of Education for the Handicapped, said it well:

Most teachers of the "normal" children have been trained with certain assumptions, and expect to face a certain kind of behavior from normal children. They don't expect to find the kind of behavior that they have been taught to attribute to the other ten percent. The implication in teacher-training has been that any kind of abnormal behavior is something that requires special training and special understanding.

Now, the fact is . . . the world isn't organized into 90 percent and 10 percent, or whatever percentages you want to divide handicapped and non-handicapped into. Children don't really distribute themselves into those two groups neatly. So, what regular teachers classically find is that they have a lot of children in their classes who show learning styles, behavior styles, all kinds of differences which puzzle them. So they often feel that those kids shouldn't be there, and they should be in special education, since that was the implication of teacher-training [p. 50].

Mainstreaming has highlighted the need for new kinds of teachers and new kinds of teacher preparation. In special education, there has been much greater emphasis on models that could provide the support services that would enable mild and moderately handicapped youngsters to progress in regular settings. Resource teachers, consulting teachers, and diagnostic-prescriptive teachers are examples of this new role.

There is a special need for new models for classroom teachers as well. As more and more children with special needs find their way into regular classrooms, elementary and secondary school teachers will find themselves increasingly in need of more preparation to deal with the educational challenges and issues raised by such youngsters.

The move toward mainstreaming and the resulting needs for new models of teaching has resulted in a number of new initiatives in teacher training.

Special education teacher preparation programs have begun to focus more and more on the preparation of teachers for severely and profoundly disabled children, and as mentioned above, on ways to prepare special educators to work cooperatively with their colleagues who teach in typical classrooms.

In teacher education, the move toward individualizing in the classroom has certainly been aided by the advent of mainstreaming. Further, it has been generally believed that elementary and secondary level teachers are in need of supplemental training in order best to accommodate the needs of the "special" children now entering their classes. This is being done in two ways. First, there have been massive (but undoubtedly not sufficient) efforts to provide in-service opportunities for teachers in the school. Countless workshops on Public Law 94:142, and various facets of mainstreaming have been developed and offered over the past few years.

Second, with regard to preservice teacher preparation, there have been a number of formal and informal efforts to modify the teacher training curriculum to bring it in line with the mainstreaming philosophy. Many of these efforts have developed under the aegis of the *Dean's Grant Projects*, a specially supported federal initiative designed to provide strong support for efforts to redesign teacher education in line with the push toward the integration of children with special needs.

Table 9.1 summarizes many of the critical differences between the older, more segregated (two-box) system of special education and a newer, broader range of services signified by the mainstreaming movement and the cascade model.

GUIDELINES FOR MAINSTREAMING

In this section, we describe some of the skills and attitudes necessary for good mainstreaming as well as some particular interventions that adults might make in order to smooth the path for mainstreaming. Though many of the suggestions may seem oriented toward one particular group (classroom teachers *or* special class teachers *or* school psychologists *or* resource teachers), most have applicability to wider audiences.

According to Meisels (1977), the following is a list of new attitudes and skills for mainstreaming compiled by teachers in one school:

1. Knowing how to talk to children about handicaps;
2. Teaching highly active children inner controls;
3. Learning how to support parents of special needs children;
4. Learning how to talk about handicaps with parents whose children do not have special needs;
5. Learning how to work with parents who deny their child's limitations;

Table 9.1. Prevailing and Preferred Practices in Special Education Planning.

Prevailing Practices	Preferred Practices
1. Special education is conducted mainly in separate, specialized settings, such as special classes, resource rooms, or special schools.	1. Special education is conducted as an integral part of the unified school system; as much of it as possible is made portable and provided in regular classes and schools. Specialized settings are used only for essential purposes and periods of time.
2. Special education is managed mainly by highly centralized and specialized officers of the school system, all quite distinctly set apart from the general educational leadership system.	2. The administrative management of special education, as well as instructional programs, is highly decentralized; a maximum effort is made to accommodate exceptional children in their neighborhood schools.
3. Educational programs tend to start at ages five or six for most exceptional children, with some special programs, like those for deaf children, starting earlier.	3. Special education begins at birth or as soon thereafter as it is needed.
4. Handicapped students tend to be excluded from many programs at secondary and higher levels of education, and especially from vocational education.	4. Exceptional students are given full opportunities for education in secondary and vocational schools, colleges, and expanding lifelong learning programs.
5. Placements in special settings are made on the basis of classifying children according to "categories" of handicapping conditions or giftedness.	5. Children are separated from regular classes only when necessary for specific forms of instruction; many children, consequently, even those with severe handicaps, remain in regular school settings all or most of the time.
6. Special educators, school psychologists, speech clinicians, school social workers, and other specialized staff members mainly provide services directly to children and families in schools or in clinical settings.	6. Special educators, school psychologists, speech clinicians, school social workers, and other specialized staff emphasize training as a function and they work to "give away" as many of their competencies as possible to teachers and other staff members.
7. As spaces for instruction, schools consist mainly of series of "boxes" that have little provision for variety, easy access, and flexibility.	7. Schools, as physical settings for education, provide barrier-free, safe, interesting, flexible spaces for all children, including those who are handicapped.
8. Special education financial aids to local districts are allotted mainly to programs that isolate exceptional children in separate school settings.	8. Special education financial aids are used to support all forms of special instruction, including those conducted in regular class settings.

Table 9.1. (Cont')

Prevailing Practices	Preferred Practices
9. Instructional materials for regular school programs are very limited and different from those that are available to special education instructors.	9. Adequate instructional supplies and materials are provided to all teachers, thus improving their ability to accommodate individual differences among learners.
10. Teachers "refer" special "problem children" to specialists.	10. Teachers call in specialists to help with problem children right in their classes.
11. Parents are informed, usually, about the specialized programs that are provided for their children.	11. Parents participate fully with teachers and other staff members in reaching all decisions regarding specialized programs for their children.
12. Reading instruction is conducted at multiple levels in most elementary school classrooms, but other aspects of the curriculum are standardized for all children.	12. Modern managements systems for instruction and curriculum differentiation permit a wide diversity of programing to accord with individual readiness and needs in all subjects.
13. Some children start every school year in the regular classes of their schools while others are enrolled basically only in special education programs.	13. Every child, including the handicapped, starts his first year of schooling and every successive year in a regular school program.

Source: After Reynolds, 1977a.

6. Learning how to assist parents and children through a period of hospitalization;
7. Refining skills of individualization;
8. Developing increased ability to utilize prescriptive teaching techniques;
9. Learning how to incorporate specialists into the classroom;
10. Developing behavior modification techniques;
11. Gaining awareness of physical therapy goals and techniques;
12. Becoming familiar with skills of speech therapy;
13. Acquiring familiarity with specialized medical terminology and diagnostic labels;
14. Becoming aware of the effects of medication;
15. Becoming acquainted with a number of formal and informal screening and diagnostic procedures;
16. Acquiring familiarity with state laws concerning the handicapped;
17. Coming to grips with one's own feelings concerning difference, deviance and handicaps [p. 8].

Another format for assessing a "regular" teacher's readiness for mainstreaming was devised by Lay-Dopyera (1981). "Questions to Ask in Assessing a 'Regular' Teacher's Readiness for Mainstreaming" (see Table

Table 9.2. Questions to Ask in Assessing a "Regular" Teacher's Readiness for Mainstreaming.

Note to the user: you may quite legitimately disagree as to whether some or all of the items are likely to be related to success in mainstreaming. You may also feel other items should be included. Revise as you wish to suit your own perceptions better.

Item	Responses
Do you know where to go (resource person or agency) to obtain general information on specific handicapping conditions?	List each resource person or agency mentioned:
Do you know who to contact to receive help with specific questions regarding program concerns for children with special needs?	List each person or agency mentioned:
In what instructional areas do you routinely provide for instruction and involvement on multiple levels?	List each instructional area mentioned and the number of different levels identified in each area:
Do you routinely group (place in subgroups to work together) children according to criteria other than academic achievement?	List each of the criteria mentioned by which subgroups are formed:
Do you have accessible an array of different kinds of instructional materials at various levels for the instructional areas emphasized in your classroom?	List each of the instructional areas for which this is the case:
In what instructional areas are you capable of providing an appropriate program for an individual child without need for commercially prepared materials (texts, workbooks, teachers guides, kits, etc.)?	List each of the instructional areas for which this is the case:
In which instructional areas do you keep individual records for children regarding their progress?	List each of the instructional areas for which this is the case:
Do you work closely with parents in accomplishing objectives emphasized in the classroom? How many of the parents of your children do you talk with on a weekly basis?	List the number of children (in current classroom) for whom the teacher has frequent parent contact (at least weekly) for the purpose of involving parents in accomplishing objectives emphasized in the classroom:
Why do you think "mainstreaming" is valuable?	List the reasons given:

Comments:

Source: Lay-Dopyera, 1981, pp. 51–2.

9.2) is a self-administered, open-ended questionnaire that helps teachers clarify some specific elements of the mainstreaming process, recognize the strengths they bring to mainstreaming, and augment their skills, in areas where they may have had less experience.

Both Meisels' list of skills and attitudes and Lay-Dopyera's questionnaire provide useful information to teachers and others preparing for participation in a mainstreaming program. An additional source of relevant information is the National Support Systems Project (NSSP) at the University of Minnesota which has been heavily involved in the provision of technical assistance to mainstreaming projects for a number of years. Recently, the NSSP has been developing a series of competency clusters for teacher preparation. Though not yet available in final form, the competencies and their subtopics, summarized in Table 9.3, provide useful specifics for consideration in our mainstreaming efforts.

As we can see, the competency clusters emphasize the elements that many would agree make up a good teacher for any youngster. Having a knowledge of curriculum, competency at teaching basic skills, skills in the area of classroom management, understanding of the consultation process, the ability to develop positive relationships with students and parents, and the capacity to encourage students to build positive peer relationships are all essential aspects of good teaching which are repeated in good mainstreaming. In addition, some knowledge of handicapping conditions and an understanding of the referral process would certainly be useful for those adults involved in mainstreaming. Finally, skill at individualized teaching may be the key to all teaching and an adherence to professional values is a quality we should expect from all adults who work with troubled children.

One especially critical competency area (#6 in Table 9.3) has to do with maximizing positive student-student relationships. Considerable attention has been paid to the need to provide positive peer experiences in mainstream programs and Meisels (1977) offers the following guidelines to teachers and others working toward this goal:

1. Arrange with parents for special needs and nonspecial needs children to play together outside of school;
2. Individualize the curriculum for all children, not just the special needs children;
3. Establish respect for individuals as the prime classroom value;
4. Create a safe, protected environment so that children can risk forming relationships;
5. Explain individual differences to children in a neutral, value-free manner;
6. Read aloud books and stories that deal with differences;
7. Answer children's questions directly and honestly;
8. Reinterpret actions for children in behaviorally observable terms: e.g., "His legs don't work very well," or "It's hard for him to hold your hand without squeezing it."
9. Encourage children to use behavioral explanations rather than labels;
10. Design and guide positive interactions between children based on a common interest or curricular experience;

Table 9.3. Recommended Competencies for Mainstreaming.

1. Curriculum	The preparation of all teachers should include the study of and firsthand experience with curricular principles, guides, and structures from preschool through secondary school levels. The means and procedures by which curriculum is developed, adopted, and changed should be understood and there should be practice in designing and modifying curriculum and materials, especially to suit the individual needs of students.
2. Teaching Basic Skills	The preparation of all teachers should include necessary elements to assure competency in teaching the basic skills (defined to include literacy, life-maintenance, and personal-development skills).
3. Class Management	All teachers should be proficient in class management procedures, including a variety of ecological interventions, group techniques, crisis interventions, etc.
4. Professional Consultation and Communication	It is essential now that all teachers have opportunities to master the knowledge and practices involved in effective consultation and other forms of professional communication. All teachers should be skilled at group problem-solving and conflict resolution.
5. Teacher-Parent-Student Relationships	All teachers should have skills and sensitivity for dealing with parents and siblings of handicapped students; they should have knowledge of family life and skill at parent interviewing.
6. Student/Student Relationships	All teachers should be able to convey to students positive attitudes about skills necessary for productive interactions with mainstreamed peers.
7. Exceptional Conditions	All prospective teachers should have preparation in understanding exceptional children, in school procedures for accommodating children's special needs, and in the functions of specialists who serve exceptional children. Moreover, opportunities for direct experience with the children and with specialists should be provided.
8. Referral	Teachers need to learn the procedures for referrals, the responsibilities involved, and the ways to capitalize on referral resources on behalf of better education for individual pupils.
9. Individualized Teaching	All teachers should be competent in the assessment of the individual student's educational needs and in adapting instruction to the individual. Teachers should have working knowledge of the IEP development process.
10. Professional Values	Professional educators' values ought to reflect a primary emphasis on the needs and rights of individual students. Teachers should be knowledgeable about school law and codes of ethical behavior established by the teaching profession.

Source: After Reynolds, 1980.

11. Encourage all children to talk about feelings such as fear and anger—and help them begin to understand and govern these emotions;
12. Encourage spontaneous dramatic play and role playing to help non-handicapped children identify with the experience of special needs children (e.g., using crutches, walkers, hearing aids, crawling or limping);
13. Create opportunities for all parents to meet with each other to discuss their reactions to mainstreaming [Meisels, 1977, p. 8].

MODELS FOR MAINSTREAMING

Beery (1972) has described a number of successful mainstreaming programs. Some especially interesting examples, based on Beery's description are discussed below.

1. *The Diagnostic-Prescriptive Teacher Model.* This model is based upon two premises: (1) the child is not defective, but the educational system in which he finds himself is; and (2) teachers would be more willing to deal with children with behavioral and learning problems if they had practical information on how to attack the problem. The Diagnostic-Prescriptive Teacher (DPT) is conceived of as a change-agent within the school who can assist teachers in teaching *all* children and help them adjust to children's individual needs. The DPT is a full-time school-based teacher who specializes in educational diagnosis and programming for those children who present problems in learning and/or behavior.

2. *The Helping or Crisis Teacher Model.* This model was developed primarily by Fritz Redl, utilizing the concept of life-space interviewing or crisis intervention as it applies within the school setting. The two major goals of this model are to provide the child with perceptual training and to teach him coping. Redl defines a crisis as "a juicy episode of chronic maladaptive behavior." This episode can involve fighting, aggression, withdrawal, or depression. Once this behavior is targeted, a teacher can wait for an appropriate episode to see if some insight can be promoted, by talking issues through, and helping the youngster to understand his own behavior. Redl calls this sequence the clinical exploitation of life events.

Because the regular classroom teacher lacks the time to do the crisis intervention, the employment of a helping teacher is needed. This crisis teacher can be used in a crisis in two ways, he or she can take the class while the teacher handles the life-space interview, or the child can be sent to the crisis teacher with a brief description of what has been going on.

3. *The North Sacramento Project.* This project provides a model for integrating children with special needs into the regular classroom. Two experimental classes were set up by a university professor in a local public elementary school, each containing six children with special needs, three

labeled EMR and three educationally handicapped. It was found that the structure of the classes led to more progress for *all* of the children in the class than in their previous classes.

The classes are constructed so that teacher aides can be utilized if needed. The classes take advantage of children as resources. Most of the work that the children do on a daily prescription basis is either self-corrected or peer corrected. Every child in the class finishes around 20 or 25 papers per day in the various academic areas: spelling, arithmetic, reading, social studies and science. The reading program utilizes both peer and cross-age tutoring which is carefully analyzed and periodically checked. There are no row desks; the children work together.

Each child is able to function on his own and it is made worthwhile for him to manage his own behavior. The teachers rarely use something as token as M & Ms, but rely more on praise, check marks, awarding of free time, and activity centers.

Since the passage of Public Law 94:142 and the dramatic increase in mainstreaming programs, many of the most important aspects of the three examples described above have been combined into a helping teacher or resource teacher role. While the roles might be defined differentially by various schools or districts, we can consider them together in terms of their relationship to the mainstreaming process.

The resource/helping teacher provides a broad range of services and functions in a number of roles. For example, resource/helping teachers:

1. Assist classroom teachers in dealing with emergency situations with disturbed children.
2. Help teachers better understand and program for difficult youngsters.
3. Follow up crises in an attempt to help youngsters understand their own behavior.
4. Coordinate school and community resources in planning for troubled children.
5. Provide individualized tutoring or small-group instruction in a resource room or in the regular classroom.

According to Nyquist (1977), in an official New York State Education Department position paper:

Clearly, the resource room is a very constructive way to approach mainstreaming. This approach has the specificity needed to go to the heart of a child's problem to find a remedy, and, at the same time, it is flexible, and can be adapted to any number of different school systems. For the special educator a resource program offers distinct advantages. Not limited to a small number of children, the resource teacher helps many children throughout the school. By its nature, this approach avoids the labeling and stigma of many special education programs. The plan attacks a child's particular educational problem rather than labeling him abnormal. Because a child does not have to be labeled to receive special help, the plan encourages the identification and remediation of large numbers of children in the public schools who have difficulties but receive no special help [pp. 7–8].

Good resource programs, then, according to Nyquist, demonstrate the four elements necessary for successful mainstreaming: *preparation* (of teachers, parents, children, and school and district administrators); *pacing* (finding the optimal rate for integration and choosing youngsters and settings for maximal teacher-student-setting match); *specificity* (diagnosing/prescribing/developing materials/evaluating: individualized educational planning); and *flexibility* (openness to ideas, suggestions, and the eternal possibility of change) (Nyquist, 1977, pp. 9–11).

PROBLEMS AND CRITICAL ISSUES

Tension is rife these days at the Calvin Coolidge Elementary School in Grand Falls. The two third grade teachers, Emily Frazier and Warren Norton, aren't speaking, and principal Fred B. ("We're all members of one big educational team!") Hotchkiss has applied for early retirement.

It all began when the Grand Falls school board enthusiastically adopted the Weighted Pupil Plan to determine classroom size. Using the plan, teachers judge their pupils on the basis of "instructional problems" and assign each pupil to one of 14 categories ranging from "Normally Achieving" with a weight factor of 1.0 to "Monolingual Foreign Language", which earns a student 2.5 on the Weighted Pupil Plan scale.

The plan's noble goal is to do away with the traditional system of determining the number of pupils in a classroom simply by counting the number of heads. [T]he fortunate teacher with 25 students who spoke only Lithuanian would, under the plan's perspective, face a classroom jammed with the equivalent of 62½ pupils and would thus be entitled to whatever extra instructional assistance the school district could bestow.

And therein lie the roots of the dispute at Coolidge. Unfortunately, funds were available to hire only three teacher's aides for the third grade. The competition between Miss Frazier and Mr. Norton for the services of the aides was understandably fierce [Hoppe, 1978, p. 96].

While laced with obvious hyperbole and exaggeration, the situation described above is based on all-too-real experience. As the editor's note which preceded the article stated:

The unsettling aspect of the following story is that it's based on an actual program. The Denver Class Size Reduction Plan was designed as a method for determining class size and how teacher aides should be distributed among the various classrooms; the quotes from the plan, as used in the following story, are authentic [p. 96].

In turn, this one example is representative of the strategies devised to remedy one significant issue raised by the mainstreaming movement: how to assign youngsters to classrooms equitably. This is a concern not only for the education of children with special needs but also for the education of so-called "typical" youngsters. The implication is that if mainstreaming brings youngsters with serious individual needs into regular classrooms, then teachers will need to spend more and more of their time with such children. Since there are only so many hours to each school day, ultimately the needs of the typical children are likely to be neglected.

The issue of equitable assignment is problematic for teachers as well. Some agree with the implication described above, others simply feel unable to meet the needs of disabled children no matter how much time is available. In many places, teachers' unions have incorporated "number of handicapped children per classroom" into their negotiations with their districts.

Even for teachers who seem more able or more willing to participate in the mainstream process, the issue of exactly how completely to be involved remains open. As Reynolds (1977b) noted:

About half of my special educator friends these days seem to be out giving lessons to the masses on individualized education programs (IEP's). Without even trying, I have been shown at least six sets of transparencies, listened to endless audio cassettes on the requirements of Public Law 94-142, and I have been guided through several versions of "sure fire" forms to satisfy all of the new regulations.

What I see and hear seems well designed to keep teachers out of jail—to comply with the law, that is—but usually I sense little vision of how people might come together creatively to design environments for better learning and living by handicapped students [p. 60].

Silverman (1978) also raises problems with the mainstreaming process for behaviorally disturbed children and relates some of his experiences with severely troubled youngsters in a psychiatric hospital-based special preschool program. It is Silverman's contention that youngsters who made good progress in his preschool program and later in primary-level special classes may have been irreparably damaged by the school's insistence on mainstreaming.

It may be instructive to consider one of Silverman's examples—the case of Amy is summarized on the next page.

AMY

Amy C., now 14 years old, was referred to the Program when she was five and having difficulty adjusting to a normal kindergarten class. At that time, her parents described her as having three cycles of behavior: 1) withdrawal in her morning school situation, 2) aggressive, destructive behavior on return home and 3) "high, silly moods after dinner at night." When not withdrawn she was said to be aggressive and destructive and to have tantrums. She was also said to be given to bizarre behavior, particularly in public.

In the course of the evaluation that took place at this time, Amy impressed her six examiners as an anxious, withdrawn, unrelating girl who was selectively mute and bizarre.

At the start of her three-year stay in the Program, Amy cried a great deal and often talked to her mother, who was not present, typically doing so in high pitched tones. She also exhibited a good deal of bizarre behavior, for example, grabbing the air, suddenly getting up and running in and out of a room, smelling everything within reach and the like. Gradually, she became much more relaxed and came to exhibit far fewer bizarre mannerisms but continued to be an attention seeking child. For a long time she remained on the periphery of her group and had great difficulty relating to children and adults. Gradually, both in her group and in individual therapy, she grew more communicative and made some feeble efforts at expressing her feelings.

During this time, her mother attended a mothers' psychotherapy group that met weekly and her parents attended family conferences once each month. While the C. family was a troubled, complex one both parents came to cope with Amy better and to feel that their family situation had eased considerably. By the end of Amy's stay in the Program she was still a rather remote, occasionally bizarre girl but she was much improved and finally came to be able to relate to adults with some warmth. She made progress in the academic area as well but her learning always seemed to take place on a rather concrete level and her cognitive short-comings remained evident to the end of her stay.

Amy was 8½ when she was discharged from the Pre-School Program into a self-contained special education classroom in her local community. She did well in that protected setting, progressing academically and presenting tolerable problems at home. The next year, however, she was placed in a regular classroom where she encountered great difficulty in getting along with other children. They teased and picked on her, referring to her as "the crazy C. girl." (One is tempted to agree with her mother in feeling that Amy was "thrust out too soon.") Amy's difficulties in a normal school setting became worse and the C.'s sought help at the Bradley Child Guidance Clinic.

There despite intensive work with Amy and her family, she again grew more shy and withdrawn and was totally lacking in playmates. She resumed her wars with her mother by hurling obscenities at her. She again became obsessed with elimination and began once more to withhold. She started eating with her hands and grew fearful that she was going to be poisoned, by toothpaste or by getting soap in her mouth. When things reached these dire proportions, Amy was referred to the Bradley In-patient Service. Amy was hospitalized for fifteen months and once again received intensive treatment. Once again, Amy grew better. She stopped hurling obscenities, she ate reasonably, her fear of poisoning left, and she generally grew less bizarre and more relating. She was able to manage home visits and generally came to function on a much more acceptable level. Gradually, with a good deal of preparation and support, Amy was reintroduced to her family and to a private school setting. When last heard from, she was making an acceptable adjustment [pp. 64–5].

Silverman believes that since Amy was fortunate enough to receive and apparently profit from early intervention, progress should have been more continuous. Though she was able to demonstrate her ability to function academically and behaviorally in the self-contained special class, Silverman states that "The girl was obviously unable to cope with the demands of a normal school environment and the system was apparently not flexible enough to provide her with the greater protection she needed" (p. 65).

While much of what Silverman says may be accurate and though we would also agree that Amy was "thrust out too soon," we find it impossible to accept Silverman's conclusions and the implications he raises relative to the mainstreaming process.

Mainstreaming does *not* mean the integration of *all* youngsters into regular classrooms. Public Law 94:142 does not require school districts to move youngsters from more restricted settings to regular classrooms at the first sign of progress. There is nothing in the federal legislation or in the concept of mainstreaming to document Silverman's contention that "one would expect the seriously behaviorally disturbed child with needs for long-term help to receive a thin rehabilitative diet—and even this would be in danger of coming to an end with the first signs of improvement" (p. 63-4).

Finally, and also contrary to Silverman's assertion that the concept of least restrictive environment forces seriously disturbed children to adapt to normal school settings (and to suffer the consequences when this proves impossible), McDaniels (1978) notes that the appropriate section of the federal law reads as follows:

(B) procedures [must be established] to assure that, to the maximum extent appropriate, handicapped children . . . are educated with children who are not handicapped, and that special classes, separate schooling, or other removal of handicapped children from the regular educational environment occurs only when the nature of severity of the handicap is such that education in regular classes with the use of supplementary aids and services cannot be achieved satisfactorily. [Public Law 94:142, Sec. 612(5) (B)].

The phrase, "to the maximum extent appropriate" is obviously vague, implying as it does a clinical and educational judgment. If Amy was reintegrated too soon, it was the result of an inappropriate decision—a bad judgment—not because the concept of mainstreaming forced her into this traumatic experience. Judgments are imperfect by definition; none of us makes the right decision every time nor is there any evidence available to demonstrate that more appropriate judgments are made in segregated than in integrated settings.

The problem in mainstreaming is the same as in all other human service decision-making processes: too many assumptions go unchallenged and too many decisions are made on the basis of inaccurate and/or incomplete information. Systems interpret too rigidly guidelines that call for creative and flexible problem solving.

Silverman is quite right in pointing to the inflexibility of the system which surrounded Amy, and unfortunately other youngsters have been caught in the same dilemmas. But the answer is not to abandon the notion that children are entitled to an education in the least restrictive setting appropriate to their needs. It is important to have goals and it is imperative that we continue to help troubled youngsters who have difficulty "connecting" to the world around them learn and grow in their ability to relate to others and to have as rewarding a life as possible. All disturbed children may not be good candidates for regular classroom participation without considerable assistance. On the other hand, however, all youngsters who have been labeled "emotionally disturbed" or "behavior disordered" do not also have to be consigned to life as a chronic patient.

It is useful to remember Nyquist's elements for successful mainstreaming: preparation, pacing, specificity, and flexibility. While most if not all of those elements were apparently missing from Amy's situation, one hopes they are present in many other youngsters' systems. Mainstreaming gives the public schools the responsibility to provide individualized educational programs for all disabled youngsters and to do so in the least restrictive setting appropriate to their needs. While this obviously encourages integration of youngsters with special needs into regular classrooms, the law is quite clear in its implication that youngsters be served in less "normal" settings if regular class participation with appropriate support services and supplemental assistance is not sufficient.

CONCLUSIONS

According to Zigler and Muenchow (1979),

> Mainstreaming must be considered in context: Ten years ago, less than half of the estimated 8 million handicapped children in the United States were receiving special education services, and 1 million handicapped children were excluded from the public school system entirely. . . . The passage of the Education for All Handicapped Children Act of 1975, which guarantees a "free appropriate public education" in the "least restrictive environment" to all handicapped children, therefore represents a major landmark in entitlement legislation [p. 993].

In order for the practice of mainstreaming to approach its promise, however, a number of things must happen. Zigler and Muenchow (1979) discuss the need for better research on all aspects of the mainstreaming process, as is implied by the title of their article, "The Proof is in the Implementation."

Beyond the need for more and better information, however, is the requirement that we reconceptualize our perception:

> [Our] viewpoint must switch from the present fix on pathology, which points the accusing finger of cause at the child, to approaches which emphasize the fact that the problem is not in the child, but in the mismatch which exists between the child's needs and the opportunities we make available to nurture his self-realization. . . .
> Traditional mass instructional practices are incompatible with mainstreaming concepts. The degree to which mainstreaming can occur and be successful relates directly to the accommodative ability or accommodative power of the educational environment to respond to all children in all curricular areas [Meisgeier, 1976, p. 246].

Table 9.4. Mainstreaming Is/Mainstreaming Is Not.

What Mainstreaming Is:	What Mainstreaming is *NOT*:
• enlarging the stream of regular education and changing the nature of the regular classroom to be more accommodating to all children.	• changing the special child so that he will fit back into the unchanged regular classroom.
• looking at the educational needs of children instead of at clinical or diagnostic categories or labels.	• the wholesale return of all exceptional children in special classes to regular classes.
• providing the most appropriate education for each child in the least restrictive setting.	• permitting children with special needs to remain in regular classes without the support services they need.
• looking for and creating alternatives that will help general educators serve children with learning and adjustment problems in regular settings.	• ignoring the need of some children for a for a more specialized program than can be provided in the general education program.
• uniting the skills of general education and special education so that all children may have equal opportunities.	• less costly than serving children in special self-contained classrooms.
• the development of individual education programs or prescriptions for each handicapped child.	• a guarantee of high-quality education.
• training regular teachers to become more knowledgeable and resourceful in dealing with exceptional children.	• an argument for the elimination of the identification process or for the support of a "sink-or-swim" approach that would result from the discontinuation of special education.
• changing special education roles to incorporate more emphasis on indirect support services.	• to be assessed in terms of convenience or efficiency, but rather through its effects on children.
• a means—not an end in itself.	• the law, Public Law 94:142.

Source: After Glatter, 1977.

In fact, mainstreaming remains a concept with different meanings for different people. Though it is probably impossible to develop a definition with anything like universal agreement, it is important that we continue our efforts to clarify the implications of such a potentially powerful idea. We therefore close this chapter with Table 9.4, which lists some aspects of what mainstreaming is and describes some misconceptions about what mainstreaming is not. Each reader can undoubtedly add his or her own conceptions to both sides of the table.

10
Prevention

Our laws and public policies affirm the principle that every American child should have the opportunity to realize his or her full potential. Appropriate mental health care can be essential for the realization of this potential.

As the Commission traveled throughout America, we saw and heard about too many children and adolescents who suffered from neglect, indifference, and abuse, and for whom appropriate mental health care was inadequate or nonexistent. Too many American children grow to adulthood with mental disabilities which could have been addressed more effectively earlier in their lives through appropriate prenatal, infant, and early child development care programs.

Troubled children and adolescents, particularly if they are from racial minorities, are too often placed in foster homes, special schools, mental and correctional institutions without adequate prior evaluation or subsequent follow-up. Good residential facilities specializing in the treatment of special problems are in short supply.

Services that reflect the unique needs of children and adolescents are frequently unavailable. Our existing mental health services system contains too few mental health professionals and other personnel trained to meet the special needs of children and adolescents. Even when identified, children's needs are too often isolated into distinct categories, each to be addressed separately by a different specialist. Shuttling children from service to service, each with its own label, adds to their confusion, increases their despair, and sets the pattern for adult disability [Report of the President's Commission on Mental Health, 1978, pp. 6–7].

Veronica's Short, Sad Life—Prostitution at 11, Death at 12
The first time Veronica was arrested she was 11 years old. The charge
was prostitution. Before another year passed, the police, unaware of
her real age, arrested her 11 more times for prostitution.

At the age of 12 Veronica was dead—killed in a mysterious plunge last
July from the 10th floor of a shabby midtown hotel frequented by
pimps.

Veronica's death, which is being investigated as a possible murder, is
one more grim crime statistic to the police. But Veronica's life, and
her encounters with the city's social service and criminal justice
systems in the last year, illustrate the problems and dangers confronting
thousands of runaway girls and boys who turn to prostitution to survive alone on the streets of New York.

Six public and private agencies were partly aware of Veronica's difficulties and were supposedly providing aid. But none of the agencies
knew her entire history and none intervened quickly enough to rescue
her. . . .

The six agencies . . . now cite bureaucratic barriers and communication breakdowns for their failure to act more effectively.

"You can't tell me appropriate intervention couldn't have saved her
life," said the [director of a program for runaway youth]. "The
juvenile-justice and child-welfare systems in the city are chaotic. Programs just don't exist and everyone knows it" [The New York *Times*,
Monday, October 3, 1977].

The quotation from the president's commission that opened this chapter
paints a very bleak picture. Veronica's story adds real-life horror and is unfortunately repeated thousands of times each year. Newspaper accounts,
school records, court files, mental health clinic notes, social service
documents, and the like are filled with case histories similar to the one
described here. The problems of inappropriate and inadequate services provided in piecemeal fashion and at the wrong time are all too well known to
human-service workers. The frustrations created when our very best efforts
fail are equally familiar to adults who work with troubled children.
   When we consider the scope of the "disturbed child" problem, and the
fact that our direct services are often not available to those who need them
most and least effective for those who do manage to receive them, we arrive
at the inescapable conclusion that the remedial intervention direct-service
model we've utilized for so long does not, and in fact cannot ever hope to

deal effectively with the magnitude of needs associated with children who are labeled emotionally disturbed. Instead, the quotations at the beginning of this chapter only reemphasize the importance of the much-debated mental health concept known as prevention. For an increasing number of educators and psychologists who work with troubled children, prevention is regarded as the last hope for impacting on the scope of the problem called emotional disturbance. Such persons might find it easy to agree with Albee (1977) who said:

> Finally, I am convinced that primary prevention is the only meaningful long-term answer to the problems of emotional distress and personal unhappiness in our society [p. 10].

This chapter will examine some major definitions of the various levels of prevention, describe some of the critical needs for preventive activity, delineate the major assumptions behind a preventive model, focus more specifically on the kinds of preventive programs that have been and are being developed (with special attention to some programs that might serve as models), and finally will try to identify some major implications of a preventive approach for the variety of persons who work with troubled children. We begin with some definitions of the field.

DEFINITIONS

Prevention has been defined in a variety of ways, but no single statement more accurately reflects the current state of the prevention field than that made by Cowen (1978), who said that prevention is really "a beautiful, mushy, abstract term." Cowen's meaning, of course, is that there has been considerable difficulty agreeing on definitions of prevention and also on the kinds of programmatic interventions mandated by a focus on the prevention of emotional disturbances. Indeed there are problems with a preventive model (as we shall see later in this chapter), but there is also great potential in the area of prevention for work with troubled children and troubled systems.

The most traditional definition of prevention stems from the work of Gerald Caplan (1964) and distinguishes three levels of preventive activity; primary, secondary, and tertiary. According to Caplan, primary prevention aims at reducing the incidence of new cases of mental disorder in the population by combatting harmful forces which operate in the community and by strengthening the capacity of people to withstand stress. Another definition is that of Bower (1964), who defined primary prevention as "any specific biological, social, or psychological intervention which promotes or enhances mental and emotional robustness, or reduces the prevalence and/or incidence of learning and behavior disorders in the population at large" (p. 1). Finally, a third definition of primary prevention comes from Cowen (1978) who said that "Primary prevention seeks to forestall the development of pathology—or better yet to build health from the start" (p. 53).

We can see from the above definitions that there are two critical dimensions to primary prevention. First, primary prevention focuses on the "population at large." Second, primary prevention is concerned with eliminating the causes of emotional disturbances and ultimately with reducing the incidence of new cases of emotional disorders.

Secondary prevention, as defined by Caplan, aims at reducing the duration of cases of mental disorder which occur in spite of the programs of primary prevention. By shortening the duration of existing cases, the prevalence of mental disorder in a community is reduced (p. 89). According to Cowen, the goals "are to identify signs of maladjustment as soon as possible and to introduce prompt correctives to short circuit negative outcome" (p. 53).

Secondary prevention, then, is concerned with efforts aimed at particular, identifiable, vulnerable groups in society. The goals of such efforts are to reduce the seriousness and/or the duration of the already identified difficulties (or potential difficulties) in order to prevent more serious emotional troubles in the future.

Tertiary prevention is directed at reducing the likelihood that individuals who are already experiencing emotional difficulties will become even more severely disabled. Thus, Caplan says that tertiary prevention aims at reducing the rate of residual defect which is a signal to mental disorder. It seeks to ensure that people who have recovered from mental disorder will be hampered as little as possible by their past difficulties in returning to full participation in the occupational and social life of the community. (p. 113).

Tertiary prevention, then, is aimed at minimizing permanent disability and reducing the residual effects of emotional difficulties. The focus of such activities is essentially on treatment and rehabilitation programs. Table 10.1 summarizes these definitions and provides some examples.

More generally, Bower has suggested that the aim of prevention is to encourage the full development of the human being as a rational, creative, and self-actualizing organism. Bower went on to state that the goals of prevention might be twofold: (1) to effect a flexible coping ability in individuals (as opposed to rigid defending); and (2) to increase the immunity of children through modeling and support in typical developmental crises in life.

Similarly, Rappaport (1977) has said: "The aim is not prevention of illness but rather promotion and spread of already existing strengths of a community" (p. 526-7). Finally, the President's Commission Report (1978) states that "our working definition of prevention embraces a broad range of activities which attempt to help individuals avoid becoming patients" (p. 51). Helping people avoid becoming mental patients is really the key concept in the prevention of emotional disorders. What is the rationale for such a concept? What are the particular purposes implied in efforts to help people avoid becoming patients? These are some of the questions addressed in

Table 10.1. Definitions and Examples of Preventive Programs.

Primary Prevention:	What is done for population at large	Eliminating causes	Reducing Incidence of New Cases
Secondary Prevention:	What is done for identifiable vulnerable groups	Reducing Seriousness	Reducing Duration
Tertiary Prevention:	What is done by way of treatment and rehabilitation	Reducing Residual Effects	Minimize Permanent Disability

Programs in Primary Prevention	Programs in Secondary Prevention	Programs in Tertiary Prevention
A program of group sessions for parents of new-born disabled children.	Counseling services for mothers experiencing post-partum depression.	A program for halfway house residents to familiarize them with local transportation systems and local shopping facilities.
Providing consultation to a marriage counseling service based at a local church	A 24-hour emergency home visiting team.	
A program training exgang members to become gang workers.	A program at a school for blind children to offer emotional first-aid to children in need of psychological support.	A Saturday night social program for adult mentally retarded clients of the center.
Organizing a tenant's rights group at a neighborhood housing project.	A round-the-clock consultation service for general practitioners who have individual cases with emotional problems.	A program of vocational and aptitude testing for all newly released outpatients with appropriate referrals for training and job placement.
Working with PTAs of the local schools developing drug abuse prevention programs.	A training program for local police in handling persons with symptoms of emotional disorder.	A program to escort patients discharged from the inpatient unit to their first appointment for after-care.
Developing and staffing a prenatal care program for unwed adolescents.		
A program with local primary school teachers to sensitize them to the problems of the single parent family.	An open house at the local mental health center with tours and presentations in order to inform area residents about treatment services available.	A training program for paraprofessional staff of mental hospitals to enable them to teach patients self-care, homemaking, and budgeting.

Table 10.1 (Cont.)

Programs in Primary Prevention	Programs in Secondary Prevention	Programs in Tertiary Prevention
Offering discussion groups for men and women coping with issues raised by the women's liberation movement.	A program management level personnel at local industries about symptom recognition and referral techniques.	A program working with boarding home proprietors on the problems of after-care patients housed in their homes.
A program offering consultation to private nursing homes on ways to enrich the social experience of patients.	A training program for nurses at a local general hospital about methods of identifying symptoms of emotional disorder among their patients.	A program for families of discharged patients about the needed supportive role of the transition period.

Source: Examples after Perlmutter, Vayda, and Woodburn, 1976, pp. 536–37.

the following section focused on the need for the development of preventive programs.

WHY DO WE NEED PREVENTION?

1. *Mental health care is expensive.* In the late 1950s, approximately 1.7 billion dollars a year was expended for mental health services in the United States. By 1976, that figure increased tenfold to approximately 17 billion dollars per year. That kind of expenditure, at a time when money is no longer so readily available and efforts are being made to conserve resources of all types, is simply prohibitive. It should also be pointed out that more then 50 percent of mental health care expenditures have typically been channelled to institutional services, a tradition that is being challenged on a number of fronts today.

Despite the expenditure of this increasing amount of money, it is quite clear that the field has lacked the funds necessary to meet the needs of its clients. The effects of inflation, combined with the notion that a continuation of this geometric increase in funds for mental health services is unlikely, may mean that the cost of providing even current levels of mental health care has become too expensive for current society to undertake.

2. *Mental health care is not typically effective for the most disturbed people.* It has been reported that approximately half of the persons discharged from mental institutions are typically readmitted within one year. Despite massive efforts by scientists working from a number of different theoretical perspectives we have clearly failed to find answers to the problems presented by the major mental illnesses. Specific efforts with young people have, on the average, proven no more successful than more general efforts.

Despite all the attempts to develop and implement effective programs for troubled youngsters, there are currently more disturbed children than there have ever been before.

What all this points to is what has been recognized by many for some years, that the track record of even our most respected clinical approaches at its very best must be considered mediocre. In other words, prevention is aimed at helping people avoid becoming patients because the evidence indicates that once they do become patients, it is not very likely that their problems will be remediated.

3. *Even if it were effective, mental health care is not universally available.* Despite the intentions of the community mental health center movement, sizable numbers of people remain underserved. It has also been noted that mental health help may be both least available and when it is available, least appropriate where it is most needed. That is to say, minority groups, poor people, and persons with handicapping conditions continue to remain underserved populations with regard to appropriate mental health care. Perhaps most unfortunately, in many incidences mental health care has continued to remain divorced from efforts to impinge on the major social problems of our day.

4. *The mental health system has too few trained staff to handle the mental health needs of the community.* According to most recent estimates, between 5 and 15 percent of children between the ages of three and fifteen years of age are labeled emotionally disturbed. Furthermore, the President's Commission Report (1978) indicates that up to 25 percent of the population shows signs of emotional disorder at any given time. What we have to contend with in the provision of services to troubled children is a chronic and continuing major imbalance between the demand for appropriate services and the supply of appropriately trained persons to provide such services.

Further, it should be emphasized that according to all the best estimates of both the emotional needs of persons and the numbers of people being trained to work in the variety of roles that touch upon the lives of troubled persons, it seems clear that there will *never* be enough trained staff to handle the extent of the "emotional disturbance" in our society. In other words, even if we were accurate in our identification of persons with potential emotional difficulties, we could never expect to have the staff available to treat (even if we could do that effectively) the numbers of persons we would identify.

5. *The mental health system has always been oriented to repairing casualties.* From all that has been discussed above, it should be clear that we reach far too few people far too late. As Cowen (1978) has said, at a time when all of us are concerned with the conservation of energy, we seem to have designed a mental health system that gets minimal mileage per gallon. A preventive focus would hope to decrease the number of casualties in need of repair.

Despite what seems to be a dramatic need for preventive programs now, it is interesting to note that prevention is not really a new concept. The following quote from Harry Stack Sullivan, was published in 1931:

> Either you believe that mental disorders are acts of God, predestined, inexorably fixed, arising from a constitutional or some other irremediable substratum, the victims of which are to be helped through an innocuous life to a more or less euthanasic exit . . . or you believe that mental disorder is largely preventable and somewhat remediable by control of psychosociological factors [p. 991].

What Sullivan was discussing in that passage might be regarded as the first of five major assumptions behind the notion of prevention. Those assumptions are listed below.

1. Social emotional disorders are preventable.
2. Early experiences influence later life adaptations.
3. The investment of time and resources with young children yields a better investment/pay-off ratio than with older children or adults.
4. Early detection and intervention lower the probability of more serious later problems.
5. Unattended early problems lead to more serious problems later.

The ways in which these assumptions are built into preventive practices are described in the remainder of this chapter.

PREVENTIVE PROGRAMS

Table 10.2 outlines two major types of prevention-focused programs currently being developed. When we think about actually doing prevention there are really only two major kinds of interventions to be considered. One kind of program is oriented toward reducing the quantity or intensity of psychological stress in the community, while the other is more oriented to increasing an individual's capacity to resist the existing stresses. In other words, if we're concerned about helping people avoid becoming mental patients, there are really only two things for us to do: reduce the amount of stress that impinges upon people, and/or increase each individual's ability to withstand the stress in the system within which he or she lives.

Reducing the Psychological Stress in the Community

Essentially, there seem to be three basic strategies to reduce a community's stress level (and the corresponding negative impact that stress has on individual members of that community).

Table 10.2. Types of Prevention Programs.

I. Reduce the quantity or intensity of psychological stress in the community		
A. Support Basic Societal Units	B. Community Education	C. Total Use of Community Strengths
Developmental day-care programs School-based prevention programs Efforts to influence total school educational milieu, Develop "Growth inducing school environments	Classes: parenting; Prenatal preparation; Improving public understanding of Mental Health and Disturbances	Building home-school links National Center for Prevention

II. Increase individual's capacity to resist existing stresses	
A. Build General Competencies in Each Child	B. Identify and Build Specific Strengths in Each Child
Affective education programs Primary group experiences in schools Teaching prosocial behavior	Regular child health and developmental assessments School focus on strengths.
C. Find Innovative Ways to Provide Basic Tools to Each Child	D. Build Competencies in Individual Adults
Creative use of curriculum, group process, communication skills, and independent living programs.	Consultation with teachers, support for classroom teachers, counseling parents to foster healthy mental development.

1. **Support to basic societal units.** Instead of focusing on individuals, even the general population of individuals, this strategy focuses on the units in which we spend such great portions of our lives. If the stresses existent in the systems where we live are reduced, it seems likely that considerable emotional disturbance can be avoided. For families, these efforts might include better financial support to stabilize the lives of those in need of monetary assistance, more attractive community programming that would encourage families to spend more of their leisure time together and more attention paid to the role of the parent by other community institutions. For schools, this strategy essentially involves the building of healthy classrooms and the provision of support to teachers and other school staff members necessary to accomplish that task. Programs incorporated under this heading might include: school-based prevention programs, developmental day-care programs, and other efforts to influence total educational milieus.

2. **Community Education.** We need to see people as learners throughout their lifetimes and to provide them with the support they need to pursue their learning interests. Further, we could upgrade the general education level of society by providing effective and relevant programs of community education. Finally, such a system of community education would serve as an effective vehicle for transmitting information about mental health–related issues to the society at large. Activities might include classes for the general public or for identified target groups on issues such as parenting, prenatal preparation, where to find psychological assistance in the community, etc.

3. **Total Utilization of Community Strengths.** One factor in the creation of emotionally disturbed persons in our society is the lack of continuity between available services. As a result, people who are clearly in need of services often fall into the cracks and remain unserved. A more continuous sequence of available services would be a great boon to the effectiveness of clinical treatment.

Correspondingly, a more integrated effort on the part of major societal systems could provide a geometrically increased support system for society at large. That is to say, the same financial expenditure could provide more education, more recreation, more important involving social experiences for more people if community strengths were better integrated. Examples of programs subsumed under this strategy might include: efforts to build links between major societal units (e.g., home-school, neighborhood–community center), as well as more comprehensive efforts to coordinate services (e.g., the development of a National Center for Prevention).

Increasing Individual Capacity to Withstand Stress

We can identify four major strategies for increasing the capacity of individuals to withstand the stresses that exist in daily living.

1. **Building general competencies in each child.** This strategy involves the teaching of important life skills to each child in the way most likely to have a positive impact. Activities that might be included here would be the development and use of affective education programs in schools, other efforts to provide youngsters with primary group experiences in schools or neighborhood centers, and general efforts to teach "prosocial" behavior.

2. **Identifying and building specific strengths of each child.** This subcomponent involves conscious efforts to help children understand their particular abilities and develop them to the fullest extent possible. Programs incorporated under this strategy might include the regular use of developmental assessment techniques designed to provide a comprehensive picture of an individual child's abilities at a given time, and a more specific school focus on building educational programs based on individual children's abilities.

3. **Finding innovative ways to provide basic tools to each child.** This strategy recognizes the commonality of some needs across children and the critical importance of helping youngsters learn appropriate and effective ways to satisfy those basic needs. Such a strategy could incorporate programs that use curriculum creatively to focus on the teaching of independent living skills to all youngsters, improving interpersonal communication skills and understanding, learning how to be an effective member of a group process, and so on.

4. **Building competence in individual adults.** This strategy reemphasizes the ecological viewpoint which views each child as an inseparable part of a mini-social-system and consequently implies that strengthening of specific competencies in particular adults can have dramatic implications for the prevention of emotional disturbances in children. Program examples here might include consultation with teachers, counseling parents to foster healthy development in their youngsters, and the like.

MODEL PREVENTION PROGRAMS

While there are a great many programs concerned with the prevention of emotional difficulties in youngsters, it is difficult to identify specific model programs in this area for a number of reasons. Many programs have a variety of objectives, only some of which are preventive in nature. Other programs may be so narrow that they do not qualify as models for more than a small number of the persons who work with troubled children and troubled systems. In fact, it is unlikely that there really are true models in this area at present, but the following programs are offered as examples of what might look like model programs to persons involved in this field. Some of the programs are more specific than others and some of the programs are more concerned with various aspects of prevention than others. For example, some of the programs outline new roles for workers with troubled children while others focus more clearly on redevelopment of traditional roles and settings. Each of the programs does have implications for both educators and psychologists, one reason for including them as examples in this section.

Primary Mental Health Project (PMHP)

The primary mental health project begun approximately 20 years ago by Emory Cowen and colleagues in Rochester, New York has served as the model for a great variety of early secondary prevention programs. Cowen (1978) has summarized much of the history and critical factors in the development of the primary mental health project which began when efforts to provide psychological services to schools resulted in two surprising findings: first, that youngsters being referred for psychological assistance in the sixth, seventh, or eighth grades had already accumulated considerable documentation indicating that there were clear emotional difficulties as far back as kindergarten or first grade; and second, that teachers were sometimes spending as much as 50 percent of their time working with three or four maladapting youngsters in a class of 25 to 30 students. These observations led Cowen and his colleagues to conclude that help for maladapting school children was either not available at the most appropriate time, or at least not available in the amount needed. Consequently, a decision was made to focus all available professional resources in the primary grades in an effort to emphasize early detection and intervention in problems of this sort.

For the first year of the project efforts were made to answer two questions: (1) could project personnel accurately identify high risk children in the early school years? and (2) would a preventive approach for such children help? The issues were researched carefully, and two major conclusions were drawn:

1. Children with high risk of school failure could be accurately identified in the first three school years, and;
2. If nothing were done for such children, they were likely to follow a downward spiral ending up in a variety of unfortunate outcomes.

Personnel of the primary mental health project have spent the last 15 years or so working to develop the most effective ways to provide programs for the youngsters identified as having severe early needs in school. At this point the primary mental health project is located in more than 25 schools in the Rochester area, serving approximately 12,000 children in all. In addition, the project has served as the model for similar programs in a variety of other geographical locations around the United States.

Cowen (1978) has summarized project procedures in a series of five points. They can be stated as follows:

1. Brief, objective, standardized measures have been developed for rapid and accurate early identification of youngsters whose school functioning is ineffective. It is important to know that these screening measures consider children's resources as well as their school adjustment problems.
2. Each primary mental health project school employs a group of about five half-time child aids who serve as helping persons for the youngsters in need of assistance.
   Most program referrals come from classroom teachers and run the
   ut from hostile and aggressive behaviors to timid and withdrawn
   s to more pure educational problems. Following referral, joint

review of each particular child situation is undertaken and ultimately an intervention built around regular contacts between the child and the program aid is designed.

4. Communication lines among all the adults who work with an individual child are kept open and an exchange of information is frequent. The main goal of the program efforts of each child is to restore children to effective classroom functioning as soon as possible.
5. The primary mental health professional's role differs considerably from more traditionally defined school psychology positions. For example, much less of the mental health professional's time is devoted to direct, one-to-one service with children. On the other hand, considerably more time and effort goes into training, consultation, and resource-providing activities for other school personnel.

More than 16 separate outcome studies have documented the effectiveness of the primary mental health project in a number of areas. Further, Cowen and his colleagues have been able to show through cost-benefit analysis that for roughly a 40-percent increment in service costs, effective school mental health services have been expanded by more than one thousand percent (Door, 1972).

Although the primary mental health project has continued to grow and change according to the results of their programmatic research, Cowen (1978) has identified four essential structural features of this program:

1. There has been an unchanging emphasis on very young children.
2. Continuous efforts have been made to utilize systematic early detection procedures to identify school adjustment problems as soon as possible.
3. Carefully selected, well-trained, closely supervised, nonprofessional child aides have been recruited and utilized to deliver prompt and effective helping services to more and young school children in urgent need of such help.
4. School mental health professional's role has been changed in the direction of what Cowen calls "quarterbacking functions."

Finally, while the primary mental health project stands out as a model of secondary prevention programming, Cowen (1978) is quick to point out that no matter how effective the primary mental health project becomes, it remains a better job of restoration. There is an urgent need, he points out, to attend to a more basic question which he defines as "how can settings and experiences be designed to favor health and growth from the start?" That is to say, efforts like PMHP notwithstanding, increased attention must be paid to the problems of primary prevention.

Program for the Treatment and Education of Autistic and Related Communications Handicapped Children (Division TEACCH)

Division TEACCH is the first statewide program in America for severely disturbed youngsters. The program grew out of a research project conducted by Eric Schopler and his colleagues in North Carolina in which it was documented that parents of severely troubled youngsters could function as co-therapists or educators with their own children. As a result of that finding, special clinical and classroom procedures, organizational structures, and guidelines for parents involvement were all developed and proved quite effective. Ultimately, parents and professionals combined to push for legislation mandating this kind of service on a statewide basis and the program was formed.

Currently, the program operates in the following way:

> Parents bring their children to the center for a diagnostic evaluation used for determining appropriate special education approaches and behavior modification techniques. These are written up in home programs used by parents for their child at home. These home programs are based on our psychoeducational assessment and also on what parents have learned from their socialization struggles with the child. Home programs are demonstrated by therapists to parents observing through a one-way screen. Parents also demonstrate their use of the home program while therapists observe. Parents and teachers carry on a dialogue in this manner, working toward developing the optimum individualized educational approach for each child and family [Schopler, 1978, p. 79].

While Schopler's program may be seen to fit most easily into the definition for tertiary (or possibly secondary) prevention, Schopler describes its preventive aspects in another way. Over ten years experience with the program, Schopler and his colleagues have found that the major source of severe emotional disturbances in the children they see and maladjustments in the families they serve can be traced back to two general conditions: (1) the misunderstanding of both the child and his parents; and (2) the lack of programs and resources necessary for meeting the child's special needs. That is to say, what the division TEACCH program can prevent, according to Schopler and colleagues, is: (1) the typical increase in disturbance suffered by persons with special emotional needs as the result of the failure of society to make appropriate programs and support services available; and the negative effects of the myths stemming from beliefs, attitudes, and ˙es of the past that stand in the way of preventing the kinds of severe ˙l problems children in his program demonstrate. Further, ˙d his colleagues believe that the way to prevent these kinds of difficulties from worsening is by the provision of service through an educational program model.

The division TEACCH experience provides considerable support for the ecological perspective on disturbed behavior. It is critical to emphasize Schopler's conclusion that even in the case of seriously troubled youngsters, the major source of disturbance may be traced to inadequacies in the ecosystem, lack of appropriate programs and resources, and community misunderstanding of children and parents. In other words, it is not the isolated, bizarre behavior of an identified child that constitutes the disturbance but rather the failure of society to provide a match for the needs of that youngster and his family that defines the disturbance.

As we have described earlier, interventions must focus on the disturbed ecosystem in order to have an impact and the division TEACCH program has demonstrated the effectiveness of such an approach to work with troubled children and families. By working to reduce the discordance which is typically found in the systems surrounding children labeled autistic, division TEACCH has undoubtedly prevented the occurrence of more, and more serious, emotional disturbances.

One of the unique aspects of the division TEACCH program is the strong emphasis on parent involvement both in understanding the difficulties presented by their youngsters and in developing and implementing appropriate programs for their remediation. Schopler (1978) has listed seven preventive aspects of parent involvement:

1. Minimum disruption of parent/child bonds.
2. Maximum social support at points where parent/child bonds are threatened.
3. Reducing impractical suggestions by professionals which come from lack of familiarity with the families home life details.
4. Reducing differences in understanding and planning for each child.
5. By actively including parents in plans for needed services not only do parents provide most effective help, they also improve the chances for giving priorities to the child's most important needs.
6. Treatment solutions become less irreversible for the child.
7. The stresses and strains on both child and family from not having appropriate help are reduced and unnecessary institutionalization can be avoided [p. 92].

The division TEACCH effort has been able to document its effectiveness in dispelling myths about untestability and parent involvement while at the same time preventing the continual misunderstanding of the severely troubled youngsters that the program trys to serve.

Systems-Oriented Resource Teacher

In Chapter 5, we discussed the importance of the increasingly popular resource teacher role. The resource teacher can provide direct services to children, both individually and in groups of various sizes, and may also serve as consultant to the other adults who work with children with special needs. In a given school, the resource teacher typically interacts with children, classroom teachers, specialists, administrators, and members of the surrounding community and can become a critical link in the planning and implementation of successful educational programs.

If viewed from an ecological perspective, the role of resource teacher carries great potential both for delivering appropriate direct services to disturbed children and for effecting necessary system changes through a variety of more indirect-service functions (consultation, in-service education). The all-too-frequent adoption of a direct-service-only model, however, makes it impossible for resource personnel to become meaningfully involved in preventive activities and programs. This is especially frustrating because of the critical position of resource teachers at the interface of so many of the systems that impinge on the lives of disturbed children. While there are a variety of models that could be developed for the involvement of resource teachers in preventive activities, the systems-oriented resource teacher role described in Chapter 5 may serve as one example. Instead of focusing exclusively on direct service, such a role mandates an emphasis on indirect services, such as consultation, in-service education, and coordination, in addition to the more typical resource teacher responsibilities.

By focusing on indirect-service roles and by becoming skilled in content areas such as comprehensive psychoeducational planning, affective education, the identification and utilization of community resources, teaming or multidisciplinary efforts, and interpersonal communication, resource teachers should not only improve their effectiveness with identified youngsters, but also prevent many additional children from reaching the point where they too would be referred for direct-service help.

Specifically, there are a number of ways in which resource teachers might become involved in preventive activities in their schools. Such activities might include:

- Helping teachers incorporate affective education programs into their regular classroom routines.
- Facilitating the sharing of ideas among teachers for modifying learning environments and matching teaching styles to the range of children's learning styles.
- Working with administrators to develop early intervention programs for the school's youngest groups of children.
- Providing information to parents about ways to build youngster's strengths and reduce weaknesses.

• Helping to develop effective home-school relationships and communication.

If resource teachers could assist school staff members in their efforts to understand better, accept actively, and more successfully develop and implement educational programs for youngsters with a wide range of ablities and interests, they would surely prevent the occurrence of a number of emotional disturbances. The acceptance of individual differences and the ability to implement programs that can help all children increase self-understanding and self-control are important aspects of both the systems-oriented resource teacher role and the prevention of emotional disturbance.

A Competence Building–Resource Enabling Model

In an effort to summarize what we know about the advantages and disadvantages of a preventive approach, Cohen (1978) has said:

> What can we now say about the concept of prevention? On the one hand, it is a notion with a great deal of intellectual and moral appeal. By proposing that we deal directly with the root causes of disability and dysfunction, it offers an attractive alternative to our current system of trying to mend and maintain those who suffer because their needs have not been met. The preventive model also represents a comprehensive and systematic approach for dealing with individuals and their environment in a humane and holistic manner.

> On the other hand, the preventive model is plagued by a number of serious difficulties. In addition to being beset by philosophical debate and political conflict, the preventive approach also shoulders the unenviable burden of having to compete for scarce financial resources, with its only collateral being a tenuous promise to reduce the incidence of future problems [p. 123].

Though Cohen emphasizes the need to retain the basic thrust of the preventive approach, he also calls for a new framework for the application of the preventive viewpoint:

> (O)ne that incorporates the major features of the preventive model into a positive comprehensive approach that enhances the competencies of individuals, while increasing the tolerance and receptivity of communities to those who do not conform to conventional standards of "normality" [p. 124].

Cohen goes on to propose such a model based on three critical concepts: needs, resources, and competence. The essential features of his (Cohen & Devine, 1977) competence building–resource enabling model follow:

1. People grow and develop positively when their basic (biological, psychological, spiritual, social) needs are being satisfied.
2. The fulfillment of these needs depends upon the availability of relevant

resources in the community and upon the individual's ability to gain access to and utilize those resources. Positive mental health may be viewed as the existence of both of those conditions.

3. When basic needs are not met, people may experience frustration, distress, and a generalized inability to cope with the everyday demands of life. Ultimately, this condition may lead to diminished self-esteem, demoralization, helplessness, and the loss of functional ability.

4. Within this needs-based framework the job of the human-service system is to (1) assess the degree to which needs are being met in the community; (2) identify and develop resources appropriate to the unmet needs; (3) assist and support those individuals who do not have the skills necessary to successfully pursue these resources, and (4) work to increase the level of tolerance and acceptance of the community toward those who have already suffered because of the long-standing inaccessibility of resources to them.

In an effort to demonstrate the manner in which the competence building–resource enabling model would operate, Cohen has also provided the following hypothetical example. The strategies and interventions suggested here represent some but certainly not all of the activities that would follow from a positive and proactive preventive model.

The Case of Jane A.

Jane A. is a 15-year old school dropout who lives with her mother and four brothers and sisters, all of whom are younger than Jane. Her father, a perennially unemployed laborer, who frequently hit his wife and children when he drank excessively, disappeared when Jane was 8 years old.

When she was 6, Jane had her first difficulty in school. Undernourished and overtired from being kept awake at night by the endless fighting of her parents, she was brought to the attention of the school principal for her inability to attend to the first-grade teacher. Her parents, immersed in their own difficulties, reacted defensively when they discussed Jane's problem with the principal. They left the school in awkward silence, the situation unresolved. A short time later, Jane was assigned to a class of "slow learners" where she remained through the seventh grade, sinking deeper and deeper into a pattern of self-doubt, confusion and declining motivation. When she was 12, Jane began missing school occasionally. At age 14, neither willing nor able to keep up with her seventh grade work, Jane stopped coming to school altogether.

At first, she tried to find a job, but after several unsuccessful attempts, she became discouraged and stopped looking. During the day, when most of her friends were in school, she would pace about her family's four-room railroad flat until the screaming and crying of her youngest siblings and the demands of her mother drove her into the street.

One day, while walking downtown, she met Dawn, another 15-year-old.

Dawn shared with Jane her discovery that shoplifting was a good diversion from the lonely vigil of aimless drifting. The two girls quickly became partners.

Today, Jane was caught shoplifting a cardigan sweater from a discount clothing store. She was arrested and brought to the Public Safety Building. For Jane, the arrest represented the latest episode in a long series of failures [After Cohen, 1978].

Table 10.3 presents a summary of the critical needs and situations that occurred as Jane was growing up. The last column in Table 10.3 suggests some of the activities that might have been implemented during the course of Jane's development, activities that might have prevented Jane from sinking deeper and deeper into her current situation.

A review of Table 10.3 indicates the variety of ways in which interventions into Jane's system at earlier times in her life might have prevented or at least reduced some of her difficulties. While it appears that Jane surely has a problem now, some of her earlier inappropriate behaviors can accurately be viewed as a little girl's reaction to a troubling situation. Interventions were needed in other aspects of the system (e.g., to help Jane's parents resolve their conflicts more constructively) that may have resulted in a more harmonious ecosystem for Jane. When those interventions did not occur, Jane's system continued to deteriorate. Not only were Jane's present difficulties not prevented, they were very likely exacerbated by the failure of family, school, and social agencies to develop a program to meet Jane's needs.

SOME PROBLEMS WITH PREVENTION

The above discussion has focused on critical elements of a preventive model for work with troubled children. Though there is great potential in possible effectiveness of prevention in efforts with troubled youngsters and the systems that attempt to serve them, a number of problems with prevention are listed below:

1. There is currently, despite many efforts to produce one, no single national strategy or coordinator for prevention.
2. In addition, there is no concerted effort to document what we already know about prevention.
3. Preventing mental illness means attempting to build better mental health in our community, but we have a very difficult time agreeing on a definition of mental health.
4. It has proven very difficult to demonstrate the positive effects of the preventive programs that do exist.

Table 10.3. A Competence Building–Resource Enabling Approach to the Case of Jane A.

Critical Situation or Event	Unmet Need	Competence-Resource Goal and Suggested Strategies
Jane's inability to attend in first grade	biological:rest and nutrition	—support and counseling for parents to reduce frustration and fighting and to help them meet their own needs
		—school breakfast and lunch program
		—nutritional education program in school
	coping with emotional conflict and frustration	—parent education programs (e.g., Parent Effectiveness Training)
		—increased awareness and skill for teacher in areas of child development and interpersonal effectiveness-through consultation and in-service education
		–affective education for Jane to help her develop emotional discharge and coping skills, as well as building positive interpersonal relations
		—restructure early-grade classroom and curriculum to allow for more active learning
Transfer to "slow learners" class	adequate self-esteem	—reduction of stigmatization and increased "normalization" of school setting through elimination of tract system and special classes. Integration of all students into regular classes through the use of resource teachers and other assistance to primary teacher
		—provide opportunity for mastering non-academic competencies (e.g. social and motor skills)
	cognitive and academic development	—provide supplementary attention and cognitive stimulation through a one-to-one relationship (e.g. big sister program, tutor)
Father leaves home; Jane takes on additional responsibilities at home	appropriate childhood social development	—provide additional support for mother through coordinated efforts of various human service agencies (e.g. social services, home aides, vocational preparation). This would not only help mother, but might also relieve Jane's burden, so she could pursue age-appropriate social experiences
		—provide positive social and recreational outlets through neighborhood or community center. This would also make available other supportive adult role models for Jane

Table 10.3 (Cont.)

Critical Situation or Event	Unmet Need	Competence-Resource Goal and Suggested Strategies
Loss of interest in school	adequate cognitive stimulation and positive sense of purpose and belonging	—availability of alternative curriculum options within mainstream of regular school for those not interested in traditional orientation
		—supplementary work orientation experiences within school program
		—non-school opportunities to be involved in productive learning and service activities (e.g. dramatics, gymnastics, "rent-a-kid" projects)
Arrested for Shoplifting	positive self-identity and social role	—personal advocacy for Jane through judicial diversion program which would assist Jane in becoming involved in an appropriate educational-vocational program, as well as providing support and counseling for her
		—development of additional vocational training and job opportunities for youth. This would involve public education efforts directed at potential employers, in addition to increased allocation of vocational funding

Source: Cohen, 1978, pp. 130–32.

5. There is considerable resistance to the idea of prevention, much of which is based on growing mistrust of professionals.
6. There is at least a perception currently existing that prevention and the kinds of programs it requires will be too expensive.
7. Prevention is low on everyone's hierarchy of needs—i.e., it always takes a back seat to what has become known as "the clinical press."
8. In a given school or agency serving troubled children, no one is typically responsible for prevention.
9. There is an illusion that prevention is simple.
10. Society may "need" its mentally ill; it will be very hard to change our tendency to "blame the victim."

The President's Commission (1978) has identified six major research questions which must be addressed in the very near future if the problems with prevention delineated above are ever to be effectively reduced:

1. What groups are at high risk of developing emotional disturbances?
2. What factors contribute to the risks?
3. Can we effectively reduce or eliminate the most significant factors?
4. Does eliminating them effectively lower the rate of emotional disturbance?
5. If so, are the costs of intervention justified by the benefits obtained?
6. Are the programs responsive to the principles governing the rights of individuals and of society?

IMPLICATIONS AND CONCLUSIONS

There are two primary conclusions to be drawn from our discussion of prevention with special relevance for educators and psychologists involved in work with troubled children, especially in school-based programs.

First of all, we must at the very least learn to prevent the kinds of emotional disturbances that are created and exacerbated by life in schools. While the reticence of some school people to become involved in the conditions of a child's "outside life" that are contributing to his difficulties may be understandable, we should not defend those who refuse to admit and work at eliminating the school's role in producing emotionally disturbed children.

There are two parts to this. First, we must modify our school settings in an effort to prevent the kinds of severe negative emotional impact which schools, as we have come to know them, have on great numbers of children. Second, we can prevent the artificial production of disturbed children by being much more careful about using the "emotionally disturbed" label.

Second, and more proactively, we must begin focusing our efforts on the development of positive growth-inducing school environments. We need to understand better—more precisely, more completely—the effects schools have on children. We need to delineate our mental health objectives for youngsters and try to match them to the environments that can best suit those needs.

How can we prevent the negative effects of school experience from increasing the numbers of disturbed children? What steps must we take to foster the creation of more positively oriented models of mental health? First of all, we can recognize the reality of some problems with the preventive model and target our interventions to remedy those issues which we can most competently affect. For example, though it may not be in our power to create a national center for prevention, it is possible for individual psychologists and educators to take on the often unaccepted responsibility for coordinating preventive efforts in a particular setting. Similarly, although it is difficult to document the general, overall effectiveness of a preventive program, it is possible (as Cowen and others have done) to calculate cost-benefit ratios and other indices that describe the effectiveness of particular preventive activities clearly and openly.

Second, we can begin to address ourselves to the critical questions raised by the president's commission and repeated above concerning the future of prevention as a workable concept. Though the commission's report contained a strong endorsement for prevention, it also indicated that there were some very critical questions to be answered by preventive efforts in the next few years. If individual educators and psychologists cannot work together toward the development of solid responses to those questions, we may be contributing to the demise of the prevention concept.

Third, we can pay more careful attention to the experiences recounted by those involved in programs for troubled youngsters. Elsewhere we have described our efforts in one comprehensive program for troubled children and families and concluded:

> *For troubled children of multiple-problem families, intervention—even the best conceivable kind of intervention—at age 6 or 7 or 8 (let alone age 11 or 12) may be too late.*

> All too often we entered situations where the odds seemed hopelessly stacked against us. Some of the six and seven year old youngsters we served had already been labeled (psychiatrically and otherwise) and gained reputations (often deserved, sometimes not) as "the worst kid in school," "the terror of the block," etc. In addition, we met parents whose frustration with their children and the institutions that should have been (but often weren't) serving their children had caused them to give up on their 6 and 7 year old youngsters.

> Sometimes intervention had a lasting effect on such situations. More often, our interventions had a temporary effect which seemed to dissipate when our support was withdrawn. Frequently, it seemed to us, our efforts had the most impact when they included successful attempts to help parents understand and foster healthy mental development in their children or when they improved the coordination of services to a family, etc. Such services could fall under the rubrick of prevention . . . "a broad range of activities which attempt to help individuals avoid becoming patients." (President's Commission Report, p. 51)

> Prevention may be the most effective and, in the long run, least expensive way to improve the likelihood of satisfying and productive lives for these children [Apter et al., 1979, p. 64, emphasis added].

We must also attend more clearly to some program elements that are critical to preventive efforts. A partial list follows.

Skills and Supports for Children

Two major components in the prevention of emotional disturbances are the offering of support to the person in need and the facilitation of skill development and refinement (e.g., cognitive, affective, and behavioral skills). Many programs have discovered the importance of providing both psychological support and specific content area skills for the prevention of later disturbances.

It is important to emphasize the implication of children's needs for skills and supports to our thinking about prevention. Many children who, at great human and financial costs to society, have ended up in institutions, could with continuous support avoid the increasing disabilities often brought on by institutionalization and live productively in the mainstream of community life. Those same youngsters might have been prevented from needing institutionalization at all if someone had succeeded in helping them learn appropriate skills in their very early years.

Skills and Support for Adults

The relationship between work with adults and the prevention of emotional disturbances in children has been discussed earlier in this chapter. It is important to point out here that adults have the same needs for skills and supports demonstrated by children. Oftentimes, the kind of assistance (gaining access to appropriate services, getting some help at thinking through a problem with a child, finding out where to begin the search for a job) that can be provided by a teacher, psychologist, social worker, or other worker can serve as the support needed to ultimately prevent later difficulties. Sometimes, even the best support system is insufficient because adult skills need to be improved in order to become marketable assets.

Resource Networks

Natural support systems are increasingly being viewed as one critical aspect of providing for the mental health needs of children. The President's Commission (1976) discussed natural support systems in the following terms:

> Personal and social supports existing in neighborhoods and communities are great resources in American society for maintaining Mental Health and preventing development of serious mental and emotional disabilities. Families, friends, neighbors, schools, churches, self-help groups, volunteer associations are where we turn when we have problems. Without impairing the autonomy, natural strengths, and effectiveness of these supports, we need to enhance their ability to contribute to the Mental Health of friends, neighbors and families [p. 10].

Better understanding and utilization of natural support systems would certainly improve society's ability to provide appropriate preventive services to children and adults. It is also important, however, to develop new support networks designed to provide assistance to both consumers and providers of helping services. Teachers who incorporate troubled youngsters into their classrooms and families striving to maintain their children at home both need support in order to be effective.

A preventive approach is complex; it requires a variety of services aimed at a number of target populations. In addition, in order to approach maximal impact, services must be provided in a coordinated manner. At the present time, many of the services that might be offered to a troubled child and family are provided on a fragmented and disconnected basis. Oftentimes such a failure to coordinate efforts magnifys the family disturbance instead of preventing it from worsening.

Improving our abilities to provide skills and supports for children and adults, offer comprehensive and coordinated services, and utilize resource networks productively are critical activities that mandate striking changes in the way human-service workers approach their jobs. Such an emphasis also calls for change in societal values and makes Bloom's (1971) discussion of the primary issue in moving toward a preventive orientation an appropriate way, not to end, but to continue thinking about the prevention of emotional disturbances:

> The fundamental issue in primary prevention may very well be whether our society will permit mental disorders to be prevented. We may discover that the motive of preventing mental disorders may conflict with other motives, for example, the wish for privacy and anonymity and the strong desire to be left alone. At the organizational level, we must recognize that our society and its social institutions are based upon the assumption that mental disorders will occur, that special facilities for the treatment or the storage of persons who fail to survive our primary social institutions need to be constructed and manned. Finally, there may be some fundamental truth in the commonly held belief that we all need to be able to identify persons less fortunate and less productive than ourselves. From this point of view, it may be that preventive efforts will fail because, simply stated, our society needs its mentally ill. Thus, to consider seriously that emotional disorders can be prevented in significant numbers without requiring some painful adjustments in societal values, community organization and professional practices may be quite naive. Successful preventive programs require increased capacity on the part of our primary institutions, our homes and schools most particularly, to retain their members instead of ejecting them [pp.3–4].

11

Ecological Research and Interventions: Directions for the Future

In 1976, Wilbert McKeachie constructed a revised version of William James' "Talk to Teachers" (1922). Based on a more ecological orientation and on the assumption that the interesting features of cognitive systems are not context-free, McKeachie's talk to teachers would include the following:

1) Human beings are learning organisms—seeking, organizing, coding, storing, and retrieving information throughout their lives.
2) More emphasis needs to be placed on the social milieu of learning; the role of the school, the family, and the community in a child's development.
3) The importance of identifying critical elements of the skill or knowledge to be learned.
4) The value of teaching strategies for learning subjects as well as the content of those subjects.
5) The notion that learning something in the classroom has different consequences from learning by experience, or learning from peers.
6) The importance of "talking, writing, doing, interacting, and teaching others" for student learning.
7) The general idea that teachers are models for students and the specific importance of support and encouragement for student learning.
8) An emphasis on flexibility of approach to match student and teacher characteristics, curriculum goals, etc.
9) Increased emphasis on situational variables and the value of humanizing

our learning situations through individualized instruction, smaller schools, etc. [McKeachie, 1976, p. 826].

McKeachie's talk to teachers serves a dual role at the beginning of this chapter. First, it demonstrates how "systems" thinking can be utilized to make even very cognitive content more applicable. Second, it represents an example of the kind of efforts we need in both our research and our program planning activities. In this chapter, we will explore the utility of ecological principles in both of these critical areas.

RESEARCH

Gibbs (1979) has summarized recent calls for ecological reform in psychological research:

> The most popular reformist plea in contemporary psychological research is the call for ecologically oriented inquiry. In perception and memory, in learning and development, in social influence and attitude change, one hears the same lament of trivial and irrelevant research and the same plea for sensitivity to the contextual continuities and potentialities of human behavior. . . . The general claim of the ecological reformers is that empirical psychologists have become so enamored of laboratory precision that they have lost their sense of the human problem, that generalization to the authentic significance of the person in the real environment has been sacrificed to the quest for certainty in our knowledge [p. 127].

Gibbs points out that the ranks of ecological reformers include some prominent names in a number of research areas in modern psychology. Included on his list are cognitive psychologists (Neisser, 1976; Jenkins, 1974), learning researchers (Herrnstein, 1977; Rogers-Warren & Warren, 1977), developmental psychologists (Bronfenbrenner, 1977; Kuhn, 1978; McCall, 1977; Wohlwell, 1973), and social psychologists (McGuire, 1973; Abelson, 1976; Mussen, 1977).

Finally, Gibbs discusses at length what he terms the authenticity-certainty research polarity and finds that neither element is sufficient by itself as the basis for a comprehensive strategy of psychological research. He therefore proposes the adoption of a transactional, ecologically oriented inquiry model that "reflects an interplay between the features and phases associated with deduction (theory, manipulation, control) and those associated with induction (holistic data, ecological validity, discovery orientation)" (p. 135). It is only through the adoption of this strategy, according to Gibbs, that the tension between certainty and authenticity can be reduced and the advantages of each dimension can be developed to their fullest.

For Bronfenbrenner (1977), the decision is between rigor on the one hand and relevance on the other. And relevance, Bronfenbrenner notes, includes not only the objective elements of an environment but also the perceptions of persons within those systems. The transactional inquiry model proposed by Gibbs (1979) comes to mind with Bronfenbrenner's conclusion that "In ecological research, the principal main effects are likely to be interactions" (p. 518).

Bronfenbrenner (1977) proposes that research efforts be organized around an experimental ecology of human development in order to more thoroughly examine the changing relationships between persons and environments. As a beginning, Bronfenbrenner (1977) offers nine propositions for systems research (see Table 11.1).

As we can see in Table 11.1, Bronfenbrenner has provided us with a set of guidelines for future research along ecological lines. Research conducted in accordance with these propositions would chart new directions and expand our knowledge of the realities in which children grow and develop. For example, the first proposition in Table 11.1 (reciprocity) draws a contrast between the traditional unidirectional research model and the preferred ecological experiment that is designed to focus on reciprocal relationships.

Similarly, Wahler et al. (1977) point out that the standard applied behavioral analysis model is limited by its focus on a single dyad (teacher-child, parent-child) interaction. After reviewing a series of such studies, Wahler et al. (1977) concluded: "Looking at these studies as a group, it seems logical to assert that no perspective that accounts for a single pair of interacting variables (e.g. teacher-child) can explain the functioning of what is essentially a social system—such as a classroom or a family" (p. 213). Instead, Wahler et al. propose an alternative way to examine behavioral data:

> The systems approach, as we define it, understands the world as comprised of systems and subsystems that function as wholes and must be understood as wholes. Borrowing a bit from the Gestalt psychologists, this system model argues that parts never explain the wholes, borrowing from Roger Barker (1968), the approach argues that behavior must be studied in its context to be understood [p. 215].

Wahler et al. differentiate between three subsystems within their systems approach: the child as a behavioral system, the primary group as a behavioral system, and the community as a behavioral system. Research efforts need to focus on each of those subsystems and ultimately on the integration of data from each of those subsystems, if we are to understand troubled systems.

Similarly, Swap (1978) has proposed three nested subsystems (behavior settings, patterns of behavior across settings, community and culture) each

Table 11.1. Principle Propositions of Ecological Research.

1. Reciprocity	In contrast to the traditional, unidirectional research model typically employed in the laboratory, an ecological experiment must allow for reciprocal processes; that is, not only the effect of A on B, but also the effect of B on A. This is the requirement of reciprocity.
2. Recognizing the functional social system	An ecological experiment requires recognition of the social system actually operative in the research setting. This system will typically involve all of the participants present, not excluding the experimenter. This is the requirement of recognizing the totality of the functional social system in the setting.
3. Beyond the dyad	In contrast to the conventional dyadic research model, which is limited to assessing the direct effect of two agents on each other, the design of an ecological experiment must take into account the existence in the setting of systems that include more than two persons (N + 2 systems). Such larger systems must be analyzed in terms of all possible subsystems (i.e. dyads, triads, etc.) and the potential second- and higher order effects associated with them.
4. Indirect impact of physical factors	Ecological experiments must take into account aspects of the physical environment as possible indirect influences on social processes taking place within the setting.
5. Interactions between settings	In the traditional research model, behavior and development are investigated in one setting at a time without regard to possible interdependencies between settings. An ecological approach invites consideration of the joint impact of two or more settings or their elements. This is the requirement, wherever possible, of analyzing interactions between settings.
6. Higher order effects	The design of an ecological experiment involving the same person in more than one setting should take into account the possible subsystems, and associated higher order affects, that exist, or could exist, across settings.
7. Ecological transitions	A fruitful context for developmental research is provided by the ecological transitions that periodically occur in a person's life.
8. Larger contexts	Research on the ecology of human development requires investigations that go beyond the immediate setting containing the person to examine the larger contexts, both formal and informal, that affect events within the immediate setting.
9. Transforming experiment	Research on the ecology of human development should include experiments involving the innovative restructuring of prevailing ecological systems in ways that depart from existing institutional ideologies and structures by redefining goals, roles, and activities and providing interconnections between systems previously isolated from each other.

Source: After Bronfenbrenner, 1977a.

of which lends itself to particular kinds of research activities, as described in Table 11.2.

In her effort to develop a framework for the integration of ecological research findings, Swap (1978) reviewed data from a variety of sources and concluded that "different techniques were effective or ineffective with different children at different times" (p. 189). Swap decried the fact that what we currently know about children's development is based too firmly in contrived laboratory situations and proposed the kind of multisetting, multimethod approach represented in Table 11.2.

The critical point of Swap's position is that our research efforts must avoid a single-minded (and simplistically naive, by ecological standards) search for a "master solution" to the problems presented by troubled children. Swap notes that this is a problem for studies directed at the community/culture level as well as those focused more specifically on behavior settings. Casting your research efforts to a wider field, without incorporating a framework for studying and understanding the complex transactions within a system, does not by itself represent good ecological research. On the contrary, Swap (1978) suggests that we can avoid the fruitless search for a master solution by learning to do the kind of ecological research that will help us "identify significant generalizable patterns when small numbers of subjects participate in multiple settings" (p. 191).

Wicker (1979) reviewed recent developments in ecological psychology and proposed two new approaches to research in community and organizational settings. Similar to Swap (1978), Wicker (1979) suggests that though ecological theory views behavior settings as elements of larger systems,

Table 11.2. Potential Areas for Ecological Research Efforts in Three Subsystems

Subsystem	Potential Areas for Research
Behavior Setting	Characteristics of children. Characteristics of significant others. Characteristics of the physical milieu. Characteristics of program, space, and time.
Patterns of Behavior Across Settings	Identified child in different milieus. Handicapped and nonhandicapped children in different milieus. A single variable in multiple milieus with multiple methods.
Community and Culture	Formal structures. Informal structures. Physical characteristics.

Source: After Swap, 1978.

research has not typically focused on these connections and linkages. Consequently, Wicker believes that ecological researchers should, first of all, consider directing their attention to behavior-setting linkages, interpersonal links (to what extent are participants in setting A acquainted with participants in setting B?), shared leadership (in what settings does this occur and what is the impact?), shared clienteles, economic dependencies, flow of information, flow of goods and services. Secondly, Wicker proposes that researchers study the life cycles of behavior settings, the circumstances surrounding the initiation of settings, adaptation to external conditions, factors leading to termination, and the like.

Like Swap, Wicker criticizes the focus of ecological research and suggests the new directions listed above. Wicker also notes (as Swap implied) that ecological research may involve more than the unobtrusive observation of environments suggested by Barker (1965, 1968). Instead, Wicker suggests a radical departure for the ecological psychologist's role: "that ecological psychologists develop a technology for deliberately intervening in behavior settings to improve setting functioning and to increase the satisfaction and well-being of the people (both staff and clients) who occupy them" (p. 762).

While Wicker's point is well taken and ecological researchers may need to develop more active roles in some situations, we would be wise to remember Barker's (1968) dictum that "ecological psychology is a transducer science" (p. 143). Barker (1968) describes two roles for the psychology researcher: the psychologist as operator (O) and the psychologist as transducer (T). In the O role, researchers act on their environment and study "psychological units arranged in accordance with the curiosities of the psychologist" (Barker, 1968, p. 143). By acting as an operator, Barker notes, the psychologist achieves control that allows a focus on the situations or elements of most concern to the researcher.

On the other hand, when the psychologist assumes the role of transducer, the research objective is to "preserve phenomena that the psychologist as operator carefully alters, namely psychologist-free units" (Barker, 1968, p. 143). Barker makes a strong case for the fundamental difference between O-data and T-data. Using the concept of intelligence as an example, Barker notes that despite the huge amount of O-data amassed by the administration, scoring, and analyses of millions of intelligence tests, the science of psychology has provided little if any information (T-data) about the intellectual demands of living environments or the reactions of children and adults to those demands.

Similarly, Barker notes that while contrived studies of frustration in children produced certain O-data, T-data (Fawl, 1963) indicated that "frustration was rare in children's days, and when it did occur it did not have the behavioral consequences observed in the laboratory" (Barker, 1968, p. 44). Barker concluded that while the O-experiments may have simulated theoretical frustration, they apparently did not represent real-life frustration very accurately.

While it may be appropriate to consider ways in which the researcher can combine O and T roles in particular studies then, it is imperative that we maintain our focus on studying the way systems actually work. For troubled children, we have described the critical importance of systems analysis to the understanding of emotional problems and ultimately for the remediation of such difficulties. Wicker suggests that it may be appropriate at some point to test out our system interventions and to evaluate their effectiveness. That is certainly a desirable new phase in ecological research and will surely be facilitated by the adoption of the multisetting, multimethod transactional approach suggested by Swap (1978).

EXAMINING ENVIRONMENTS

While the overriding principle of ecological research must continue to be the study of interactions within systems, it is clear that an expanded emphasis on the environmental aspects of the person-environment relationship is needed. While we have amassed great quantities of information about individual troubled children, we have been much less thorough in our efforts to understand troubled systems.

Sommer (1977) expressed concern about his perception that psychological research was becoming less generalizable each year, as psychology continually increased its committment to laboratory studies and lagged farther and farther behind in the development of field methods. While he did not advocate abandoning the laboratory, Sommer suggested that a better balance between field and laboratory studies would benefit psychology by enabling us to study the ways in which people actually behave in their natural environments.

Sommer (1977) presents a strong argument for the development of a "Psychology of Natural Behavior," as he points out the importance of understanding natural environments:

> The ability to "read" environments is the basis of the naturalist's craft. One is able to examine a living room, classroom or street corner in terms of constraints this puts upon behavior, the kind of actions it facilitates, encourages, demands. There are lessons in the kind of furniture in a person's living room, how it is arranged, how it is cared for, the decorations, the location of the television set or stereo, and so on. One can also "read" a city park, prison or restaurant interior, in each case attending to somewhat different items. Experience in making observations and comparing different settings provides clues as to what is important. Frequently the omission of something (the

absence of books in a living room, or the absence of wall decorations in a college classroom), is as significant as what is there [p. 1].

Gump (1975) has also noted that our lack of understanding about educational environments leads to an inability to agree upon conceptualizations and definitions of environments. Further, Gump pointed out that our lack of understanding of environments is an obstacle that pervades the social sciences and quoted Schulman (1970) to confirm the point: "Social scientists are dramatically impotent in their ability to characterize environments. Generally they don't even try" (p. 374).

According to Gump (1975), the environmental research that has been done has focused essentially on two kinds of environments: the physical and the phenomenological or perceptual. Neither one is sufficient, in Gump's view, for the study of ecological systems and he proposes an alternative conceptualization of environment for use in research efforts. Gump's conceptualization is based on Barker's work (described earlier) and includes the following four components:

1. The physical milieu.
2. The program, operations, or "standing pattern of behavior."
3. The fit between the milieu and the program.
4. The boundaries.

For an example in an educational setting, we can see that the school library is a *milieu*, pupils doing research constitutes one *program*, the fact that the pupil's task is facilitated by the library's structure (access to materials, workspaces, etc.) is representative of the *fit* (or synomorphy) between milieu and program, and regular school hours may serve as a *boundary* (after school, the milieu may be used for a different program).

Kounin (1975) notes that the kind of ecological study of classrooms suggested by Gump's conceptualization places great value on completeness. In his own work, this kind of completeness has helped Kounin discover, for example, that the "success" of a formal classroom lesson is related to two systems elements: the delivery of signals that support appropriate behavior, and the prevention of inputs that encourage inappropriate behavior.

In a study with more specific relevance to troubled children, Pastor and Swap (1978) used an ecological approach to examine the placement of children labeled emotionally disturbed in regular classrooms or special classes. In addition to looking very carefully at the children in their study, Pastor and Swap also examined a variety of evironmental features of the two kinds of settings. They concluded that the small number of youngsters responded differently in different settings, and that "the impact of each program was different for each child and related to the interaction between the child's temperament and behavior problems, characteristics of teachers and peers, and environmental variables'' (p. 215). Pastor and Swap suggested that some of the environmental variables that emerged in their study be subject to more extensive examination in future research with troubled children and the systems that surround them.

Curran and Algozzine (1980) studied the degree to which teachers' ratings of children are related to teachers' tolerance of childrens' behaviors. They concluded that:

> The level of a teacher's tolerance for a specific set of behaviors was shown to be related to the teacher's rated interaction potential for a hypothetical child thought to exhibit the behaviors. As such, the results partially support an important assumption underlying ecological theory; that is, certain levels of differential attitudes toward behaviors did result in differential interaction potentials [p. 173].

Both the Curran and Algozzine (1980) and the Pastor and Swap (1978) studies serve as examples of the kind of ecological research needed to study a critical ecological assumption, i.e. that a better *fit* between teacher and child can reduce the incidence of emotional disturbances (ecologically defined) in classrooms. Studies such as these are worthy first steps in a research process which is aimed at developing a more substantive data-based foundation for the ecological point of view.

The need for a more ecologically oriented research base has been a much-discussed topic in recent years. In addition to the documentation provided above, Belsky and Steinberg (1978) have called for an ecological approach to future research on day care, and Gump, Schoggen, and Redl (1957) have demonstrated the utility of an ecological approach to a residential setting (in this case, a summer camp program) for children. Most recently, Belsky (1980) has used Bronfenbrenner's work as the basis for an ecological integration of research in the area of child maltreatment. Through a very careful and comprehensive analysis of a wide range of research findings, Belsky has developed a strong position that

> (C)onceptualizes child maltreatment as a social-psychological phenomenon that is multiply determined by forces at work in the individual (ontogenic development) and the family (the microsystem), as well as in the community (the exosystem) and the culture (the macrosystem) in which both the individual and the family are embedded [p. 320].

Finally, the need for a broader, more ecological research base also has implications for public policy. Brim (1977) has called for the establishment of a national observatory to be responsible for the ongoing and longitudinal study of the development of children in their natural environments. The Carnegie Council on Children (Kenniston, 1977) noted that

> Some traditional American views we conclude, severely hamper our national efforts to help children and parents. They obscure the "ecology of childhood"—the overall social and economic system that exerts a crucial influence on what happens to parents and children. Until policy makers and planners shift their focus to the broad ecological pressures on children and their parents, our public policies will be unable to do much more than help individuals repair damage that the environment is constantly reinflicting [p. xiii].

INTERVENTIONS

One recurrent problem with nonecological intervention strategies is described by Stephens (1976) in a discussion of mainstreaming:

> While deficiencies in students are being recognized, those deficiences inherent in general and special education programs are often ignored. Without significant modifications in the preparation of teachers, teacher educators, and other school personnel, mildly handicapped children who are mainstreamed will again become victims of a general education system which has been unable to deal adequately with more normally functioning students [p. 148].

Stephens decries our tendency to blame students when in fact they may be victims of a system or program whose deficiencies are ignored. Morse (1976) raises the same issue with regard to teachers, noting that we tend to blame teachers for what are really program inadequacies:

> Perhaps we have been making the teachers the scapegoats. . . . We focus on the competency of the teacher and the accomplishment of successful prescriptions when the real issue is elsewhere. . . . It is dismaying to see teachers described as incompetent when anyone who has been in the business knows that the program is so incomplete that recovery would be a miracle. . . . Yet time after time, in my experience, it is the limited program rather than limited teacher which spells defeat. Every child is in a milieu and is undergoing milieu experience. The experience in his milieu may be positive or negative but there it is. Teacher competency must be replaced by program competency if we are to be honest. The list of those special educators in our field who have begun to work on total program competency in place of teacher competency is not very long [p. 87].

The ecological perspective described throughout this book asserts the ineffectualness of planning interventions without consideration of context and system variables. In order to productively incorporate those variables into our planning efforts, we must understand them more completely. As Willems (1977) has noted:

> Before we can be truly effective in designing and affecting human living condi-
> tions and alleviating human suffering, we must know much more about the
> principles that characterize and govern the systems into which such designs
> and alleviating efforts must, of necessity, intrude [p. 44].

While Willems' words may seem to have most relevance for future ecological research efforts described in the first part of this chapter, they raise one critical implication for future interventions. In Willems' words again:

> (I)t just may be that in the long run, the most direct and efficient path toward
> scientific understanding of behavior will involve the timely recognition and ac-
> ceptance of complexity within an ecological perspective [p. 44].

In fact, the future of ecological intervention strategies is staked to our willingness to accept the complexity of troubled systems. While this brings complications to the roles of all those who work with troubled youngsters, we can no longer pretend that such complexities do not exist in the systems of the youngsters we serve. We have seen that when interventions on behalf of troubled children ignore the surrounding programs and systems, the likelihood of success is minimized. Complex though they may be, troubled systems are real, and it behooves us to accept that reality and incorporate it into our intervention planning efforts without further delay.

There are two general ecological beliefs that can assist our intervention plans: behavior is largely controlled by the setting in which it occurs, and correspondingly, a change in the setting will likely result in changed behavior. As Barker once noted, the best way to predict human behavior may be to know in what setting it occurs. While some documentation for the strength of this concept known as "place dependency" exists, we need to know much more completely the effects of various settings on the behavior of both typical youngsters and those labeled disturbed.

More specifically, Newbrough et al. (1978) have outlined some implications of Kelly's ecological principles for intervention planning. Those guidelines, along with the principles from which they emanate, are summarized in Table 11.3.

As we can see in Table 11.3, the principle of interdependence, or the interrelatedness of system elements, makes it important for us to understand the relative contributions of system variables in order to intervene effectively. It is equally important to identify the level of adaptation required by the various settings in which an individual typically functions. In addition, we

Table 11.3. Ecological Principles and Implications for Interventions.

Principle	Implications for Intervention
Interdependence: The basic elements of a system (the persons, roles, settings, and rules) are interrelated. Whenever any element of a system is changed, there are alterations in the relationships between all other elements.	1. One should know the system before intervening to change it. 2. To understand a behavior, one must look at the relative contribution of both person and setting variables.
Adaptation: The process by which individuals and the species as a whole attempt to meet the demands of the environment for survival. Each setting requires specific adaptive capabilities.	1. To understand an organization or a setting, one must describe the adaptive skills it demands. 2. It is important to consider the extent to which the personal characteristics of an individual are adequate for meeting the demands of the particular environment. 3. It is useful to compare the adaptive skills required by the various settings (school, neighborhood, home) in which the individual functions, in order to determine if these make conflicting demands on the individual.
Cycling of resources: The use and transformation of energy during the life cycles of the organisms that live in a certain environment.	1. Before designing an intervention, it is important to evaluate the manner in which the system defines and distributes its resources. 2. One needs to investigate new ways in which the system can use its resources to facilitate human development. An attempt should be made to identify and mobilize existing resources that are not being used.
Succession: Although an organization may appear to be in a steady state a longitudinal time perspective reveals that it is in a continual process of change, responding to continual inputs and adaptations.	1. A time perspective is necessary to understand an organization and to anticipate the rate and direction of its change.

Source: After Newbrough et al., 1978.

should know how adaptable an individual can be, how well he or she can respond to the demands of new and different environments.

The third principle outlined in Table 11.3 refers to the ability of a system to use its energy efficiently. With regard to intervention planning, this notion implies both a need to investigate the system's current effectiveness, and, when appropriate, the development of new ways to utilize unused existing resources.

Finally, the principle of succession notes that systems are dynamic, always involved in a continual process of change. It is therefore important to add the perspective of time to our efforts to understand systems.

An example of the use of ecological principles for future program planning may be useful at this point. If we were, for instance, concerned about the mainstreaming of troubled children into regular classrooms, we might focus on a problem such as: "How should classrooms be set up to provide effective educational programs for all their students, including those with special needs?" Ecological theory would propose the following guidelines for work on such a problem:

1. *Avoid overpopulation induced stress.* Even if class size is set at an unalterably high number, formats can be developed to help youngsters feel a part of a smaller reference group. For example, each classroom could be informally divided into smaller working groups for regular portions of each day.

2. *Bonding reduces inappropriate behavior.* Aggressive actions and the tendencies of groups to exclude unwanted numbers ("expulsion reaction") can be minimized by efforts to pair or bond youngsters into satisfactory peer relationships.

3. *Children must have some function in the classroom.* It is important for each individual to see himself and be seen by others as being a responsible participant in classroom life.

The incorporation of ecological notions, such as those described above, into intervention planning efforts truly takes the onus of disturbance off the child. Rather than continue to argue over whether to intervene at the personal or environmental levels, ecological interventions point the way to a more comprehensive and productive interactional focus for our intervention efforts. Implications of an ecological basis for the future of human services are described in the final section of this chapter.

VIEWS TO THE FUTURE

At the conclusion of the comprehensive study of child variance referred to earlier, Rhodes (1975) offered the following speculations for consideration as predictions for the future:

1. There will be the beginning of profound and radical changes in human services in the next decade. The crisis in human care giving will lead to a variety of dramatically different models.
2. The basic relationship between caretaker and care recipient will change.

Whether teacher-student, therapist-patient, counselor-client, etc., the traditional unidimensional roles in these relationships will move in the direction of more bilateral relationships.

3. Within the next decade, a new perception of human services will emerge and will result in experiencing ourselves and others to new depths. Our belief in the concept of "normality" will begin to erode.

4. There will be an acceleration of the declassification effort. Our classification systems will continue to break down despite the opposition from individuals and groups whose power is controlled by ties to a particular category.

5. There will be increasing pressure toward deinstitutionalization. State-operated institutional programs will continue to have their populations reduced, and more and more buildings will be abandoned. Ultimately, care-taking functions may be removed from the state and taken over by more logical reference groups—unions, cultural organizations, and the like.

6. There will be strong moves to debureaucratize care giving, including some efforts to deprofessionalize human-service delivery. Instead there will be increasing efforts by small groups of people to care for one another through personal pledge, not public contract.

Rhodes (1975) concluded that:

> Generally, then, the trend of caring and care giving will be away from separation, differentiation and therapeutic isolation. The wholistic philosophy, the total view, the ecological perspective will begin to assert itself as a dominant force in caring [p. 99].

While many of Rhodes' predictions seem to have been realized, his overall vision of a world in which deviance can be known and even celebrated remains unfulfilled. The ecological tone of his speculations about the future, however, has surely been felt in the years since the study of child variance was concluded and continues to show promise for the future.

Another more sobering vision of the future has been provided by Edelman (1981):

> The already great needs of children will only increase in the 1980s. More children will be born at risk and a greater number of families will undergo economic, psychological, and emotional stress. Therefore, in the next decade more children will need the support and protection of their relatives, their churches, their community and state and federal governments in order to grow up strong and healthy [p. 111].

Edelman points out that since children are such an easy group for politicians to ignore ("They do not vote, lobby, or make campaign contributions") and since inflation has been eroding the power of human-service dollars while Congress considers cutting those funds back even further, millions of children do not have access to the services needed to satisfy even very basic needs.

The task, for those of us who are concerned with increasing the strength of the systems that surround children, then, according to Edelman, is to fight the myths that work against children and their families. Those myths are summarized below.

1. *Only other people's children have problems.*

    All youngsters are touched by current concerns and it is in each of our best interests to attend to the needs of society's children.

2. *Families are self-sufficient; they should take care of their own children.*

    The nuclear family (father works, mother stays at home to care for two normal children) represents only 1 out of every 17 families in America today. All families need some form of assistance from time to time.

3. *No one should take responsibility for children except their parents.*

    Such an attitude allows those whose work impacts on children to pass the buck; to blame parents (or the children themselves) for their own failure to develop shared solutions to child and family system problems.

4. *Helping children whose families cannot fully provide for them condones and rewards failure and erodes American family values.*

    Ignoring the plight of children whose parents, for one reason or another, may be unable to provide adequately for them, hurts innocent youngsters and ultimately contributes to the deterioration of society.

5. *Child advocates want the government to take control over families and children's lives.*

    The issue is not whether government interferes since it already does; the issue is to find ways for government policies to help families help themselves.

6. *Meeting childrens' needs and protecting their rights will divide families and pit parents and children against each other.*

    The best way to help children is to help families; to help parents act effectively in their relationships with their children.

7. *Children's issues should be above the political process.*

    The political process is the way to achieve change for all issues, including those related to children.

8. *Providing needed services is too expensive.*

In fact most services to children and families, especially in light of the later costs they may prevent, are very good investments for the recipients of services *and* for taxpayers [after Edelman, 1981, pp. 111–13].

Dispelling the myths, and improving the situation of children in America requires action and Edelman suggests that the following actions be taken:

1. Take children's interests into our own hands.
2. Be specific and break down the needs of children and family into manageable pieces.
3. Stay away from rhetoric and general labels.
4. Become hard-nosed and tough in pursing children's interests.
5. Gain greater technical knowledge of how bureaucracies work.
6. Coalesce around a few key children's issues.
7. Persist [pp. 115–16].

Edelman's position, which focuses on the unfortunate situation of some youngsters and utilizes advocacy to mobilize societal resources to rectify identified problems, represents the "thesis" position described by Rhodes. The antithesis position would question the seemingly endless nonproductive care giver–care receiver encounters and the valuing of "normality." Instead, antithesists argue that the kind of change needed is in our attitudes toward deviance:

We should not try to wipe out variant conditions. Instead of making war on these conditions we should try to understand their meaning to us. . . . We must not lock deviance out, but bring it in our midst to teach us what we should know about ourselves, and allow us to experience the rich range of what we are and could be [Rhodes, 1975, p. 90].

From an ecological perspective, both positions are valid. We do need to modify our attitudes about deviance; the rights of people with special needs to live and work and go to school in the mainstream of community life demand a change in our attitudes about differences. The key to such a change may be found in the ecologist's belief that deviance is defined by faulty interactions, failures to match between person and environment.

We need also to mobilize resources to improve the lives of children in our society. Following the guidelines suggested by Edelman will lead to the development of healthier settings in which children can live and grow. From the ecological viewpoint, such settings have the dual advantage of improving the likelihood that environments will match the needs of children more effectively and that children will not always have to shoulder the blame when disturbed interactions occur.

In the final analysis, an ecological orientation provides an overarching framework which can encompass views as disparate as the two described above; help us understand and create new ideas for resolving critical problems in our efforts to serve troubled children; explain the differences between troubled and troubling (disturbed and disturbing) youngsters and provide guidelines for working with both groups; and demonstrate the importance of attending to adults' needs in order to impact on children. Perhaps most of all, the ecological perspective offers the promise, as yet unfulfilled, for creative productive responses to the problems of troubled systems.

References

Abelson, R.P. Script processing in attitude formation and decision-making. In Carroll, J.S. & Payne, J.W. (Eds.), *Cognition and social behavior.* Hillsdale, NJ: Erlbaum, 1976.

Abeson, A., Bolick, N., & Hass, J. *A primer on due process: Education decisions for handicapped children.* Reston, VA: Council for Exceptional Children, 1975.

Ackerman, N. *The psychodynamics of family life.* New York: Basic Books, 1970.

Albee, G. The relation of conceptual models to manpower needs. In Cowen, E.L., Gardner, E.A., and Zak, M. (Eds.) *Emergent approaches to mental health problems.* N.Y.: Appleton-Century-Crofts, 1967.

Albee, G. Letter to the editor, *APA Monitor,* February 1977.

All our children. *Behavior Today,* September 26, 1977, **8,** (31), 1.

Andornico, M., Fidler, J., Guerney, B., & Guerney, L. The combination of dyadic elements in filial therapy. *International Journal of Group Psychotherapy,* 1967, 17, 10–17.

Apter, S.J. Applications of ecological theory: Toward a community special education model for troubled children. *Exceptional Children,* March 1977, **43,** (6) 366–73.

Apter, S. (Ed.) *Focus on prevention: The education of children labeled emotionally disturbed.* Syracuse: Publications in Education (Syracuse University Press), 1978.

Apter, S.J.; Apter, D.S.; Trief, P.M.; Cohen, N.; Woodlock, D.; & Harootunian, B. *The BRIDGE program: Comprehensive psychoeducational services for troubled children and families.* Final report of NIMH grant (MH 22358), Syracuse (New York): 1979.

Atkinson, L. Treatment of deviance by the legal-correctional system. In Rhodes, W.C. & Head, S. (Eds.), *A study of child variance. Vol. 3: Service delivery systems.* Ann Arbor: Institute for the Study of Mental Retardation and Related Disabilities, 1974.

Attneave, C.L. Social networks as the unit of intervention. In Guerin, P.J. (Ed.), *Family therapy: theory and practice.* New York: Gardner Press, 1976.

Auerswald, E.H. Interdisciplinary versus ecological approach. In Ackerman, N. (Ed.), *Family process.* New York: Basic Books, 1970.

Badger, E.D. A mother's training program: A sequel article. *Children Today,* 1973, 1, 7–11.

Ballard, J. & Zettel, J. Public Law 94:142 and Section 504: What they say about rights and protections. *Exceptional Children,* 1977, **44** (3), 177–85.

Barker, R.G. Explorations in ecological psychology. *American Psychologist,* 1965, **20,** 1–14.

Barker, R.G. *Ecological psychology.* Stanford: Stanford University Press, 1968.

Barnes, C., Eyman, W., & Bragar, M. *Teach and Reach: An Alternative Guide to Resources for the Classroom.* Syracuse: Human Policy Press, 1977.

Baruch, D.W. *New ways in discipline.* New York: McGraw-Hill, 1949.

Bednar, M.J. & Haviland, D.S. The role of physical environment in the education of children

249

with learning disabilities. (A Position Paper.) New York: Center for Architectural Research, 1969.

Beery, K. (Ed.) *Models for mainstreaming.* San Rafael, CA: Dimensions Publishing Co., 1972.

Belsky, J. Child maltreatment: An ecological integration. *American Psychologist*, 1980, **35** (4), 320–35.

Belsky, J. & Steinberg, L.D. The effects of day care: A critical review. *Child Development*, 1978, **49**, 929–49.

Bennett, L.M. & Henson, F.O. *Keeping in touch with parents: The teacher's best friend.* Austin: Learning Concepts, 1977.

Bersoff, D.N. School psychology and state divisions of special education: A suggestion for change. *Journal of School Psychology*, 1971, **9** (1), 58–60.

Blau, T.H. Diagnosis of disturbed children. *American Psychologist*, 1979, **34** (10), 969–72.

Bloom, B.L. Strategies for the prevention of mental disorders. In *Issues in Community Psychology and Preventive Mental Health* (Task force on Community Mental Health of Div. 27 of the American Psychiatric Association). New York: Behavioral Publications, 1971.

Bower, E. Primary prevention in the school setting. Reprinted by U.S. Dept. of H.E.W. from Bower, E. (Ed.), *Orthopsychiatry and Education.* Detroit: Wayne State University Press, 1971.

Bower, E.M. Primary prevention of mental and emotional disorders: A frame of reference. In *The protection and promotion of mental health in schools.* Mental Health Monograph #5, U.S. Dept. of H.E.W., NIMH, January 1964.

Bower, E.M. & Lambert, N.M. In-school screening of children with emotional handicaps. In Long, N., Morse, W., & Newman, R. (Eds.), *Conflict in the Classroom*, Belmont, CA: Wadsworth, 1971.

Bricker, W.A. Competence as a key factor in the study of children's deviant behavior. Paper presented to Tennessee Association of Mental Health Centers, Nashville, October, 1966.

Brim, O. Brim urges observatory to study kids. *APA Monitor*, April 1977, **8**, 4.

Bronfenbrenner, U. Toward an experimental ecology of human development. *American Psychologist*, 1977a, **32**, 513–31.

Brookover, B. et al. *American psychologist, Self-concept and school ability.* E. Lansing, Mich.: Michigan State University, 1965.

Brown, G.B. & Palmer, D.J. A review of BEH funded personnel preparation programs in emotional disturbance. *Exceptional Children*, November, 1977, 169–74.

Brownbridge, R. & Van Fleet, P. (Eds.), *Toward community action. Investments in prevention. The prevention of learning and behavior problems in young children.* Washington, D.C.: Office of Education, Bureau of Research, 1967.

Byrne, S. Nobody home: The erosion of the American family (A conversation with Urie Bronfenbrenner). *Psychology Today*, 1977, 41–7.

Calvert, D. Dimensions of family involvement in early childhood education. *Exceptional Children*, 1971, **37**, 655–59.

Cantrell, M.L. Incidence of children's inappropriate behavior as a function of skill/demand discrepancies. Mimeo, Peabody College, 1974.

Cantrell, R.P. & Cantrell, M.C. Preventive mainstreaming: Impact of a supportive services program on pupils. *Exceptional Children*, 1976, **42** (7), 381–86.

Caplan, G. *Principles of preventive psychiatry.* New York: Basic Books, 1964.

Caplan, G. *The theory and practice of mental health consultation.* New York: Basic Books, 1970.

Carroll, A.W. The classroom as an ecosystem. *Focus on Exceptional Children*, 1974, **6**, 1–11.

Cavior, E.C., Schmidt, A., & Karacki, L. *An evaluation of the Kennedy youth center differential treatment program: In program and 12 month post-release outcome for Kennedy youth center, Ashland, and Englewood.* Washington, D.C.: Research Office, U.S. Bureau of Prisons, October 1972.

CCBD-BEH Dialogue Continues. *CCBD Newsletter* (Dembinski, R.J., Ed.), October 1979, **18** (1), 1-2.

Challenges for children's mental health services. McLean VA: MITRE Corp., 1977.

Cherry, T.J. The Oregon child study and treatment centers. *Child Care Quarterly*, 1976, **5** (2), 146-54.

Children in adult jails. Boston: Children's Defense Fund, 1978.

Chinn, P.C., Winn, J., & Walters, R.H. *Two-way talking with parents of special children.* St. Louis: Mosby, 1978.

Cohen, H., Filipczak, J., & Bis, J. *Case I: An initial study of contingencies applicable to special education.* Silver Spring, MD: Institute for Behavioral Research, 1967.

Cohen, R. Prevention reconsidered: Assets, liabilities, and alternatives. In Apter, S.J. (Ed.), *Focus on prevention: The education of children labeled emotionally disturbed.* Syracuse: Publications in Education (Syracuse University Press), 1978.

Cohen, R. & Devine, M.E. A needs-based service delivery model for community mental health centers. In *Sourcebooks on paraprofessionals in community mental health centers.* Berkeley: Social Action Research Center (for National Institute of Mental Health), 1977.

Cohen, S. *Family reactions to the handicapped child.* New York: Hunter College of the City University of New York, 1974.

Cole, J. & Magnussen, M. Family situation factors related to remainers and terminators of treatment. *Psychotherapy*, 1967, **4**, 107-09.

Coletta, A.J. *Working together: A guide to parent involvement.* Atlanta: Humanics Limited, 1977.

Conoley, J., Apter, S., & Conoley, C. Teacher consultation and the resource teacher: Increasing services to seriously emotionally disturbed children. In Wood, F. (Ed.), *Education of Seriously Emotionally Disturbed Children and Youth.* Reston, Va: CEC, 1981.

Council for Exceptional Children. Resource programs—A cooperative venture. *Exceptional Children*, 1976, **43** (1), 54.

Cowen, E. Prevention in the public schools: Strategies for dealing with school adjustment problems. In Apter, S.J. (Ed.), *Focus on prevention: The education of children labeled emotionally disturbed.* Syracuse: Publications in Education (Syracuse University Press), 1978.

Craw, G.A. *Children at risk: A handbook of the signs and symptoms of early childhood difficulties.* ERIC Document (ED 157 607). 1976

Curran, T.J. & Algozzine, B. Ecological disturbance: A test of the matching hypothesis. *Behavioral Disorders*, 1980, **5** (3), 169-74.

Daly, P. B., Davis, M.L., Daily, L., & Fixson, D. *A comprehensive early intervention program for families with problem children.* Father Flanagan's Boys Home, Lincoln, Nebraska: 1977.

D'Angelo, R. & Walsh, J. An evaluation of various therapy approaches with lower socioeconomic group children. *Journal of Psychology*, 1967, **67**, 59-64.

Dee, G. The effects of parent-group counseling of children with school and adjustment problems. *DAI*, 1970, **31**, 1008A.

Deno, E. Special education as development capital. *Exceptional Children*, 1970, **37** (3), 229-37.

Dokecki, P. & Hutton, R. Critique of Mental Health services: Case for the liaison perspective presented to 85th Annual Meeting of American Psychiatric Association. In Himmelsbach, J. (Chair), Ecological approaches to service delivery: New roles for community psychologists. San Francisco, August 27, 1977.

Door, D. An ounce of prevention. *Mental Hygiene*, 1972, **56**, 25-7.

Dunn, L.M. *Exceptional children in the schools.* New York: Holt, Rinehart, & Winston, 1973.

Eaves, R.C. & McLaughlin, P.M. A systems approach for the assessment of the child and his environment: Getting back to basics. *Journal of Special Education*, 1977, **11** (1), 99–111.

Edelman, M.W. Who is for children? *American Psychologist*, 1981, **36**, 2, 109–16.

Eisenberg, L. Possibilities for a preventive psychiatry. *Pediatrics*, 1962, **30**, 815–28.

Erikson, E.H. *Childhood and society* New York: Norton, 1950.

Evans, S. The consultant role of the resource teacher. *Exceptional Children*, 1980, **46**, (5), 402–04.

Eysenck, H.J. The effects of psychotherapy. In Eysenck, H.J. (Ed.), *Handbook of abnormal psychology*. New York: Basic Books, 1961.

Farris, R. & Dunham, H. *Mental disorders in urban areas*. Chicago: University of Chicago Press, 1939.

Fawl, C.L. Disturbances experienced by children in their natural habitats. In Barker, R.G. (Ed.), *The stream of behavior*. New York: Appleton-Century-Crofts, 1963.

Feagans, L. Ecological theory as a model for constructing a theory of emotional disturbance. In Rhodes, W.C. & Tracy, M.L. (Eds.), *A study of child variance* (Vol. 1). Ann Arbor: Institute for the Study of Mental Retardation and Related Disabilities, 1972.

Firestone, P., Kelly, M.J., & Fike, S. *Are fathers necessary in parent training groups?* Children's Hospital of Eastern Ontario and Carleton University Departments of Psychology, 1977.

Forness, S.R. The mildly retarded as casualties of the educational system. *Journal of School Psychology*, 1972, **10** (2), 117–24.

Fowler, D.E. *Experiential innovations in teaching visiting teachers*. Paper presented to the annual meeting of the American Personnel and Guidance Assoc., 1970.

Fox, R.S., Schmuck, R., Van Egmond, E., Ritvo, M., & Jung, C. *Diagnosing professional climates of schools*. Fairfax, VA: NTL Learning Resources Corporation, 1975.

Gallagher, J.J. The special education contract for mildly handicapped children. *Exceptional Children*, 1972, **38**, 227–35.

Gallessich, J. A systems model of school consultation. *Psychology in the Schools*, 1972, **9**, 13–15.

Gallup Poll, *Phi Delta Kappan*, September 1979.

Gardner, J.E. *Paraprofessional work with troubled children*. Venice, CA: Children's Center for Educational Therapy, 1975.

Garmezy, N. DSM III: Never mind the psychologists; Is it good for the children? *Clinical Psychologist*, 1978, **31** (3), 4–6.

Garrigan, J.J. & Bambrick, A. Family therapy for disturbed children: Some experimental results in special education. *Journal of Marriage and Family Counseling*, 1977, **3** (1), 83–92.

Gatti, F. & Coleman, C. Community network therapy. *American Journal of Orthopsychiatry*, 1976, **4**, 608–17.

Gentry, N.D. & Parks, A.L. *Education of the severely/profoundly handicapped*. Austin: Learning Concept, 1977.

Gerard, R.E. *Differential treatment: A way to begin*. Washington, D.C.: Bureau of Prisons, Dept. of Justice, 1970.

Gibbs, J.C. The meaning of ecologically-oriented inquiry in contemporary psychology. *American Psychologist*, 1979, **34** (2), 127–40.

Glasser, W. Class meetings and schools without failure. Laverne, CA: Laverne College Center, 1971.

Glatter, P. *What mainstreaming is/what mainstreaming isn't*. Mimeo. Syracuse: Syracuse University Dean's Grant Project, 1977.

Gluck, M., Tanner, M., Sullivan, O., & Erikson, P. Follow-up evaluation of 55 child guidance cases. *Behavior Research and Therapy*, 1964, **2**, 131–34.

Gorham, K.A., DesJardins, C., Page, R., Pettis, E., and Scheiber, B. Effect on parents. In

References

Hobbs, N. (Ed.), *Issues in the classification of children* (Vol II). San Francisco: Jossey-Bass, 1975.

Graubard, P.S. Children with behavioral disabilities. In Dunn, L. (Ed.) *Exceptional children in the schools.* New York: Holt, Rinehart, & Winston (1973).

Gray, S. & Klaus, D. Early training for culturally deprived children. Nashville: George Peabody College, 1963.

Gronlund, N.E. *Measurement and evaluation in teaching.* New York: Macmillan, 1976.

Grosenick, J.K. & Huntze, S.L. National needs analysis in behavior disorders: Columbia, Mo: University of Missouri-Colombia, Dept. of Special Education, 1979.

Guerney, B. Filial therapy: Description and rationale. *Journal of Consulting Psychology, 1964,* **28,** 304-10.

Guerney, L., Stover, L., & Guerney, B. The efficacy of training procedures for mothers in filial therapy. *Psychotherapy,* 1967, **4,** 110-15.

Gump, P.V. Education as an environmental enterprise. In Weinberg, R.A. & Wood, F.H. (Eds.), *Observation of pupils and teachers in mainstream and special education settings: alternative strategies.* Minneapolis: Leadership Training Institute, 1975.

Gump, P., Schoggen, P., & Redl, F. The camp milieu and its immediate effects. *Journal of Social Issues,* 1957, **13** (1), 40-46.

Hammill, D.D. & Bartel, N.R. *Teaching children with learning and behavior problems.* Boston: Allyn & Bacon, 1978.

Haring, N. The emotionally disturbed. In Kirk, S. & Weiner, B. (Eds.), *Behavioral research on exceptional children.* Washington, D.C.: Council for Exceptional Children, 1963.

Hartman, A. The generic stance and the family agency. *Social Casework,* April 1974, 199-208.

Hartman, A. The ECOMAP: An ecological framework for assessment and intervention. In Newbrough, J.R.; Walker, L.S.; & Abril, S. Workshop on Ecological Assessment. Presentation to the National Association of School Psychologists, New York, March 23, 1978.

Heller, K. & Monahan, J. *Psychology and community change.* Homewood, IL: Dorsey Press, 1977.

Herrnstein, R.J. Doing what comes naturally: A reply to Professor Skinner. *American Psychologist,* 1977, **32,** 1013-16.

Hewett, F.M. *The emotionally disturbed child in the classroom.* Boston: Allyn & Bacon, 1968.

Hewett, F.M. & Taylor, F.D. *The emotionally disturbed child in the classroom: The orchestration of success.* Boston: Allyn & Bacon, 1980.

Hobbs, N. Helping disturbed children: Psychological and ecological strategies. *American Psychologist,* 1966, **21,** 1105-15.

Hobbs, N. *The futures of children.* San Francisco: Jossey-Bass, 1975.

Hobbs, N. Families, schools, and communities: An ecosystem for children. *Teacher's College Record,* 1978, **79** (4), 756-766.

Hobbs, N. Perspectives on re-education. *Behavioral Disorders,* 1978, **3** (2), 65-6.

Hoppe, A. How to weigh a pupil—And solve the class size problem. *Learning,* 1978, 96-8.

Hunt, J. Parent and child center: Their basis in the behavioral and educational sciences. *American Journal of Orthopsychiatry,* 1971, **41,** 133-38.

Jahoda, M. *Current concepts of positive mental health.* New York: Basic Books, 1958.

James, W. *Talks to teachers on psychology: And to students on some of life's ideals.* New York: Holt, 1922. Originally published, 1899.

Jenkins, J.J. Remember that old theory of memory? Well, forget it! *American Psychologist,* 1974, **29,** 785-95.

Johnson, S.M., Bolsted, O.D., & Lobitz, G.K. Generalization and contrast phenomena in behavior modification with children. ERIC Document (ED 101 832), 1975.

Jones, M. *The therapeutic community.* New York: Basic Books, 1953.

Juul, K.D. *Educational and psychological interactions: Models of remediation for behavior disordered children.* Bulletin No. 62 from the Dept. of Education and Psychological Research, School of Education, Malmo, Sweden, July, 1977.

Kaplan, F. & Sarason, S.B. (Eds.) *The psychoeducational clinic: Papers and research studies.* New Haven: Dept. of Psychology, Yale Univ. in conjunction with Mass. Dept. of Mental Health, 1967.

Karnes, M. An approach for working mothers of disadvantaged preschool children. *Merrill-Palmer Quarterly*, 1968, **4**, 173–84.

Karnes, M. *A new role for teachers involving the entire family in the education of preschool disadvantaged children.* Unpublished manuscript, University of Illinois, 1969.

Karnes, M.B. & Zehrback, R.R. Flexibility in getting parents involved in the school. *Teaching Exceptional Children*, 1972, **5**, (1), 6–19.

Kauffman, J.M. *Characteristics of children's behavior disorders.* Columbus: Charles E. Merrill, 1977.

Kauffman, J.M. Where special education for disturbed children is going: A personal view. *Exceptional Children*, 1980, **46**, (7), 522–26.

Kelly, E. Parental roles in special education programming: A brief for involvement. *Journal of Special Education*, 1973, **7**, 357–64.

Kenniston, K. & The Carnegie Council on Children. *All our children: The American family under pressure.* New York: Harcourt, Brace, Jovanovich, 1977.

Kirk, S. *Educating exceptional children.* Boston: Houghton-Mifflin, 1972.

Knoblock, P. An alternative learning environment: Its impact on prevention. In Apter, S.J. (Ed.), *Focus on prevention: The education of children labeled emotionally disturbed.* Syracuse: Publications in Education (Syracuse University Press), 1978.

Koppitz, E.M. Strategies for diagnosis and identification of children with behavior and learning problems. *Behavioral Disorders*, 1977, **2** (3), 136–40.

Kounin, J.S. *Discipline and group management in classrooms.* New York: Holt, Rinehart, & Winston, 1970.

Kounin, J.S. An ecological approach to classroom activity settings: Some methods and findings. In Weinberg, R. & Wood, F. (Eds.), *Observation of pupils and teachers in mainstream and special education settings: Alternative strategies.* Minneapolis: Leadership Training Institute, 1975.

Kroth, R.L. *Communicating with parents of exceptional children.* Denver: Love, 1975.

Kuhn, D. Mechanisms of cognitive and social development: One psychology or two? *Human Development*, 1978, **21**, 92–118.

Laten, S. & Katz, G.A. *A theoretical model for assessment of adolescents: The ecological/behavioral approach.* Madison: Madison Public Schools, 1975.

Lay-Dopyera, M. Questions to ask in assessing a "regular" teacher's readiness for mainstreaming. In *Mainstreaming children with special needs: An independent study guide,* Syracuse: Division for the study of Teaching, School of Education, Syr. Univ. 1981, pp. 51–2.

Lessing, E. & Schilling, F. Relationship between training selection variables and treatment outcome in a child guidance clinic: An application of data-processing methods. *Journal of American Academy of Child Psychiatry*, 1966, **5**, 313–48.

Letulle, L.J. Family therapy in residential treatment for children. *Social Work*, 1979, **24** (1), 49–51.

Levine, M. Problems of entry in light of some postulates of practice in community psychology. In I.I. Goldenberg (Ed.) *Clinical psychologists in the world of action.* Lexington, Mass.: D.C. Health, 1973.

Levinson, P. The next generation: A study of children in AFDC families. *Welfare in Review*, 1969, **7**, 1–9.

Lewin, K. Psychological ecology. In Cartwright, D. (Ed.), *Field theory in social science: Selected theoretical papers by Kurt Lewin.* New York: Harper & Row, 1951.

Lightfoot, S.L. Family-school relationships. *Citizen Action in Education*, 1981, **8** (1), 6–7.

Linton, T.E. The educateur model: A theoretical monograph. *Journal of Special Education*, 1971, **5**, 155–90.

Lobitz, G.R. & Johnson, S.M. *Normal versus deviant children: A multi-method comparison.* ERIC Document (ED 099 128), 1974.

Long, N. *Direct help to the classroom teacher.* Washington, D.C.: Washington School of Psychiatry, 1966.

Long, N.J., Morse, W.C., & Newman, R.G. *Conflict in the classroom.* Belmont, CA: Wadsworth, 1965.

Lowitt, M.F., Leifer, A., Cochran, N., & Weene, K. Family psychopathology in parent-child relationships. *Proceedings of the Annual Meeting of the American Orthopsychiatric Assoc.,* Washington, D.C.: 1975.

MacKay, L. Ecological Mapping. Presentation to the National Association of School Psychologists, N.Y., March 23, 1978.

MacKeith, R. The feelings and behavior of parents of handicapped children. *Journal of Developmental Medicine and Child Neurology*, 1973, **15**, 524–27.

Mager, R. *Preparing instructional objectives.* Palo Alto, CA: Fearon, 1972.

Magne, O. *A new concept of handicap.* Department of Educational and Psychological Research, School of Education, Malmo, Sweden, Reprint 233, December, 1977.

Martin, E. Quoted in Long, K., *Johnny's such a bright boy, what a shame he's retarded.* Boston: Houghton Mifflin, 1977.

Mathis, H. Training a "disturbed" boy using the mother as therapist: A case study. *Behavior Therapy*, 1971, **2**, 233–34.

McCall, R.B. Challenges to a science of developmental psychology. *Child Development*, 1977, **48**, 333–44.

McDaniels, G. Mainstreaming—not exactly new. *American Psychological Association Monitor*, May 1978, 9, 5, p. 2.

McGowan, R. Group counseling with underachievers and their parents. *School counselor*, 1968, **16**, 30–5.

McGuire, W.J. The yin and yang of social psychology: Seven Koan. *Journal of Personality and Social Psychology*, 1973, **26**, 446–56.

McKeachie, W.J. Psychology in America's bicentennial year. *American Psychologist*, 1976, **31** (12), 819–33.

Meisels, S. First steps in mainstreaming: Some questions and answers. Media Resource Center, *Young Children*, 1977, **33** (1), 4–13.

Meisgeier, C. A review of critical issues underlying mainstreaming. In Mann, L. & Sabatino, D. (Eds.), *The third review of special education.* New York: Grune & Stratton, 1976.

Mercer, J.R. A policy statement on assessment procedures and the rights of children. *Harvard Educational Review*, 1974, **44**, 328–44.

Miller, B.L. & Wilmshurst, A.L. *Parents and volunteers in the classroom: A handbook for teachers.* San Francisco: P & E Research Assocs., Inc., 1975.

Miller, S. Exploratory study of sibling relationships in families with retarded children. Unpublished dissertation. Columbia University, 1974.

Mischler, E.G. & Waxler, N.E. *Interaction in families: An experimental study of family processes in schizophrenia.* New York: Wiley, 1968.

Montgomery, M.D. The special educator as consultant: Some strategies. *Teaching Exceptional Children*, Summer 1978, 110–12.

Morrison, G.C. & Smith, W.R. *Emergencies in child psychiatry. A definition and comparison of two groups.* Paper presented to the annual meeting of the American Orthopsychiatric Association, New York: 1970.

Morse, W. Self-concept in the school setting. *Childhood Education*, 1964, **41**, 195–198.

Morse, W. Worksheet in life-space interviewing for teachers. In Long, N., Morse, W., &

Newman, R. (Eds.), *Conflict in the classroom*, Belmont, CA: Wadsworth, 1965.

Morse, W.C. The education of socially maladjusted and emotionally disturbed children. In Cruickshank, W.M. & Johnson, G.O. (Eds.), *Education of exceptional children and youth* (2nd edition). Englewood Cliffs, NJ: Prentice-Hall, 1967.

Morse, W. Competency in teaching socio-emotional impaired. *Behavioral Disorders*, 1976, 1 (2), 83-7.

Morse, W. Serving the needs of individuals with behavior disorders. *Exceptional Children*, 1977, **44**, 155-164.

Morse, W., Bruno, F., & Morgan, S. *Training teachers for the emotionally disturbed: An analysis of programs*. Ann Arbor: University of Michigan, School of Education, 1975.

Morse, W., Cutler, R., and Fink, A. Public School classes for the emotionally handicapped: A research analysis. In Long, N., Morse, W., and Newman, R. (Eds.) *Conflict in the classroom*. Belmont (CA): Wadsworth, 1965.

Morse, W.C., Smith, J.M. & Acker, N. Videotape training packages in child variance. *The ecological approach: a self-instructional module*. Ann Arbor: University of Michigan, School of Education, 1978. Mimeo.

Mour, S.I. Teacher behaviors and ecological balance. *Behavioral Disorders*, 1977, 3 (1), 55-8.

Mussen, P. (Ed.) *Handbook of research methods in child development*. New York: Wiley, 1960.

Nathan, P.E. Diagnostic and treatment services for children: Introduction to the section. *American Psychologist*, 1979, **34** (10), 467-68.

Neisser, V. *Cognition and reality: Principles and implications of cognitive psychology*. San Francisco: Freeman, 1976.

Newbrough, S.R., Walker, L.S., & Abril, S. Workshop on ecological assessment. Presentation to the National Association of School Psychologists, New York, March 23, 1978.

Newcomer, P.L. *Understanding and teaching emotionally disturbed children*. Boston: Allyn & Bacon, 1980.

New York State Guidelines for carrying out the responsibilities of the Committee on the Handicapped. New York State Education Department, July 1978.

New York *Times*. Veronica's unhappy life: Prostitution at 11 and dead at 12. November 3, 1977.

Nyquist, E. *Mainstreaming: Idea and actuality*. Albany: State Education Dept., 1977.

O'Dell, S. Training parents in behavior modification: A review. *Psychological Bulletin*, 1974, **81**, 418-33.

Oxman, L. The effectiveness of filial therapy: A controlled study. Unpublished doctoral dissertation, Rutgers University, 1971.

Pastor, D.L. & Swap, S.M. An ecological study of emotionally disturbed preschoolers in special and regular classes. *Exceptional Children*, 1978, 213-15.

Paroz, J., Siegenthaler, L.S., & Tatus, V. A model for a middle-school resource program. *Journal of Learning Disabilities*, January 1977, **10**, (1), 7-15.

Pate, J. Emotionally disturbed and socially maladjusted children. In Dunn, L. (Ed.), *Exceptional children in the schools*. New York: Holt, Rinehart & Winston, 1963.

Patterson, G., Jones, R., Whittier, J., & Wright, M. A behavior modification technique for a hyperactive child. *Behavior Research and Therapy*, 1965, **2**, 217-26.

Paulson, M.J. et al. Suicide potential and behavior in children ages 4 to 12. *Suicide and Life-Threatening Behavior*, 1978, **8** (4), 225-42.

Perkins, J. Group counseling with bright underachievers and their mothers. *DAI*, 1970, **30**, 2809A.

Perlmutter, F.D., Vayda, A.M., & Woodburn, P.K. An instrument for differentiating programs in prevention—Primary, secondary, and tertiary. *American Journal Orthopsychiatry*, 1976, **46** (3) 533-41.

Pooley, R.C. *The Pendleton project: Semi-annual narrative report*. Virginia Beach, VA:

Virginia State Division of Justice and Crime Prevention, 1976. (ERIC Document Reproduction Service No. ED 140 134.)

President's Commission on Mental Health. *Preliminary report to the president.* Washington, D.C.: 1976.

Public Law 94:142. Education for all handicapped children act. *Federal Register*, August 23, 1977 **42** (163), 121a, 5.

Raiser, L. & Van Nagel, C. The loophole in public law 94:142. *Exceptional Children*, 1980, **46** (7), 516–20.

Rappaport, J. *Community psychology: Values, research, and action.* New York: Holt, Rinehart, & Winston: 1977.

Redl, F. The concept of the life-space interview. *American Journal of Orthopsychiatry*, January 1959, **29**, 1–18.

Redl, F. & Wineman, D. *Children who hate.* New York: Free Press, 1951.

Reinert, H.R. *Children in conflict*: Educational strategies for the emotionally disturbed and behavior disordered. St. Louis: Mosby, 1980.

Report to the president from the president's commission on mental health, Vol. I. Washington, D.C.: U.S. Government Printing Office, 1978.

Reynolds, M. *Observations on the course in special education planning held at the Federal University in Rio de Janeiro* (Brazil). Minneapolis: National Support Systems Project, 1977a.

Reynolds, M. Staying out of jail. *Teaching Exceptional Children*, Spring 1977b, 60–3.

Reynolds, M. A common body of practice for teachers: The challenge of public law 94:142 to teacher education. Minneapolis: National Support System Project, 1980.

Reynolds, M.C. & Birch, J.W. *Teaching exceptional children in all America's schools.* Reston, VA: Council for Exceptional Children, 1977.

Rhodes, W.C. The disturbing child: A problem of ecological management. *Exceptional Children*, 1967, **33**, 449–455.

Rhodes, W.C. A community participation analysis of emotional disturbance. *Exceptional Children*, 1970, **36** (5), 309–314.

Rhodes, W.C. *A study of child variance. Volume 4: The future.* Ann Arbor: Univ. of Michigan, Institute for the Study of Mental Retardation and Related Disabilities, 1975.

Rhodes, W.C. & Gibbins, S. Community programming for the behaviorally deviant child. In Quay, H. & Werry, J., *Psychopathological disorders of childhood.* New York: Wiley, 1972.

Rhodes, W.C. & Tracy, M. A study of child variance. Ann Arbor: Institute for the Study of Mental Retardation and Related Disabilities, 1972.

Ringness, T.A. *Mental health in the schools.* New York: Random House, 1968.

Rogers-Warren, A. & Warren, S.F. (Eds.). *Ecological perspectives in behavior analysis.* Baltimore: University Park Press, 1977.

Rosenblum, G. The new role of the clinical psychologist in a community mental health center. *Community Mental Health Journal*, 1968, **4** (5), 403–09.

Rubin, R. & Balow, B. Learning and behavioral disorders. A longitudinal study. *Exceptional Children*, 1971, **38**, 293–98.

Rubin, R. & Balow, B. Prevalence of teacher-identified behavior problems: A longitudinal study. *Exceptional Children*, 1978, **45** (2), 102–11.

Sabatino, D.A. School psychology—Special education: To acknowledge a relationship. *Journal of School Psychology*, 1972, **10**, 99–109.

Sagor, M. Treatment of deviance by the mental health system: structure. In Rhodes, W.C., & Head, S. (Eds.), *A study of child variance. Vol. 3: Service delivery systems.* Ann Arbor: Institute for the Study of Mental Retardation and Related Disabilities, 1974.

Salzinger, K., Feldman, R., & Portney, S. Training parents of brain-injured children in the use of operant conditioning procedures. *Behavior Therapy*, 1970, **1**, 4–32.

Sarason, S. New directions in psychological services for children with mental, emotional, and cultural handicaps. New York: *New York Society for the Experimental Study of Education Yearbook*, 1967.

Schiff, H. *The effect of personal contactual relationships on parent attitude toward participation in local school affairs.* Unpublished doctoral dissertation, Northwestern University, 1963.

Schopler, E. Prevention of psychosis through alternate education. In Apter, S.J. (Ed.), *Focus on prevention: The education of children labeled emotionally disturbed.* Syracuse: Publications in Education (Syracuse University Press) 1978

Schulman, L.S. Reconstruction in educational research. *Review of Educational Research*, 1970, **40**, 371-96.

Shaffer, P. *Equus.* New York: Avon Books: 1975.

Shakow, D. Clinical psychology 50 years from now. *American Psychologist* 1978, **33** (2), 142-58.

Silverman, M. Beyond the mainstream: The special needs of the chronic child patient. *American Journal of Orthopsychiatry*, 1979, **49** (1), 62-8.

Skinner, B.F. *Science and human behavior.* New York: Macmillan, 1953.

Sommer, R. Toward a psychology of natural behavior. *APA Monitor*, January 1977, **8**, 1.

State of New York, Office for Education of Children with Handicapping Conditions. Albany: Statement of Annual Goals (1980-81), September 1980.

Stephens, T.M. Forum. *Behavioral Disorders.* 1976, **1**, 2, 146-47.

Stickney, S.B. Schools are our community mental health centers: *American Journal of Psychiatry*, 1968, **124**, 101-08.

Sullivan, H.S. Socio-psychiatric research: its implications for the schizophrenia problem and for mental hygiene. *American Journal of Psychiatry*, 1931, **87**, 977-91.

Swanson, H.L. & Reinert, H.R. *Teaching strategies for children in conflict: Curriculum, methods, and materials.* St. Louis: Mosby, 1979.

Swap, S. Disturbing classroom behaviors: A developmental and ecological view. *Exceptional Children*, 1974, **41**, 163-172.

Swap, S. The ecological model of emotional disturbance in children: a status report and proposed synthesis. *Behavioral Disorders*, May 1978, **3**, (3), 186-96.

Tavormina, J. Basic models of parent counseling: a critical review. *Psychological Bulletin*, 1974, **81**, 827-35.

Taylor, D.A. & Alpert, S.W. *Continuity and support following residential treatment.* New York: Child Welfare League of America, 1973.

Thomas, A., Chess, S., & Birch, H. *Temperament and behavior disorders in children*, New York: New York University Press, 1968.

Thomas, E.D. & Marshall, M.J. Clinical evaluation and coordination of services: An ecological model. *Exceptional Children* 1977, **44**(1), 16-22.

Thurman, S. Congruence of behavioral ecologies: A model for special education programming. *Journal of Special Education*, 1977, **11**, 329-34.

Ullman, L. & Krasner, L. *A psychological approach to abnormal behavior.* New York: Prentice-Hall, 1969.

Unger, C. Treatment of deviance by the social welfare system: History and structure. In Rhodes, W.C. & Head, S. (Eds.), *A study of child variance, Vol. 3: Service delivery systems.* Ann Arbor: Institute for the Study of Mental Retardation and Related Disabilities, 1974.

Vogel, N.W. & Bell, E.F. (Eds.). *A modern introduction to the family*, New York: Free Press, 1960.

Wade, T.C. & Baker, T.B. Opinions and use of psychological tests: A survey of clinical psychologists. *American Psychologist*, October 1977, 874-82.

Wahler, R.G., Berland, A.M., Coe, T.D., & Leske, G. Social systems analysis: implementing an alternative behavioral model. In Rogers-Warren, A. and Warren, S.F. (Eds.), *Ecological perspectives in behavior analysis.* Baltimore: University Park Press, 1977.

Walder, L., Cohen, S., Bereiter, D., Daston, P., Hirsch, J., & Leibowitz, J. Teaching behavioral principles to parents of disturbed children. In Guerney, B. (Ed.) *Psychotherapeutic Agents: New roles for non-professionals, parents, and teachers.* New York: Holt, Rinehart, & Winston, 1969.

Wallace, G. & Larsen, S.C. *Educational assessment of learning problems: Testing for teaching.* Boston: Allyn & Bacon, 1979.

Whittaker, J. The ecology of child treatment: A developmental educational approach to the therapeutic milieu. *Journal of Autism and Child Schizophrenia,* 1975, **5** (3), 223-37.

Whittaker, J. *Caring for troubled children.* San Francisco: Jossey-Bass, 1979.

Wicker, A.W. Ecological psychology: Some recent and prospective developments. *American Psychologist,* 1979, **34** (9), 755-65.

Wiederholt, J.L., Hamill, D.D., & Brown, V. *The resource teacher: A guide to effective practices.* Boston: Allyn & Bacon, 1978.

Willems, E. Behavioral ecology. In Stokols, D. (Ed.), *Psychological perspectives on environment and behavior.* New York: Plenum Press, 1977.

Wiltz, N. Modification of behaviors through parent participation in a group technique. Unpublished doctoral dissertation, University of Oregon, 1969.

Wixson, S. Two resource room models for serving learning and behavior disorders pupils. *Behavioral Disorders,* 1980, 5(a), 116-25.

Wohlwill, J.F. *The study of behavioral development.* New York: Academic Press, 1977.

Woody, R.H. *Behavior problem children in the schools.* New York: Appleton-Century-Crofts, 1969.

Wright, H.F. *Recording and analyzing child behavior.* New York: Harper and Row, 1967.

Zigler, E., & Muenchow, S. Mainstreaming: The proof is in the implementation. *American Psychologist,* 1979, **34** (10), 993-996.

Author Index

Subject Index

About the Author

Steven J. Apter is a Professor of Special Education in the Division of Special Education and Rehabilitation at Syracuse University. Apter has also served as Project Co-Director for the Syracuse University Dean's Grant Project and directed a comprehensive NIMH demonstration project for troubled children and families (The BRIDGE Program). A Ph.D. of Syracuse University (Clinical Psychology), Apter's work has focused primarily on the implications of Community Psychology perspectives for the delivery of services to youngsters. His writing has centered on topics such as therapeutic camping, the prevention of emotional disturbances, and applications of ecological theory to the problems of troubled children. The idea for this book was developed while the author was on leave serving as Visiting Professor of Psychology at the Free University of Amsterdam in the Netherlands.

Pergamon General Psychology Series

Editors: Arnold P. Goldstein, Syracuse University
Leonard Krasner, SUNY, Stony Brook